THE PARADOX OF PROGRESS

THE PARADOX OF PROGRESS

Can Americans Regain Their Confidence in a Prosperous Future?

RICHARD B. McKENZIE

New York Oxford
OXFORD UNIVERSITY PRESS
1997

Oxford University Press

Oxford New York
Athens Auckland Bangkok Bogotá Bombay
Buenos Aires Calcutta Cape Town Dar es Salaam Delhi
Florence Hong Kong Istanbul Karachi
Kuala Lumpur Madras Madrid Melbourne
Mexico City Nairobi Paris Singapore
Taipei Tokyo Toronto

and associated companies in
Berlin Ibadan

198 Madison Avenue, New York, New York 10016

Library of Congress Cataloging-in-Publication Data
McKenzie, Richard B.
The Paradox of Progress: Can Americans Regain Their Confidence
in a Prosperous Future? / by Richard B. McKenzie.
p. cm.
Includes bibliographical references and index.
ISBN 0–19–510239–8
1. United States—Economic conditions—1981– 2. United States—
Economic policy—1993– 3. Economic forecasting—United States.
4. Pessimism—United States. I. Title.
HC106.8.M363 1997 338.973—dc20 96–23910

9 8 7 6 5 4 3 2 1

Printed in the United States of America
on acid-free paper

For Patrick and Mary Revitte

PREFACE

Conventional policy wisdom, the type emanating from Washington and many widely read authors, is that times for Americans have never been tougher. The presumption in many policy circles is that the standard of living in the country has been on a downward trend for some time. Moreover, the trend will continue without any knowable end. Our children will live less prosperous lives than we have lived, just as we are living less prosperous lives than our parents.

The central theme of this book stands in sharp contrast with the prevailing wisdom. While economic and social problems abound for many Americans, several of which are duly explored in some detail in following chapters, this book adds a measure of balance to public debates. It shows that progress for the overwhelming majority of Americans has continued unabated into modern times. Our forebears, who only several decades ago viewed many modern-day necessities as luxuries, would recognize and appreciate the advantages most contemporary Americans have. The full record of progress has gone largely unheralded. The full breadth of opportunities available for the taking by Americans have gone unrecognized.

Still, there is a prevailing paradox. In spite of the continuing progress, the economic mood of the country remains somber. Fear of a dimmer future grips many Americans. The question is Why? Why are so many Americans fearful that the American dream of a brighter future has been busted, when in fact it hasn't? The answers given here are not conventional. As commonly recognized, I understand that increasing economic insecurity has necessarily accompanied the growing competitiveness and integration of world economic activity. All American (and, for that matter, all German, Australian, and Chinese) jobs are subject to radical change over coming years. Government bean counters continue to calculate the number of "temporary workers" in the country. They don't seem to realize yet that all workers' jobs are now *potentially* temporary. However, my analysis extends the argument, maintaining that the heart of the economic plight and angst that Americans face is not *limited* opportunities, but the contrary—an *abundance* of opportunities that are emerging from a technological and economic ferment that, in retrospect, will be viewed by future historians as unequaled in the history of the human race. This ferment is, of course, reducing economic security by increasing business competitiveness; it is also increasing the competitiveness of governments and reducing governments' ability to provide their citizens with the security that they may want.

The policy pessimists recommend that governments must do more to rectify the insecurity that many Americans face. I maintain that they can't. They must and will do less. Governments are as constrained by world competitive forces as are businesses. Governments must retract their policy reaches not so much for political reasons (for example, because conservatives have beaten liberals in recent elections) but for an economic one: the financial and real (human and physical) capital that is crucial for economic development is footloose on a global scale, free to move to countries where it is treated well. Solutions for problems faced by Americans must, to an extent not fully appreciated, be private not collective. Governments are simply not as relevant to economic progress as they once were. Paradoxically, I argue that governments must now restrict their influence in the economy in modern times for much the same reasons that John Kenneth Galbraith and his followers believed decades ago that government could and should expand.

The book has an optimistic outlook. Out of the current insecurity will arise more efficient businesses and governments, and a level of prosperity that cannot be imagined or plotted today. Indeed, if our future could be imagined by anyone (or any group of policymakers in Washington), it would be less prosperous than it will likely be because the country's future would then be restricted to what could be imagined by an individual mind. As never before, the country's future will be prosperous precisely because of the widespread angst currently felt by Americans.

As always, I am indebted to Dwight Lee, who read and commented on this book. My work has benefited immensely from continuing conversations with him over the years. In fact, a portion of the book, chapter 6, is based on a paper that he and I co-authored several years ago. I am also indebted to my colleague John Whiting, who took the time to read and critique the book from the perspective of a noneconomist. My wife, Karen, and my Oxford University Press editor, Irene Pavitt, did a terrific job of correcting and smoothing the exposition. Finally, the book was written with the financial support of the John M. Olin Foundation and the Lynde and Harry Bradley Foundations, for which I remain appreciative. Patrick and Mary Revitte live a continent and an ocean away, but we have been able to maintain the type of abiding and warm friendships, linked by technology, that are at the heart of the new transnational communities envisioned in the following pages. I am pleased to be able to dedicate the book to them.

Irvine, Calif.
October 1996

R. B. M.

CONTENTS

THE PARADOX OF PROGRESS

1

PROGRESS AND PESSIMISM

Defeatism denotes a certain psychic state that has meaning only in reference to action. Facts in themselves and inferences from them can never be defeatist or the opposite whatever that might be. The report that a given ship is sinking is not defeatist. Only the spirit in which this report is received can be defeatist: The crew can sit down and drink. But it can also rush to the pumps.

Joseph Schumpeter,
Capitalism, Socialism, and Democracy

AMERICANS have historically been of two characters, each fighting with the other for control of the country's fate. On one side, Americans have been wild-eyed dreamers. The brave souls who crossed the Atlantic in the first few centuries following 1492 must have been delirious with dreams of a whole new world and a better life. How else could they have endured the treacherous journey to an unfamiliar and hostile land? The Americans who founded the country and those who followed in their footsteps endured hardships that modern Americans could not possibly imagine, but the early Americans seemed to have a common dream that life could be better. Indeed, it would get better.

Conversely, other Americans have always stood ready to find fault with their stations in life. As French historian and observer of American life Alexis de Tocqueville commented on his travels in this country,

> In America, I have seen the freest and best educated of men in circumstances the happiest to be found in the world; yet it seemed to me that a

> cloud habitually hung on their brow, and they seemed serious and almost sad even in their pleasures. The chief reason for this is that the former [oppressed people in the Old World] do not give a moment's thought to the ills they endure, whereas the latter [Americans] never stop thinking of the good things they have not got. It is odd to watch with what fervish ardor the Americans pursue their prosperity and how they are ever tormented by the shadowy suspicion that they may not have chosen the shortest route to get it.[1]

At the same time, most of the country's forebears seemed generally to perceive themselves as blessed with untold opportunities to be discovered and exploited. They knew failure firsthand, biting and frequent. They didn't like the pain of their failures any more than do contemporary Americans, but they also seemed to understand that failures were a natural part of life, of progress—a consequence of the risks that they willingly had to take to make their dreams come true.

The dual nature of the historic American character is not altogether unreasonable. Some sense of unease or dissatisfaction with current circumstances, some self-criticism, is absolutely necessary for people to move off their economic behinds. But they must also radiate some minimum sense of confidence that their moves will pay off in a brighter future.

By all widely read accounts, the current generation of Americans has lost a notable measure of the required balance in facing current and future conditions. Although the overwhelming majority of Americans have a standard of living that would have been envied by kings two centuries back, many despair at their fate in life. Many have accordingly shucked their heritage of optimism for a better future and adopted a cult of whining, of finding fault with their circumstances, and of claiming that they have been victimized by a culture that has closed off their opportunities. The so-called Generation X, that group of Americans born after 1964 who often believes that they should be entitled to the "good life" without much effort, is especially depressed. Three out of four of them, one 1994 poll reveals, believe that they will live less prosperous lives than did their parents.[2] In another 1994 poll, the Yankelovich Partners asked Americans whether things were getting better for the middle class. Thirty-four percent of the respondents said things are staying the

1. Alexis de Tocqueville, *Democracy in America* (New York: Doubleday, 1969), vol. 2, p. 536.

2. As reported in Douglas Jehl, "Clinton Urges Young to Reject Pessimism," *New York Times*, May 21, 1994, p. A15.

same; 8 percent said things are getting better; the remaining 57 percent said things are getting worse. In a 1995 Lou Harris poll, two-thirds of the respondents indicated that the American dream will be harder to achieve over the next decade than it was over the past one.[3] The pessimism is so pervasive that in a 1994 talk to UCLA students, even President Bill Clinton (who won his job in 1992 by panning the country's economic record of the previous twelve years) had to appeal to his listeners to see the world as "possibilities, not problems; to build up, not tear down; to unite, not divide."[4]

In the epigraph at the beginning of this chapter, the late Harvard economist Joseph Schumpeter notes that bad news, in itself, is not necessarily bad. What is important is how people respond to the news. Americans in the past seem to have taken the bad news of their "sinking ship" by rushing to the pumps. What is disheartening about contemporary Americans is that many have decided to sit down and drink, literally, all too ready to commiserate with others on their plight and to resign themselves to accepting their dismal fate.

In the eyes of many, Americans can be justifiably labeled a "nation of victims."[5] Far too many Americans seem to think that, for one reason or another, they are indeed victims, that they are an oppressed and suppressed people, that they have been oppressed by some other group, for example, employers, male chauvinists, Christian fundamentalists, government officials (or just the police), homosexuals (or antihomosexuals)—you name it. Blacks point to whites as a cause of their low standards of living. Women attribute their relatively low wages to the male culture in the workplace. Whites and blacks blame Jews, while Jews blame the pervasiveness of anti-Semitism. Even members of Generation X dare to claim that their weakness—their unwillingness to work hard for a living—comes from the oppression of having been given so much over the course of their short lives. Dare we entertain an "oppression of abundance"?

According to the late Aaron Wildavsky, a political scientist from the University of California, Berkeley, a tabulation of all the nation's victims adds to 374 percent of the country's population![6] The humor

3. As reported in Keith Melville, *National Issues Forum: Inequality* (New York: McGraw-Hill, 1995), pp. 10–11 (draft version).

4. Jehl, "Clinton Urges Young to Reject Pessimism."

5. See Charles L. Sykes, *A Nation of Victims: The Decay of the American Character* (New York: St. Martin's Press, 1992).

6. As reported in Paul Johnson, "Menacing Manipulators," *Insight*, September 23, 1991.

in Wildavsky's absurd calculation contains the seeds of an important reality check: Do our claims square—could they—with the facts of modern life?

Of course, there may be truth in *some* of the claims of victimization, just as there is some truth to claims that some people's fondest dreams have been shattered by turns in economic events over the past two decades. What seems to be unusual is the rapid expansion of those willing to claim victimization and to whine about their problems.[7] What seems to be new is that many Americans believe that life should be free of failures, as if it could be free of risks and uncertainties, and that the future will be dismal pretty much regardless of what they (we) do.

There has probably never been a time in which noted writers and scholars have churned out more foreboding books, with carefully crafted title words that expose their ominous tale: "great u-turn," "silent depression," "day of reckoning," "deindustrialization," "diminished expectations," "divided we fall," and "decline of great powers" (most notably, the United States). It is hard to say whether the constant flow of such readings has given rise to pervasive pessimism or whether the pessimism has given rise to the titles. Discretion suggests that writers and readers alike have been feeding on each other. Why? The answer is hardly transparent.

If Rip Van Winkle were to awaken from his long sleep today, he would surely be amazed at modern America on two counts: First, he would be astounded at the splendor of the living standard in the country; second, he would not likely understand the tenor of the times. Probably at no time in American history have more Americans lived better, but at the same time believed that the American Dream (an imagined better future for self and family) has wilted, or even that their fondest dreams have become nightmares.

Are their assessments of the future correct? If so, why? If not, why the change in outlook now? Those questions are addressed in this book mainly because it is no understatement to maintain that the country's future is dependent upon the dreams, aspirations, and expectations of the current generation, just as our current high living standard is the consequence of the dreams, aspirations, and expectations of those who have gone before. Widespread optimism can breed its own satisfaction

7. Charles Sykes adds, "By one estimate, 20 percent of Americans now claim to suffer from some form of diagnosable psychiatric disorder. . . . Dysfunction is, in every respect, a growth industry" (*Nation of Victims*, pp. 13–14).

because the optimistic people will be guided to do those things that make a bright future possible; for example, save and invest for future returns, as well as play by the rules of a decent society. By the same token, broad-based pessimism can bring forth the opposite results precisely because pessimism can cause people to live for today, to get what they can now, to play by rules that *they* concoct (not the tested rules of reasonable conduct for all), to grab what they can without regard for others or for future consequences. When people no longer believe that their futures will be better, it is altogether reasonable to expect them to spend more of their energies fighting over the *distribution* of the available income and goods and services and less on the type of *growth* that can make their futures brighter.

In the end, we all must acknowledge a central thesis of this book, that progress is not something that we can fully imagine. We are simply not smart enough, and we don't know enough to discern much about the details of the future. If we individually could imagine our futures, they would not be nearly as prosperous as they will likely be. This is because the future would be no more bright, no more sophisticated than that which we, with our limited faculties, can imagine. That is a recurring theme of this book.

My optimism is fueled by the knowledge that tens of millions of Americans have lived far better than their parents, and even far better than I could have imagined decades ago. Accordingly, I remain convinced that contrary to the prevailing view, the overwhelming majority of the country's children will live better than their parents. That is a strong statement, given the tenor of the times, but I think it is a statement that is founded on an amazing historical record of progress that has not, contrary to widespread but mistaken impressions, been broken in modern times. Americans who do not share my assessment may be surprised to learn just how much better off they are than those of 100 years ago, or even 40 or 20 years ago.

The paradox of progress in contemporary America is not that progress has continued, which it has, in spite of difficulties, but that its continuance has been accompanied by two detectable conflicting trends: rapidly expanding economic opportunities along with growing pessimism, a sense that progress has been abated and that opportunities in the future will be progressively restricted. The simple fact remains: progress has never been more possible, nor easier. Contrary to conventional wisdom, we live in fortunate times, especially when compared with our distant past. Americans need to recognize those truths and the reasons for renewed optimism that go with those truths.

A History of Dreams

In May 1609, Sir Thomas Gates left England with plans to land at Jamestown in late summer with eight supply ships. It took him more than a year to reach his destination, mainly because a storm forced him to spend the winter in Bermuda. By the time he made it to the Virginia coast, he had lost his flagship, and more than half of the colonists who boarded in England had died of starvation and disease; one man had been convicted of cannibalism.

Sir Thomas's trip was not, however, all that unusual. One historian reminds us that in those early years of discovery and conquest, it "was 'Starving Time' for Virginia, just as there were to be starving times for Bermuda, Plymouth, and Barbados, when men [and women] suffered and died, because they had not yet learned the art of colonization, and had come to America inadequately supplied and equipped and unfamiliar with the method of wresting a living from the wilderness."[8] In short, times were tough. Everything had to be done from scratch, and with little horsepower. The colonists had to dream of making the land bountiful (by first, regrettably, overpowering and suppressing the indigenous population).

Were those the "good old days"? I don't think so. Did the fact that times were tough stop many? Fortunately not. Most trudged onward.

The successful ancestors of some of the first colonialists who gathered in Philadelphia to sign the Declaration of Independence—and to pledge to one another their lives, their fortunes, and their sacred honor—were brave dreamers on more than one score. They dreamed not only of defeating one of the world's great military powers but, having done that, of entrusting the governance of a new country, not to royalty or a small core of elite compatriots, but to common folk. They imagined that certain truths were self-evident and that the "pursuit of happiness" would ultimately bear fruit, but only if the right to pursue happiness were not narrowly extended.

The founders of this country were obviously optimists. They must have figured that if people were allowed maximum freedom from the encroachment of higher authority to "do their own thing"—in effect, to pursue their own personal dreams—marvelous undreamed-of and then unknowable opportunities would unfold before future generations. In spite of understood problems with the system of govenment they constructed, they dared to think that the future of the country would be better than their fondest dreams.

8. Charles M. Andrews, *The Colonial Period of American History* (New Haven: Yale University Press, 1934), vol. 1, pp. 110–11.

Few who walked the muddy, dung-spotted streets of colonial villages or who worked in the backwoods of the colonies (which meant no farther west than western New York and Virginia) from dawn to dusk and then into the night by candlelight, often unprotected from the elements, could have imagined the progress that would be made in the ensuing two centuries. The country expanded from one sea to another, in spite of the need for long hours of backbreaking labor. Farms sprang up everywhere fertile land and water could be found, only to become so productive that fewer farms would eventually be needed. Factories with belching smokestacks replaced farms, and office towers replaced some of the factories. Wagon trains that inched across the vast hinterlands of the West gave way to steam engines that puffed along many of the same trails at then breakneck speeds. Few who rode the wagons could have ever dreamed that eventually the Rockies would be easily jumped by planes, far faster than they could get from one outpost to the next. Nevertheless, the pioneers plodded on, driven by a vision of a better life.

The history of the United States has been one of unparalleled progress, of replacement and refinement, of upward and onward, of living out the dreams of untold Americans, many of whom, before their passing, had concluded that their lives were better than their wildest dreams. Playwright George Bernard Shaw no doubt captured the world view of many ordinary but hardy American souls when he wrote, "You see things and say, why? But I dream things that never were and say, why not?"

Shaw's more important question—"Why not?"—has been parroted by presidents who wanted to make a point with eloquence, but it has also been thought, albeit with less eloquence, by hordes of Americans who unknowingly have asked "Why not?" when they refused to be slowed by the tried-and-true, the known, the safe. The country's history has been infused with a remarkable "can do" attitude that was always bolstered by dreams of "better," if not "bigger"—or, more recently for many things, "smaller" and "more powerful."

Dreams of better days in a more progressive, prosperous, and "just society" have always inspired Americans, even when the cold reality of current events might have prompted despair. Just as the country was being formed, Benjamin Franklin reflected on its likely future in a letter to George Washington:

> I must soon quit the Scene, but you may live to see our country flourish, as it will amazingly and rapidly after the war is over. Like a field of young Indian corn, which long fair weather and Sunshine had enfeebled and discolored, and which in that weak State, by a Thunder Gust, of violent wind, hail, and rain, seem'd to be threaten'd with

> absolute destruction; yet the storm being past, it recovers fresh verdure, shoots up with double vigour, and delights the eye, not of its owner only, but of every observing Traveler.[9]

Franklin was a dreamer for his times, just as poet Carl Sandburg was for a generation of Americans during this century:

> I see America, not in the setting sun of a black night of despair ahead of us, I see America in the crimson light of a rising sun fresh from the burning, creative hand of God. I see great days ahead, great days possible to men and women of will and vision.[10]

Clearly, there are those who describe the American Dream in terms of what can be bought—a house, a car, a chicken in every pot, and so forth. But *the* American Dream seems to have been far more fundamental, namely, *a predisposition to think that current conditions are not enduring, that times will get better, if only we seek to make them so.*

The Importance of Aspirations

We always live on the precipice of time, tied to a known past of ups and downs, failures and successes, always lurching forward into a future that is not so well known and can never be known with great precision. Practically the only reason that we would ever do things differently and better in the future than we have done in the past is that we have some unease, some feeling of and need for improvement, and some sense of how that improvement can be exacted. Dreams and aspirations are crucial to our development as individuals and as a nation because they are the necessary links between the known past and the unknown future. Dreams render untold futures possible (but never certain), at least in the mind. They let us see where we *could* go. They afford us the opportunity to compare where we have been with where we are going. Dreams energize the "pursuit of happiness." Because dreams always seem to render the future better than the past, they give us the drive to lurch forward with purpose, if not zest—when, in fact, we know that we would have to fall forward into the march of time no matter what.

Of course, not all American dreams have come true, but the fact that

9. In a letter to George Washington, March 5, 1780, included in *The Writings of Benjamin Franklin,* ed. Albert H. Smyth, vol. 8, p. 29 (1907).

10. Carl Sandburg, interview with Frederick Van Ryn, *This Week Magazine*, January 4, 1953, p. 11. Sandburg had used these words previously at a rally at Madison Square Garden, New York City, October 28, 1952, praising Adlai E. Stevenson during his 1952 presidential campaign (*The Papers of Adlai E. Stevenson,* vol. 4, p. 175 [1955]).

not all dreams are realized and some end up as nightmares does not diminish their importance to the history of individuals or the country. Dreams of some collide with the dreams of others, which means that our dreams must be continually adjusted to the stark reality of what has been shown to be possible. At the same time, it is in the multitude of the adjustments that we make with one another as we work together and apart that our futures can indeed be better than we could possibly have imagined. We fail frequently (or, even more frequently, do not meet with the success that is imagined) as we charge ahead, but with dreams we can put what comes—failures and successes—in a broader context, look for the balance, and seek ways of adjusting our courses for the better, with determination that we can still be on track. Sometimes, when we are truly fortunate, our lurching forward yields discoveries, valuable serendipities, that we could not have made had we not charged ahead.

Martin Luther King, Jr., electrified the masses gathered at the Lincoln Memorial one sweltering August day in 1963, when he eloquently acknowledged America's shortcomings but declared he still had a dream of going to the top of a mountain and seeing the Promised Land:

> I have a dream that one day this nation will rise up and live out the true meaning of its creed: "We hold these truths to be self-evident, that all men are created equal." . . . I have a dream that my four little children will one day live in a nation where they will not be judged by the color of their skin but by the content of their character. I have a dream today.[11]

It was the idea that dreaming of doing better despite dreadful and uncertain circumstances that caused the crowds on that August day to roar approval and that continues to cause Americans to push forward.

Jesse Owens, a black man from humble beginnings who wanted to be "the fastest man in the world, the greatest runner" and who dared to beat Hitler's best in footraces and broad jumps during the 1936 Olympics held in Berlin, was fortunate to have a coach to remind him:

> You must have a dream and a ladder to that dream.
> 1st rung is DETERMINATION
> 2nd rung is DEDICATION
> 3rd rung is DISCIPLINE
> 4th rung is ATTITUDE
> The first three rungs are important, but the fourth rung is vital.

11. Martin Luther King, Jr., "I Have a Dream" [speech delivered at the Lincoln Memorial, Washington, D.C., August 28, 1963], *Congressional Record,* April 18, 1968, vol. 114, p. 9165.

Dreams, after all, are not important because they are mere casual nighttime hallucinations that are unchecked, unbounded, and undirected. Fanciful nighttime dreams are rarely memorable beyond the waking hours. Rather, dreams befitting the dubbing of the American Dream become important when they impose an "attitude" on those who dream and who, at the same time, have the requisite determination, dedication, and discipline to pursue them. Franklin had the required attitude. King had it. Certainly, Jesse Owens had it.

Those in our history whose dreams have counted understood that dreaming meant more than twiddling thumbs, waiting for imagined ends to come true. Dreaming meant an attitude that would cause a person to make imagined results happen, in spite of all else that would deny their happening. Successful dreaming implied an obligation to be resourceful, determined, dedicated, and disciplined. Maybe too many Americans are seeking to climb Owens's ladder without remembering to step on each rung. All four rungs make the ladder worthy of the metaphor. When brave Americans signed their declaration of independence, a prosperous future was hardly guaranteed. Granted, a continent of untapped resources awaited exploration, but the resources would never be tapped by themselves. Many of the "resources" would not even be thought of as such until someone could conceive of a use for them and then do what was necessary to make use of them. But untapped resources seems a weak explanation for the widespread shift from the optimism of yesteryears to the pessimism of today. The untapped resources available and accessible to some of the poorest Americans today are surely greater than those available and accessible to most Americans, even the affluent ones, long ago. Recognizing such simple facts is a prerequisite for any reasonable reassessment of the country's future.

Many Americans appear to believe that they are being tested as no other generation has. That is pure folly—for most. Hurdles have abounded for previous generations of Americans. In colonial times, the economic standard that is now thought to reduce a person to poverty was befitting an upper-class living standard. The average living standards of most Americans in the late eighteenth century were surely lower (albeit modestly so) than the prevailing living standards of the people they left behind on the continent an ocean away.[12] By today's living standards, virtually all Americans then lived in abject poverty. After all, America was a "new world," which in less glamorous terms

12. See Alice Hanson Jones, *Wealth of a Nation to Be* (New York: Columbia University Press, 1980), chap. 3.

meant a third-world country. Dirt and disease were constant companions. Life was clearly tough and all too frequently short.

The life expectancy at the turn of the nineteenth century is not recorded. However, we do know that in the middle of the nineteenth century the life expectancy of male and female babies was, respectively, thirty-eight and forty years—*after the sciences of medicine and nutrition had improved markedly for half a century.* What are minor medical problems today (for example, appendicitis and even the common cold) could have been death warrants for early Americans. Births were the gravest of all times for both mother and child. The medical and nutrition sciences, of course, continued to improve after the mid-nineteenth century, but even by the turn of the twentieth century, life expectancy of babies of either sex had not yet reached fifty. American pessimists need to be reminded that not too long ago, times were much tougher. That transparent fact lends much needed perspective.

When the country was first organized, many probably dreamed only of staying well and having enough food in the pantry to get them through the winters. We have no solid data on living standards in colonial times, only rough estimates. The fact that many Americans had bigger thoughts of a brighter future is remarkable in itself, not to mention what they accomplished. According to historians' best estimates, in the period 1710 to 1720 annual income per capita in the colonies was probably between $600 and $900 (measured in prices of the mid-1990s), and things had probably not progressed very much by the late eighteenth century.[13] In short, today's poverty income "threshold" for a single person (below which one is officially defined to be poor) is approximately one-third of today's personal income per capita. At the time of the signing of the Declaration of Independence, however, the "average" Americans had real incomes probably no higher than one-seventeenth of today's average income—*one-sixth of today's poverty income threshold, which means that few Americans at the time of the signing were above today's poverty income threshold.*[14]

13. See Lance E. Davis et al., *American Economic Growth: An Economist's History of the United States* (New York: Harper and Row, 1972), pp. 20–21, who cites George Rogers Taylor, "American Economic Growth Before 1840: An Exploratory Essay," *Journal of Economic History* (December 1964): 427–44.

14. Alice Hanson Jones has estimated that in 1974 Americans had "real incomes per capita around 12 to 13 times as great as 200 years ago" (*Wealth of a Nation to Be,* p. 72). (Gross domestic product per capita increased by close to a third between 1974 and the mid-1990s. If incomes per capita increased by approximately the same percentage, then Americans' income per capita in 1995 was just under 17 times the level of 1774, the basis of Jones's comparison.)

Some Americans fret that our problem is lack of rapid economic growth. Maybe so, but can that be the whole story? Total national production expanded greatly between the first quarter of the eighteenth century and 1800, but only because of the rapid growth in the number of Americans, not because of rapid increases in output per person. In that early era, output per person may have grown by as little as three-tenths of a percent per year and no more than half of a percent per year, indeed meager growth rates when compared with the growth rates of the country one and two centuries later.[15] Nonetheless, in those early years economic growth during a fairly long stretch of time was, apparently, never slow enough for long enough to suppress dreams of a brighter future.

After close to a century of relatively rapid overall economic growth, national output per person in the United States in the 1868 to 1878 period was (measured in terms of 1995 prices) probably still under $2,500 a year, perhaps three to four times the average income of the late 1700s. This means that the "average" American family of four would, in the late 1800s, be living on an income equal to no more than 60 percent of today's official poverty income level. Furthermore, even achieving the below-poverty incomes, no doubt, required Americans at the turn of the century to spend far more hours at work (upward of 50 percent more) than contemporary Americans must now spend to achieve much higher incomes. Moreover, the quality of goods and services available at the turn of the century was substantially inferior to the goods and services that can be purchased today. The difference in quality then and now is apparent when it is realized that indoor plumbing was rarely found in homes even a hundred years ago, and even most dreadfully poor people today have running water and flushing toilets.[16]

When thinking of life in early America, it may be understandable that many contemporary Americans think of the pleasant life that George Washington lived at Mount Vernon or that Thomas Jefferson lived at Monticello, but those palatial living conditions were only rarely duplicated elsewhere. In the last half of the eighteenth century, Americans had, on average, incomes that would yield living standards prevalently found today in poverty-stricken Bangladesh. After a century of progress,

15. Davis, *American Economic Growth*, p. 22 (table 2.1).

16. In 1890, the average workweek in manufacturing was over sixty hours; the average workweek in 1992 was forty-one hours [as reported in Executive Office of the President, *Economic Report of the President: 1993* (Washington: Government Printing Office, February 1993), p. 396; and Department of Commerce, Bureau of the Census, *Historical Statistics of the United States: Colonial Times to 1970* (Washington: Government Printing Office, 1975), p. 172].

in the middle of the nineteenth century, Americans had living standards that may have afforded them the living conditions commonly found today in Mexico or Pakistan. But Americans still dreamed of doing better.

Today, social analysts and policy commentators fret that the cause of continued poverty is poverty itself. The poor have so little income, the analysts and commentators tell us, that they cannot possibly save and invest for the future. Because they cannot save and invest, the poor cannot get out of poverty. Poor parents are often poorly educated, a fact that causes many to reason that poor people do not know how to help with the education of their children, and they certainly don't have the incomes to pay others to supplement their children's education in underfunded and ill-equipped public schools crowded with other poor children. Dropouts literally breed dropouts. Poverty gives rise to its own progeny, or so the "cycle of poverty" argument goes.

There is more than an ounce of truth to what the critics argue (poverty has never made advancement easy), but there is also more than a pound of misdirection to the claims. If the critics' arguments were as sound as supposed, we must wonder how this country ever developed. The first immigrants should have remained mired in poverty. Almost all were poorer than today's poor families. Many were poorly educated (although many had important skills, honed in their home countries) by the standards of their day. Clearly, growth in the American economy was spurred by many favorable conditions, for example, a tremendous amount of fertile but uncultivated land at a time when agriculture dominated economic life. But there must have been something other than a relative abundance of key resources at the disposal of earlier Americans. What to do with all the resources the wilderness contained was a question that, at the time, had no ready-made answers. People had to develop the answers by taking the necessary initiative.

Granted, today's rich and poor alike face a daunting economic "wilderness" covered, in places, with bewilderingly sophisticated production techniques. However, even the poor have many favorable economic conditions, not the least of which is a social safety net that can cushion their falls if, or when, they fail. Fertile land may be beyond their reach, but land is no longer important to most of the likely pursuits the poor might consider. Furthermore, many other resources crucial to modern production (not the least of which are computer chips) are no less readily available than was fertile land a century ago. Indeed, many important resources are cheaper today (especially when compared with incomes) than were the important resources a half century ago, and they are getting cheaper, relentlessly.

Loss of Power

If progress has continued for so long, what then is the source of the angst? An important part of the answer is that Americans today are being confronted, as are other peoples around the world, with some new realities, namely a loss of power of former economic power centers—governments as well as business and labor organizations—to control economic and social events.

After World War II, America ruled supreme. The United States was then the chief economic and military power in the world. Granted, many people were convinced that the Great Depression, during which a quarter of the labor force was unemployed and national production plummeted to two-thirds its previous peak, would be revisited. Most thought that the transition from a defense-based economy would be difficult and long. Few realized the extent of the domestic and international pent-up demand for goods and services Americans could not buy during the war. Most understood that the European and Japanese economies had been devastated by the war, with factories and office towers across those lands in shambles, but many did not realize the extent to which Americans would be called upon to feed and rebuild both the defeated and victorious countries.

Contrary to common expectations, the American economy took off after World War II with barely a detectable recession, fueled by both domestic and foreign demand. The economic expansion continued throughout the 1950s and 1960s with only four minor and short-lived downturns. Real worker wages rose in line with unbroken productivity growth. The country's major firms could, with a degree of confidence, call many of the economic shots in their markets. U.S. firms had reason to believe that they could extend their economic clout by simply extending their scale and scope of operations, controlling themselves by the techniques of "scientific management." Former Harvard economist John Kenneth Galbraith could, in the 1950s and 1960s, wax eloquently about the emergence of the "new industrial state," or how the 500 or so largest firms in the country could manage their markets to maximize the profits of their stockholders. Governments had to gain power, according to Galbraith and his followers, to countervail against the growing power of corporations.

Moreover, the intellectuals and policy practitioners seriously believed, following the theories of John Maynard Keynes, that the federal government could manage the national economy, smoothing out the business cycles with higher growth rates resulting (if investment were stimulated with the proper mix of fiscal and monetary policies). If industries didn't do what the government wanted, then the government could simply force the industries to do what was in the national purpose through some new regulatory scheme. Government could also, or so many came to believe in the 1960s, regulate the distribution of income through a variety of poverty and social relief programs. Poverty could be whipped under the banner of the "Great Society." If the Soviets wanted to engage the country in a space race, we could take the challenge and beat them hands down. Firms expanded to the level of multinationals. Governments at all levels expanded rapidly in real dollars and as a percentage of gross domestic product through the 1970s. Those were heady times, perhaps too much so.

However, the tide of national confidence began to turn in the 1960s. Some ill-equipped foreign troops running around the Vietnamese jungle proved to everyone that our military power was not all powerful. The Vietnam War had been an obvious drag on the U.S. economy for years, and the drag became more onerous in the first few years of the 1970s. The military buildup in Vietnam exacted an obvious toll on the ability of the American economy to produce consumable goods and services. The growing domestic dissension over the war meant that more Americans were manning the antiwar demonstrations and fewer were hitting their books and manning their workstations. In the early 1970s, America was a nation divided on many fronts. Wage growth suffered, without much question, as a consequence. Perhaps the national unity, and sense of collective national will, suffered as well. The country lost a measure of control over its fate.

By the 1970s, the dictates of Keynesian economics had proven unproductive, perhaps counterproductive, in regulating the national business cycles. Politicians had begun to pervert Keynesian economics, using its policy prescriptions—lower taxes and increased spending to stimulate the economy—as a means of running up federal deficits, of spending more than was collected in taxes. Inflation began to mount and, by the late 1970s, seemed to be spiraling out of control.

In August 1971, then President Richard Nixon sought to control the prices of practically all goods and services in the American economy in the vain hope that he could suppress the escalating pace of inflation (which, incidentally, was running at only the modest annual rate of less than 5 percent during the first half of 1971). The price controls that were retained through various phases of decontrol until the late 1970s served only to disrupt many people's economic plans and to impose unnecessary hardships on many Americans, especially those who found their costs had risen but who could not raise their prices. Without question, many precious resources in the early 1970s were diverted from truly productive uses, such as research and construction, to truly wasteful purposes of dealing legally and illegally with the official price controls—and with escalating inflation rates that continued in spite of them. The message of the control efforts was simple: No one really knew how to control economic events.

The Organization of Petroleum Exporting Countries (OPEC) compounded the country's adjustment problems in the early 1970s by organizing its first oil embargo with the intent of driving up the price of the energy that had been propelling the growth of all western economies, not just the American economy. The OPEC oil embargo was surely grounded in the efforts of a relatively small group of countries, which controlled a lion's share of the world's known oil reserves, to flex their monopoly muscle.[17]

The oil embargo hurt the American economy by reducing the availability of a cheap source of energy that literally fueled economic growth, but the American policy response compounded the harm. The additional energy price controls and rationing systems that were subsequently put into force, all in the name of preventing price-gouging (and not totally abandoned until the 1980s), ensured that the supply of energy and economic growth would be curbed more than necessary, given the actions of OPEC. Many Americans realized then that their livelihoods were vulnerable to foreign forces that did not have to invade the usual way, with guns, tanks, and planes. Foreigners could subdue the country, at least partially, through the impairment of the economy and the draining of the nation's income through price increases.

Beginning in the 1970s, major American firms began to falter when faced with foreign competition. By the mid-1980s, Galbraith's theories appeared silly. Large firms were no longer growing; many were radically downsizing, cutting tens of thousands of jobs at a time. Gargantuan firms were being controlled by the very markets they were supposed to dominate. The "new industrial state" was being reengineered. Labor unions were becoming more or less inconsequential in controlling the fate of their workers. Instead, the fate of unions was being contained by international competitive forces.

17. As *Wall Street Journal* editor Robert Bartley argues, OPEC's efforts to raise the price of oil were probably also related to the freeing of the dollar in 1971, after which the OPEC countries saw the purchasing power of a barrel of oil extracted from their underground reserves fall by half (*Seven Fat Years* [New York: Free Press, 1992], pp. 31–33).

By the 1980s, many government efforts to relieve social problems had proven to be unproductive—if not as counterproductive as Keynesian economics was in solving business cycle problems. The hundreds of billions of dollars spent on trying to pull the poor out of their dire straits may have been contributing to the breakdown of the last vestiges of control by families and communities on what people, especially the young, do. The heady days of the late 1940s, 1950s, and 1960s came to an end with the recognition that people and governments were no longer in charge of unfolding economic and social events, but were being controlled by detached, unseen, untouchable, and hard-to-quantify forces of the global economy. In turn, the global economy was being driven by technological developments that had lives of their own, not controllable by individual or collective actions.

Clearly, we live in an "age of diminished expectations," as Stanford economist Paul Krugman argues, but only because we have just passed through an era of exaggerated and unsustainable expectations.[18] This line of argument has more recently been developed at length by *Washington Post* columnist Robert Samuelson.[19] Our expectations must be tempered by the circumstances we face, but that is not to say that we can't expect more progress. Paradoxically, the power lost by former economic power centers has not been gained by new centers; the power has been dissipated. However, new economic opportunities and more growth can be seen in the dissipation of economic power.

Concluding Comments

It should now be apparent that I don't share the dreadful outlook for the American economy that has been carefully crafted by legions of writers and speakers. A part of my optimism has arisen from my investigation of a number of the pessimistic claims regarding America's economic past and future, many of the results of which have been published elsewhere and are surveyed with extensions in following chapters.[20] In chapter 2, I seek to demonstrate how difficult it is for contemporary commentators to accurately predict the future by going back a hundred years and examining the predictions that commentators of the 1890s made for the 1990s.

18. Paul Krugman, *Peddling Prosperity: Economic Sense and Nonsense in the Age of Diminished Expectations* (New York: Norton, 1994).

19. Robert Samuelson, *The Good Life and Its Discontents* (New York: Times Books, 1995).

20. See McKenzie, *What Went Right in the 1980s.* Chapter 3 is primarily concerned with the history of progress of the last couple of decades.

The pessimists were way off base. Progress abounded. The optimists were not optimistic enough. In many important regards, the forthcoming progress exceeded their fondest expectations. The most serious error made is that human nature did not improve as predicted, but much progress occurred anyway, in spite of human nature becoming arguably worse.

I then consider in chapter 3 more recent claims regarding America's supposedly dismal economic performance in recent times to determine if the claims have merit (or to what extent they do) and if the country's future might be impaired, as claimed, because of the current dismal economic conditions. Pessimists often stress that America's future will necessarily be less prosperous than its past simply because it no longer has the necessary expansion room, or more to the point of the complaint: The country no longer has an unsettled and unexploited West. In chapters 4 and 5, I seek to put such claims in perspective, suggesting that while our unsettled western territories may have been important to our past economic development, the importance of the West to U.S. development was probably exaggerated by historians. Moreover, we must recognize that the country now has, by virtue of technology, a whole slew of "wests" to explore and develop. Indeed, it may never have been easier for young people in America to "go west," metaphorically speaking.

The U.S. is hardly without problems, and the core causes of a number of its more serious social and economic problems are duly noted. Americans will have to continue to adjust to new conditions and problems as they always have. Many of our problems are new, as will become evident in discussions of the forces of "economic tectonics" and "moral tectonics" covered in chapters 6, 7, and 8. I show that much of the angst today has emerged because old institutions, especially governments, are being forced to redefine themselves to accommodate the persistent and powerful technological and economic forces afoot in the world. In the "old America," it might have been reasonable to say that politics molded economic forces in the country; it is far more accurate today to say that economic forces are molding politics, gradually but relentlessly. In the process, Americans (and for that matter, Germans, Chinese, and Australians) are having to resurrect and fortify the principles of individual and group responsibility. Like it or not, Americans will have to accept the fact that decision making—and the benefits and costs that go with it—are gradually being devolved to more and more local levels, even back to the individual where it was a century or more ago. In the concluding chapter, I argue that much contemporary American angst emerges from the most peculiar of all sources: too many opportunities, not too few, that will inevitably spring from a growing authority of individuals to "do their own thing."

From all of the investigations covered here and elsewhere, I have learned a number of valuable lessons:

1. People—especially public commentators and scholars—tend to exaggerate the negative and overlook the positive in the economic data. Bad news sells well; good news is suppressed for what the writers believe are good journalistic and political reasons, or so it seems.
2. The economic record does not square with general perceptions. Times *could be* better for many Americans, but they *have never been better* for a substantial majority of Americans. To appropriate the title of a perceptive report on the recent economic record, "these are the good old days"—no matter what you think and no matter what you may have heard to the contrary.[21]
3. Widely accepted explanations for the deeply felt contemporary American angst are, accordingly, misleading, if not downright wrong. Contrary to conventional wisdom, the overwhelming majority of contemporary Americans have not retrogressed economically, and they will continue to move forward on economic fronts in the future. Hence, we need to look for more fundamental explanations.
4. No one has ever predicted the future very well, or else we would hardly be living in the luxury of a $7 trillion economy. Progress has almost always been more profound and uplifting than the greatest minds of the day may have thought. The predictions that commentators in the 1890s made about what life would be like in the 1990s were wide off the mark. As chapter 2 shows, those commentators were optimistic about the country's economic future, but they were still not optimistic enough. I remain convinced that in the 2090s, the commentators of that day will smile at the prevailing pessimism of today, wondering why we could not have anticipated that the future would be as bright as it actually turned out to be.
5. Paradoxically, the contemporary angst can be—should be—seen as an engine of future progress. As argued, much of the angst Americans feel is grounded in fundamental technological global changes

21. Michael Cox and Richard Alm, *These Are the Good Old Days: A Report on the American Living Standard* (Dallas: Federal Reserve Bank of Dallas, 1994).

in the world that have greatly increased the complexity of our future, which means the global changes have made our future much less knowable and much more uncertain in terms of its exact content for the current generation. But such observations do not mean that people will not find ways to exploit the complicated opportunities at hand. Through a multitude of unexpected discoveries and adjustments Americans will make with one another and with people around the globe, the future will unfold, far more complex and sophisticated and prosperous than anyone can now imagine, partly because people have been driven to find their way carefully into the uncertain and risk-filled future.

Admittedly, my optimism applies to *most* Americans. I have stressed "most" for a very good reason: Not everyone will share in the coming prosperity. Many Americans will continue to whine about their current hardship; and in the process, they will allow other Americans and people from around the globe to gain a substantial competitive advantage. Some will need a simple adjustment in their attitude and outlook. One of the more important threats to the economic vitality of other segments of the citizenry will remain the tendency of some groups (some subcultures that are no longer defined by low incomes) to discard the tried-and-true rules of decent and reasonable behavior in favor of the immediate gains that can come from breaking the "rules of the game" that necessarily hold economies, if not whole societies, together and make progress possible. These groups of Americans may very well continue to languish in difficulties as others continue to develop their global networks among people who recognize the need for constraining rules of reasonable behavior. The great division between the "haves" and "have nots" of the future will not likely be so much dependent on just how much income people now have but on just what kind of rules, if any, they are willing to accept and to concede some semblance of reasonable allegiance.

More than ever, most Americans need now to be disabused of the mythology of "bad times." The *ladder* that Jesse Owens grabbed is out there for the climbing. However, Americans—we—also need to be reminded that they—we—need to stop the whining and do the climbing. We will reach higher rungs if we climb by design, which is our choice, than if we climb by default.

2

❑ ❑ ❑ ❑ ❑ ❑ ❑ ❑ ❑ ❑ ❑ ❑ ❑ ❑ ❑

BACK TO THE FUTURE IN THE 1890s

> The next 100 years will develop changes more stupendous than have been shown by the last 100 years—in which pretty nearly every useful thing there is in the world has been invented.
>
> Charles Foster, cited in Dave Walter, *Will Man Fly? And Other Strange and Wonderful Predictions from the 1890s*

> The chief discoveries of the late Twentieth Century will consist in producing fire out of water, silver out of clay, strong and permanent buildings out of paper, a locomotive force out of gravity, diamonds out of charcoal—and making it always possible (because profitable) for an intelligent person to travel.
>
> Van Buren Denslow, cited in Dave Walter, *Will Man Fly? And Other Strange and Wonderful Predictions from the 1890s*

WHAT WILL the world be like 100 years from now? That's a tough question, but it is one that many contemporary Americans might answer with a sense of gloom, "Not very good." The question was posed to noted American commentators in the early 1890s, and their answers were surprisingly upbeat.

As happened to be the case when the question was asked, the World's Columbian Exposition, which showcased the technological marvels of the day, was scheduled to open in Chicago in May 1893. In anticipation of the opening, the American Press Association of New York City asked seventy-four prominent Americans of very diverse occupations—including theologians, humorists, politicians, journalists, and poets—to predict what life would be like in America in the 1990s. Their essays were carried in many of the country's major daily newspapers and in hundreds of weekly newspapers. Understandably, most of their predictions were wide off the mark; that is, we now live in a world that is far more advanced on a technological scale and far less advanced on a human scale than the commentators anticipated a century ago.

The gap between the commentators' best predictions and the reality we live ought to bring home an important lesson to contemporary Americans: *Times are now better than anyone ever thought they would be.* That fact might, just might, lead many to think that the future will be better than we can now imagine, in spite of all the supposed gloomy evidence to the contrary.

The State of the Nation in the 1890s

The assigned task of predicting the broad outlines, if not the details, of the future was open-ended, made daring by the transitional nature of the world and nation in the 1890s. The industrialized world had experienced a century of unprecedented economic expansion, during which the American economy grew at an average annual rate of more than 3 percent, meaning it expanded from an economy that was much smaller than the economies of European countries to one that was their rival. The "manifest destiny" of the United States once implied that the country would inevitably extend to the edges of the continent. In the late nineteenth century, the concept was gradually beginning to mean that the country had a national interest that extended beyond its northern and southern borders. By 1890, the United States had become a world power, yet it was not "fully grown," absolutely and relatively. Indeed, over the next seventy years, the United States would ratify statehood for four more contiguous states and two territories: Utah (1896), Oklahoma (1907), New Mexico (1912), Arizona (1912), Alaska (1959), and Hawaii (1959).

Two circumstances accounted for most of the economic growth in the nineteenth century: First, the national population had expanded fourteen-fold over the previous century. Second, technology had taken several leaps forward, as was evident by the several thousand-fold growth in the number of patents issued during the 1800s (from practically nothing in 1800 to more than 2,000 in 1850 to over 25,000 in 1890).[1]

1. See Department of Commerce, Bureau of the Census, *Historical Statistics of the United States: Colonial Times to 1970* (Washington: Government Printing Office, 1975), p. 959.

Many of the writers had witnessed the improvement and expanded use of the steam engine and also understood that the country's economic advance had been aided by many smaller developments. These included the invention of the cotton gin (1794), photograph (1820s), reaper (1831), and sewing machine (1851), not to mention what may appear to be minor advancements on the scale of the friction match (1827), steel-tipped plow (1838), saxophone (1846), adhesive postage stamp (1847), ice cream (1851), safety catch for elevators (1852), refrigeration system (1859), Pony Express (1860), cylinder lock (1861), paper clip (1870s), and fountain pen (1884).

At the opening ceremony for the Columbian Exposition, which ran for only six months, President Grover Cleveland pressed a button in Washington that started the machinery in Chicago, a marvel in itself. The exposition, which commemorated the four-hundredth anniversary of Columbus's Atlantic crossing, spotlighted the technological prowess of Americans, as revealed in the 260-foot Ferris wheel, the cylinder phonograph, and carbonated soft drinks that were on display for the 27 million visitors. At the time of the exposition, the first automobile powered by an internal-combustion engine had been built (1885), but "horseless carriages" were still rare. A decade would pass before Orville Wright, one of two brothers in the bicycle business (who didn't become interested in flying until 1896), would fly on December 17, 1903.

Over the preceding 100 years, the American economy had begun to shift dramatically away from its agrarian roots to an industrial base, but manufacturing employment still represented only 19 percent of the total labor force in 1890 (up from 3 percent in 1810 and 15 percent in 1850). In 1890, agriculture continued to provide jobs for 43 percent of working Americans.[2] (In the mid-1990s, by contrast, agricultural workers represented less than 3 percent of all American employees.)

Obviously, the industrialization of the American economy was not yet complete in 1890, but the trends were evident in the shift in the output shares of agriculture and manufacturing. Between 1839 and 1889, agricultural output as a share of total national output dropped from 72 percent to 33 percent, not because the country was producing fewer crops, but because the rest of the economy was growing relatively more rapidly. Manufacturing output rose during the same period from a 17 percent share of national output to 48 percent.[3]

The 100-year epoch that ended in 1890 stood witness to an equally

2. Ibid., p. 139.

3. See Robert E. Gallman, "Commodity Output: 1839–1889," in *Trends in the American Economy in the 19th Century*, ed. William Parker (New York: National Bureau of Economic Research, 1960), p. 26.

dramatic change in the outlooks of many noted thinkers. At the onset of the nineteenth century, many great minds shared dreadful visions of humankind's future, following the lead of the Reverend Thomas Robert Malthus. In 1798, he had postulated population growth would always tend to outstrip a country's capacity to feed its citizens. Such circumstances would press worker wages toward the subsistence level. If wages were ever to rise above subsistence, unchecked human sexual proclivities would lead inevitably to a growth in population, a greater supply of workers, and, once again, greater downward pressures on wages. Ultimately, population growth would be retarded only by pestilence and starvation. People in the future would obey the laws evident within "savage life," according to the Reverend Malthus:

> When population has increased nearly to the utmost limits of the food, all the preventive and the positive checks will naturally operate with increased force. Vicious habits with respect to the sex will be more general, the exposing of children more frequent, and both the probability and fatality of wars and epidemics will be considerably greater; and these causes will probably continue their operation till the population is sunk below the level of the food; and then the return to comparative plenty will again produce an increase, and, after a certain period, its further progress will again be checked by the same causes.[4]

Karl Marx found this view so congenial that he predicted, in the mid-nineteenth century, a proletariat revolution and then sought to encourage just such an event.

Predicting ultimate economic calamity was as popular among the leading thinkers of the nineteenth century as it has come to be in the late twentieth century. For example, in the last quarter of the twentieth century, our media has been filled with laments that the world is running out of energy, specifically petroleum, mainly because the Organization of Petroleum Exporting Countries curbed its members' oil production in the early 1970s.

Gloomy assessments regarding the future of oil can be traced back much further. In 1891, the U.S. Geological Survey concluded that oil would never be found in Texas. President Theodore Roosevelt echoed a common prediction in 1905: "If the present rate of [petroleum] consumption is allowed to continue . . . a [petroleum] famine is inevitable."[5] In

4. Thomas Robert Malthus, *On Population* (New York: Modern Library, 1960), pp. 164–65.

5. As quoted in Charles Maurice and Charles W. Smithson, *The Doomsday Myth: 10,000 Years of Economic Crisis* (Standord, Calif.: Hoover Institution Press, 1984), p. xv.

1926, the Federal Oil Conservation Board was adamant that the United States had only seven years of oil reserve left. In 1939, the Interior Department predicted that the country would run out of oil in two decades; ten years later, it claimed that U.S. energy supplies were just about gone.[6]

The country's first "oil crisis" had nothing to do with petroleum. In the mid-1800s, a whale-oil crisis arose as the price of whale oil skyrocketed, and doomsayers were convinced that economic calamity was just around the corner, given the widespread dependence of people on whale oil for light, cooking, and heating. The crisis was ameliorated by crude-oil exploration that resulted in bringing in the first successful oil well (August 27, 1859, in Titusville, Pennsylvania, where oil was found in commercial quantities at a depth of only 69 feet). Around the turn of the twentieth century, the country had a timber crisis because rapidly expanding railroads had absorbed 25 percent of the U.S. timber supply for their crossties. When the last tree was cut, the country would surely go into a tailspin—because then trains could not run and houses could not be built—or so the critics of the day mistakenly thought.[7]

It appears that most Americans paid little heed to the doomsayers, however, in spite of the reoccurring bank panics and recessions and fears about the unknown economy. Instead, they diligently went about their business, responding to the economic incentives close at hand, making a living, finding or developing substitutes for the resources that were becoming progressively scarcer—and, in the process, proving the great thinkers woefully wrong: "The genius of this new country is necessarily mechanical. Our greatest thinkers are not in the library, nor the capitol, but in the machine shop. The American people are intent on studying, not the hieroglyphic monuments of ancient genius, but how best to subdue and till the soil of its boundless territories; how to build roads and ships; how to apply the powers of nature to the work of manufacturing its rich materials into forms of utility and enjoyment."[8] From 1890 to 1990, the number of patents has risen fourfold, from 25,000 to just under 100,000 (with 177,000 patent applications pending).[9]

6. Ibid., p. 12.

7. See Maurice and Smithson, *Doomsday Myth.*

8. J. Milton Mackie, *From Cape to Dixie and the Tropics* (New York: G. P. Putnam, 1864), p. 201; as cited in Lance E. Davis et al., *American Economic Growth: An Economist's History of the United States* (New York: Harper and Row, 1972), p. 244.

9. Department of Commerce, Bureau of the Census, *Statistical Abstract of the United States: 1992* (Washington: Government Printing Office, 1992), p. 535.

The Predicted State of the Nation in the 1990s

The generally upbeat mood of the 1890s was fully evident in the predictions of the seventy-four noted commentators. For example, one commentator who claimed to be both a minister and a cinematographer accurately predicted that medicine in the 1990s would achieve the exalted status of a science after "having passed through the period of preliminary experiment."[10] Another commentator, a theologian, predicted that the science of medicine would progress so rapidly that by 1990 a life span of 150 years "will be no unusual age to reach."[11]

Many of the commentators were convinced that by the 1990s human nature would be radically reformed and uplifted. In spite of millenniums of historical experience, an Episcopal bishop was confident that in another 100 years people would have learned to trust their fellow countrymen. Another commentator believed that "free and indiscriminate charity" would fade and give way to concealed aid that would cultivate self-respect and self-reliance. Many expected that by 1990 racial and religious prejudice would have been "destroyed," and it was held that labor–management conflicts would dissolve as the Golden Rule was adopted more widely in all economic spheres of life.[12]

The commentators' optimism was evident in their predictions that technology would continue to advance at an ever-faster pace, to the point that the sixteen-hour workday would be reduced to three hours with more benefits than had been received for sixteen hours in 1890. Supposedly, crime would be abolished, because criminals would be prohibited from "propagating their kind," and there would be no need for capital punishment.[13]

A shortage of trained servants was (apparently) a significant social and economic problem of the 1890s, a thought that is almost laughable in the 1990s. A poet confidently predicted that the "servant problem" would be solved by the government establishing colleges to train servants who would, as a consequence, be "more useful, better content, and more respectful and respected." A humorist who was asked to comment may have put the problem in better perspective, however, when he quipped

10. Thomas Dixon, Jr., quoted in *Will Man Fly? And Other Strange and Wonderful Predictions from the 1890s*, ed. Dave Walter (American & World Geographic Publishing, 1993), p. 10.

11. Thomas De Witt Talmage, quoted in ibid., p. 8.

12. Talmage, quoted in ibid., pp. 11–14.

13. Ella Wheeler Wilcox, quoted in ibid., pp. 20–21.

that the servant problem would remain unchanged: "Hell."[14] An economic analyst obviously came closer to the true evolution of the servant problem by predicting that servants would be supplanted by the 1990s by unspecified technologies. He predicted the "servants" of the 1990s would be turned on and off by the push of buttons.[15] (He left us to wonder if what he had in mind was anything like the dishwashers and bread machines or even the robots that are in use today.)

Several of the commentators quite accurately predicted that the costs of communicating would be lowered as modes became more convenient, improved, and more widespread. The country's postmaster general, who was one of the seventy-four commentators, predicted that the price of a stamp would fall to 2 cents (which, in 1995 dollars, was 3 cents less than the cost of a first-class stamp today, 32 cents). A naturalist predicted mail delivery by "penumatic tubes," which were a notable invention of the day in the early 1890s.[16] A poet predicted that people and goods would be moved from place to place, possibly from coast to coast, in pneumatic tubes.[17]

Most of the commentators envisioned people traveling at speeds greater than 100 miles an hour, and they seemed to think that faster travel would occur primarily because of further improvements in trains—specifically, some form of battery-operated electric trains.[18] Some commentators, however, predicted that railway and steamboat travel would be made as obsolete as stagecoach travel, because they believed that airships would be invented within the next few decades. Would people fly? You bet, but not by planes, rather by balloons, perhaps guided on their intercity travels by a line strung 100 feet above the ground, out of collision's way with rooftops and trees. A poet, an adventurer, a politician, and a naturalist did predict the development of the airplane, but most thought its development was much further than a decade away.[19]

As for the role of government, nearly half of the nineteen commentators who chose to comment on the matter predicted that by the 1990s government would be simpler and smaller than it was in 1893.[20] Although a couple of the commentators foresaw the passage of the in-

14. Bill Nye, quoted in ibid., p. 27.
15. Van Buren Denslow, quoted in ibid., p. 28.
16. Felix L. Oswald, quoted in ibid., p. 35.
17. Ella Wheeler Wilcox, quoted in ibid., p. 39.
18. Charles Foster, quoted in ibid., p. 43.
19. Foster, quoted in ibid., pp. 38–45.
20. Foster, quoted in ibid., pp. 54–61.

come tax and the expansion of government expenditures, most seem to have missed the *extent* of the expansion of government's role in the economy. At the turn of the twentieth century, total government spending represented less than 8 percent of national product, and government regulations were relatively minor. The Sherman Antitrust Act, which would seek to regulate competition in the private sector, was not passed until 1890. In 1995, federal government spending exceeded $1.6 trillion and amounted to slightly less than a quarter of gross domestic product (GDP). Federal, state, and local spending combined represented more than one-third of GDP. Government regulations in the 1990s are playing a far greater role in American business and personal decisions than they were in the 1890s.[21] However, that is easy to say, given that government regulated very little 100 years ago.

Where the Commentators Went Right and Wrong

The commentators, as a group, exhibited tremendous faith in the perfectibility of human nature and, generally speaking, underestimated technological advances in almost all areas of the sciences and the economy. As for the environment, one commentator predicted that by 1990 sewers would no longer empty into streams and send foul "vapors" into the air, a prediction that, in itself, spoke volumes about environmental conditions then.[22] Another editor/author was far less optimistic about the environment. He thought that the cutting of timber would continue until no tree was left standing. Even that commentator could see a bright side: Fewer houses would be built out of wood, so house fires would be disasters of the past and insurance companies would be forced to close up shop.[23] A humorist dared to predict (perhaps jokingly) that in 1990 less money would be spent on electing public officials.[24]

On several other counts, the commentators were fairly close to the target. A naturalist envisioned that by 1990 millions of homes would have heating and air-conditioning systems.[25] In fact, in the late 1980s less than 1 percent of U.S. homes were without heating systems and 64 percent had some form of air-conditioning (and not all U.S. houses need

21. See Melinda Warren, *Mixed Messages: An Analysis of the 1994 Federal Regulatory Budget* (St. Louis: Center for the Study of American Business, Washington University, August 1993).

22. T. V. Powderly, quoted in *Will Man Fly?* pp. 77–78.

23. John Habbenton, quoted in ibid., p. 89.

24. Bill Nye, quoted in ibid., p. 55.

25. Felix L. Oswald, quoted in ibid., pp. 88–89.

air-conditioning). A theologian confidently predicted that prisons of the 1990s would be greatly improved by the addition of "ventilation, and sunlight, and bathrooms, and libraries."[26] Indeed, no U.S. prisons today are without such amenities.

A populist editor believed that by end of the twentieth century the "economic and social questions of the day" would be covered in public school.[27] They are, in the form of lessons on the proper use of condoms, multicultural values, and drug use and abuse—often to the exclusion of basic studies. However, given widespread evidence of the deterioration of public education, especially since the 1960s, a theologian's prediction that "the stuffing machine that we call the school system, which is making the rising generation a race of invalids, will be substituted for something more reasonable" seems to be a more accurate description of how many public school systems evolved.[28]

Another commentator foresaw the development of electric "storage cells" that would make domestic life much easier. Others correctly predicted the building of the Panama Canal. Those who foresaw the development of electric modes of travel believed such methods would be used more widely than they actually are.[29] Another expected the development of a "sound book in some form," which did indeed become popular in the 1980s in the form of books on tape.[30] The secretary of the interior in 1890 imagined that much of the arid West would be farmed with the widespread use of irrigation. And yet another commentator realized that improvements in transportation would permit Florida orange growers to supply customers all over the nation with all the oranges they could eat.[31]

Instead of predictions, what many of the commentators seemed to be expressing were hopes for improvements, as they perceived them. Several reasoned that saloons would be outlawed by the end of the twentieth century (which they were, but for only a brief period), that workers would be thoroughly unionized, that brutal crimes would disappear, and that two-thirds of all lawyers would be "destroyed." (Law was then

26. Thomas De Witt Talmage, quoted in ibid., p. 20.
27. T. V. Powderly, quoted in ibid., p. 23.
28. Talmage, quoted in ibid., pp. 23–24. A growing number of critics were caustically denouncing public education on many counts in the 1980s and 1990s. See Thomas Sowell, *Inside American Education: The Decline, the Deception, the Dogmas* (New York: Free Press, 1993).
29. Warren Miller, quoted in *Will Man Fly?* p. 47.
30. John Clark Ridpath, quoted in ibid., p. 65.
31. Samuel Barton, quoted in ibid., p. 49.

believed, by at least one of the seventy-four, to be a "stupendous swindle."[32]) Ironically, the exact opposite has occurred; no industrial country has more lawyers per person than the United States.

While the commentators did foretell several technological developments, they totally missed a multitude of other tremendous developments in the scientific, social, and economic arenas, both positive and negative. Several of the commentators believed that people would fly (in a manner of speaking), but who could ever have guessed that jetting across the country in a few hours would be an everyday occurrence for tens of millions of Americans? Electric power held great promise in 1890, but the commentators certainly could not have imagined the tremendous variety of uses to which it would be applied.

No one thought to predict that running water and indoor flushing toilets would be available to practically all Americans long before the 1990s, or that the telephone (which Alexander Graham Bell had tested in 1876), radio (with the first broadcast in 1906), and television (with the first public telecasts in 1936) would dominate virtually all aspects of American life. As for fashion, the seventy-four commentators figured that dress would become simpler and would incorporate fewer buttons, but it's doubtful that anyone imagined the development of anything like Velcro (patented in 1955) as a replacement for buttons (and many other forms of fasteners).[33]

The commentators had no clue whatsoever that transistors and integrated circuits would be developed, making possible personal computers that can make hundreds of millions of calculations a second. Not one of the seventy-four commentators could possibly have predicted that whole libraries, running into the hundreds if not thousands of titles, could be crammed onto and then retrieved from a single three-and-a-half-inch silver disk, as can be done today, or that the entire Library of Congress could be imprinted on a set of disks that would require only the space of a four-drawer file cabinet.

While they understood that advances would continue to be made in the field of medicine, it is doubtful they imagined that procedures such as transplant surgery would be common in the 1990s or that eye surgery could be done with patients never spending a night in the hospital. For that matter, how many of these changes would have been anticipated even a half century ago?

32. Barton, quoted in ibid., pp. 32, 16, 22, and 73.

33. See Charles Panati, *Extraordinary Origin of Everyday Things* (New York: Perennial Library, 1987), pp. 317–18.

If the Columbian Exposition commentators were somehow to walk into a modern house, how would they view the "servant problem" of the 1990s? Undoubtedly as a joke, since housework is much less difficult and involved today than it was 100 years ago. More foods are readily available and can be stored for weeks or months with little fuss and mess. Meals can now be cooked, laundry done, and household temperature changes with the touch of a few buttons. Bread can be cooked "from scratch" by simply tossing required ingredients into a machine not much larger than the bread boxes of 100 years ago. Lawns are mowed not with sheep (as was done in the 1890s), but with machines that pull themselves. Movies are fed into homes by cable and at the discretion of the viewers. To be sure, our time travelers would undoubtedly be flabbergasted by what they would find in an ordinary, middle-income (or even many lower-income) household. Sadly, they would also be very disappointed at the way many of us have so little regard of one another, given the disrespect that abounds, the lack of common courtesies, and the growing crime rates.

Almost all in the group of writers exuded optimism, a conviction that while they did not know exactly how the world would improve, it *would* improve. In 1890, both the secretary of the treasury and an economic analyst were especially optimistic, a fact evident in the epigraphs for this chapter. A corporate executive was probably the most optimistic, waxing eloquently that there was "no limit—except the limit of the world itself—to the growth of wealth, to the augmentation of opportunity, and to the achievements of this American people."[34] A theologian feared that during the next 100 years the country would be rocked by "great calamities . . . in the form of pestilence, earthquakes, and civil strife," but even then he remained confident that progress for the country as a whole would continue practically unabated.[35]

The same level of excitement over the country's future prevailed when the World's Fair opened in New York City in 1939. This was a time when the Great Depression could still be vividly remembered, when the average family income was less than $12,000 a year (after adjusting for inflation), under today's poverty threshold, when war was breaking out in Europe, and when communism was a growing threat. Nevertheless, David Sarnoff was typical of the commentators of that era: "The promise of the future is still greater than all the glories of the past."[36] The fair

34. Erastus Wiman, quoted in *Will Man Fly?* p. 112.

35. David Swing, quoted in ibid., p. 110.

36. As quoted in David Gelernter, *1939: The Lost World of the Fair* (New York: Free Press, 1995), p. 26.

spotlighted technology developments, and the exhibitors exuded firm predictions for the future, which meant only twenty-five years hence, or 1965: The country would be crisscrossed with "superhighways." Television would be in widespread use. People would be able to buy economical, roomier, air-conditioned cars, which would enable them to live miles from work, away from the smells and sights of factories. As David Gelernter notes, from the perspective of 1939, "1960 seemed like a brilliant, glittering dream. And looking back, 1960 *was* a brilliant glittering dream. The fair kept its promise. So many of its predictions came true."[37] At the same time, even when so close at hand, the commentators of that fair, like the ones in 1893, missed some major developments, not the least of which were a host of medical developments, including the elimination of polio (a scourge in the land in 1939) and the creation of antibiotics. They overlooked altogether the development of computers. And the commentators were confident that traffic congestion could be eliminated.

Why Dreams Are So Often Surpassed

The seventy-four people asked to comment about the future in the early 1890s were dreamers, some of the country's best, which qualified them for the task. Those who made predictions in the late 1930s were equally qualified to predict the future. However, on reflection, we can intuitively understand why their best efforts do not come even remotely close to describing American lifestyles in the 1990s. Life tends to be, over long stretches of time, more advanced, and in many ways better and easier, than people's best and earliest dreams. But why has that been the case?

The answer is not as simple as it seems, mainly because of the limitations of thought itself, which is necessarily checked by the inevitable ignorance of individuals. In many regards, economic life today is far more prosperous, complex, and sophisticated for Americans than anyone could have imagined 100 years ago, and for good reason. Each prediction expressed in a commentator's essay is the product, more or less, of one person's intelligence and ignorance—of one human being who had to sit down and rely solely on his or her knowledge of the world as he or she had experienced it or could grasp it. No matter how massive a person's intelligence, experience, or distinction might be, and no matter how extensive the person's reading or the number of contacts that he or she has made, what one person can know about the world, even in consultation with others, is necessarily a trivial fraction of all that is

37. Ibid., p. 24.

known or can be learned. Indeed, the capacity of people to make correct predictions is necessarily inversely related to how much is known by all people.

The late F. A. Hayek, a social philosopher/economist, has reminded us, "Knowledge exists only as the knowledge of individuals. It is not much better than a metaphor to speak of the knowledge of society as a whole. The sum of the knowledge of all the individuals exists nowhere as an integrated whole." Hayek reckoned that the "great problem" of society is how to benefit from the totality of knowledge that "exists only dispersed as the separate, partial, and sometimes conflicting beliefs of all men."[38]

The poets, authors, theologians, and others in the group of commentators were probably exceptional in their respective fields, perhaps better qualified than most any other group that could have been assigned the task. What, then, would explain the blatant deficiencies in the predictions made by such an august group? The problem was that life had already become so prosperous, complex, and sophisticated that they could not possibly make many correct assessments. Hayek's words should remain memorable:

> The more men know, the smaller the share of all that knowledge becomes that any one mind can absorb. The more civilized we become, the more relatively ignorant must each individual be of the facts on which the working of his civilization depends. The very division of knowledge increases the necessary ignorance of the individual of most of this knowledge.[39]

Perhaps, given their limited time to think about the matter, the commentators' best approach would have been to concede, as several did, that economic life in the 1990s would likely supersede their fondest dreams.

What did happen over the subsequent century was the consequence of the (limited) intelligence of hundreds of millions of Americans who did more than dream. In spite of how little they knew of the "knowledge of society as a whole" and in spite of daunting uncertainties as to what to do with what they did know, millions of Americans worked hard and smart. Year after year for a hundred years, these millions of people separately and in conjunction with others, worked away with the limited knowledge at their disposal. The results were better than could have been imagined by any one person years before, precisely because, along

38. F. A. Hayek, *The Constitution of Liberty* (Chicago: University of Chicago Press, 1960), pp. 24–25.

39. Ibid., p. 26.

the way, no one person had the brains to imagine and then do what *all* Americans could imagine and do interacting with one another in complex ways over time.

Moreover, the collective intelligence of Americans was greater than the sum of the intelligence of the individuals. The results of their efforts were, obviously, far more creative and intellient than any one of them could possibly have imagined. This is because each person's efforts were coordinated, albeit without central direction, and the system of coordination forced them to adjust their efforts to the consequences of the efforts of many others. Individuals may have set out to accomplish their own fondest imagined end (for example, to grow a crop or to provide a service in the most productive way known), only to realize that their individual plans conflicted with others, that there were no profits to be made in what they were doing or that there were smarter or less costly ways to proceed.

Indeed, along the way, many individuals made discoveries—some by design and some by accident—or found less costly ways of doing what they were trying to do.[40] All the while, others were doing the same thing, pursuing their fondest dreams, making discoveries, and finding that there were other things that were less costly and more profitable to do. In most instances, those who developed inventions, whether small (the paper clip) or large (the radio or, even more fundamentally, the transistor) did not imagine the many uses that would be made of their inventions; they simply did not have the time to think of the same number of uses that many other people could imagine.

Those alive in 1890 (or as late as 1939) could have set out to do the best that they could, but almost all found that they had to adjust their actions in a host of new ways. The adjustment made by anyone would consequently force a multitude of small and large adjustments on others, whose adjustments would in turn force a multitude of adjustments on others, ad infinitum. No one person could possibly imagine the array of consequences beforehand that would result as adjustments were made upon adjustments. Similarly, no one person could possibly absorb the information being passed about among millions of people as they adjusted to one another, much less know how to anticipate and make all the necessary adjustments and then understand their full consequences

40. Accidental discoveries affecting many industries have fueled much economic progress. Products discovered by accident include Velcro, penicillin, X rays, dynamite, vulcanization of rubber, synthetic dyes, rayon, saccharin, iodine, and helium (Royston M. Roberts, *Serendipity: Accidental Discoveries in Science* (New York: John Wiley, 1989).

years into the future. There is an unavoidably strong evolutionary component to economic and social developments over time.

The genius of the Founding Fathers of this country is that they understood that the country's progress would require an immense number of adjustments by everyone—the kind of "microadjustments" that tolerably intelligent (and even not so intelligent) and well-meaning people are likely to make. They realized that people's efforts would have synergetic consequences, but only if they were given the freedom to operate meaningfully at the microadjustment level and only if, at the same time, people were held accountable for the adjustments they made wrongly or inappropriately; that is, if they were given the freedom to suffer the consequences, good or bad. The founders appeared convinced that "macrosuccess," as revealed in strong economic progress, would rise from the ashes of "microfailures."[41] They were willing to say in effect, "Let the evolutionary process begin." And they were right.

The founders' wisdom was to acknowledge their own limited wisdom, their inherent inability to know all that there is to know, to do all that there is to do, and to make, or just anticipate, all the adjustments required. Their wisdom was expressed in their willingness to emancipate individuals to do their own thing, to pursue their own dreams, constrained only by broad rules (written into the Constitution) that were not intended to favor anyone in particular as the adjustment process proceeded. The founders' genius lay in their recognition of the fact that individual freedom has value precisely because no one person knows very much and that they (the founders) did not know the most important thing; that is, how people would use the freedom at their disposal to make the unanticipated adjustments and to cope with the extent of their uncertainties. At any time, any one person will be ignorant of all but a trivial share of the facts and adjustments that will need to be made in the future. The founders instinctively understood the wisdom of Hayek: "If we knew how freedom would be used, the case for it would largely disappear."[42] Freedom and undreamed consequences, in other words, go hand in hand.

The founders were also wise to realize the importance of property and prices to progress. The former provides people with incentives to do all the things and make all the adjustments that progress requires. When people do things right, the value of their property rises; when they

41. The importance of failure to economic progress is covered in Dwight R. Lee and Richard B. McKenzie, *Failure and Progress: The Bright Side of the Dismal Science* (Washington: Cato Institute, 1993).

42. Hayek, *Constitution of Liberty*, p. 31.

don't, the value falls. Along the way, prices help coordinate the multitude of actions of the millions of people in this country and abroad. High prices relative to costs for some goods and services induce people to expand their energies in those endeavors; low prices relative to costs for other goods and services cause other people to contract their efforts. Throughout the 100 years following 1893, progress was made simply because a lot of people worked hard and because a multitude of prices was constantly signaling Americans how they could work smarter; that is, how they could adjust their behavior in particular ways, mainly in ways that would lower costs and increase the economic value gained from the country's limited human and physical resources.

Efficient economic activity, which is at the foundation of all growth, requires the application of an immense amount of information known only in bits and pieces to many individuals acting in their tiny corners of various national and world markets. The late Leonard Read, former head of the Foundation for Economic Education, made this point with unusual clarity in a short essay, "I, Pencil."[43]

In words ascribed to a pencil, Read recounts how no one—absolutely no one person in the world—has ever known how to make a pencil (as most pencils are made) wholly from scratch. Even for this relatively simple product, many steps are involved. Some people know how to cut the trees that are required for the wood that goes into the body of a pencil, and others know how to mine graphite, or black lead, a crystalline form of carbon that is mixed with clay to form the core of a so-called lead pencil. Neither of these groups is likely to know how to assemble a pencil, nor is it likely to know how to make the trucks that are required to deliver resources to the pencil factories or finished pencils to the stores. Someone else is needed with the know-how to make the eraser tip, and those who know how to make the eraser tip are not likely to know how to cut the wood or mine the graphite. The point of Read's story is that pencils do get made even though no one knows all there is to know about making them. They get made—somewhat miraculously—principally because markets and the prices they generate coordinate the information held in small pieces by a large number of people, enabling individuals to accomplish together what none of them could accomplish alone.

As Hayek recognized, the country's pricing system also enabled people to economize on the information they must absorb and use: "The

43. Leonard E. Read, "I, Pencil," as reprinted in *Imprimis*, vol. 21, no. 6 (Hillsdale, Mich.: Hillsdale College, June 1992).

marvel is that in a case like that of scarcity of one raw material, without an order being issued, without more than perhaps a handful of people knowing the cause, tens of thousands of people whose identity could not be ascertained by months of investigation, are made to use the material or its products more sparingly."[44] This feat is accomplished because prices summarize a great deal of information on the relative scarcity of various resources and on the trade-off that a host of people throughout the country and world are willing to make. To that extent, prices help us overcome our ignorance and enable us to accomplish far more than we could have otherwise. They ensure that the content of what people experience in the future surpasses our best predictions, that they are able to live in the future beyond their own limited means and dreams of today.[45]

The lesson is straightforward: yesterday's dreamers had no basis for making more accurate predictions about the way we now live. They literally did not know enough, nor could they have known enough. The only practical way the commentators' predictions might have come even remotely close to the reality of the 1990s is if everyone alive in the 1890s had pursued over time only those dreams related to events that were guided, directly or indirectly, by the limited knowledge of the commentators. But then, there probably would have been little progress to predict.

The former Soviet Union fell apart economically long before it fell apart politically in the late 1980s, largely because its leaders sought to ensure that the country's economic future would be guided by what the leaders knew, which was, of course, very little of all there was to be known. The Soviet leaders made a fatal mistake (founded on what Hayek dubbed the "fatal conceit"): Following the advice of Karl Marx, Soviet leaders assumed that an economy, which at a given point in time is the product of human endeavors, is necessarily a matter of deliberate human design and therefore could be subjected to useful redesign.[46] A

44. F. A. Hayek, "The Use of Knowledge in Society," *American Economic Review* 35, no. 4 (September 1945): 527.

45. Producers of radios, for example, do not need to know very much about the relative scarcities of the various resources that might go into the production of radio cabinets; all they have to do is compare a few prices and choose among them for the least expensive way of housing their radio receivers. Pricing systems permit, therefore, the use of more resources in the production of real goods and services, mainly because fewer resources are needed to collect and disseminate resources.

46. F. A. Hayek, *The Fatal Conceit: The Errors of Socialism* (Chicago: University of Chicago Press, 1988).

prosperous, complex, and sophisticated economy cannot be designed by humans, simply because of the inescapable limitations of the human beings who would be the designers. If ever an economy were "designed," it is a sure bet to be simple in design and not very prosperous for very long, because the designers will know so little of what is to be known.

The task of the Soviet designers (or planners) was made progressively less and less tenable throughout the twentieth century simply because the sum total of human knowledge continued to mount at a geometric rate while the share of that knowledge held by the Soviet designers necessarily contracted, making macromistakes and lost opportunities for advancement all the more common. The relegation of the former Soviet Union to the status of a third-world country by the last half of the twentieth century was assured when the country was forced to rely on the dreams and schemes of the few people in charge, or when the vast knowledge held separately by the millions of Soviet individuals was suppressed under the perverted banner of passing "power to the people," the exact opposite of what was actually done.

The American economy would have suffered a similar fate had we been forced to rely on the dreams of the seventy-four who were assigned the task of predicting life 100 years ago.

Today's Doomsayers: How Wrong Will They Be?

This book is predicated on the fact that during this last decade of the twentieth century, many Americans are reviving an honorable tradition; that is, they are imagining that life will get tougher. As evidenced by the array of quotes in chapter 1, many of today's commentators are predicting that resources will become scarcer and that goods and services will become less plentiful (and their growth will surely be choked). They expect incomes to fall. Sadly, many Americans today harbor little hope that their dreams will come true.

Certainly, some people's dreams won't come true, just as there have always been people who never realize their aspirations. The freedom to do what one will encompasses the whole range from all that is possible—from right to wrong—and many people will continue to do things wrong.

Each era has its own set of worries about the future. We will consider these in greater detail later. The point of this chapter is that it is reasonable for us to expect continued, undreamed-of progress in the future for the same reason the progress that has been made over the past century was greater than the seventy-four commentators could have imagined. That is, those who are making predictions today, for good and bad, hold only a tiny fraction of the usable knowledge in the country and world. They know only a smidgen of all that is known by others, and they know nothing of what others can do now with what they have and will be doing with what they will learn and obtain in the near, much less long, term. Granted, the world remains beset with problems, but Americans must remember that many people are working to solve those problems, some out of a sense of dedication to humanity, and others, no doubt, in pursuit of personal gain.

The growing shortage of whale oil in the mid-nineteenth century gave rise to the earnest pursuit of additional petroleum reserves. Shrinking forests at the turn of the twentieth century motivated farmers and lumber companies to plant trees and to begin to look for substitutes for wood. OPEC's restriction of oil supplies in the 1970s prompted exploration in other parts of the world and spurred automobile producers to build smaller, more fuel-efficient cars. The difficulties we are facing in the 1990s will be met with solutions found by people who will know things we can't know (for example, how technology will unfold and how people will adjust) and who will have strong incentives to learn more about the problems and their potential solutions than has been learned by anyone, solely or collectively, in the past.

In assessing the value of individual freedom and markets within which people will operate, all too frequently we forget that people do receive daily signals on what they are doing right and wrong and are constantly fed market-determined directions for making adjustments. Just as has been the case in the past, prices in the future will signal people to adjust and make better use of their limited knowledge and resources, which may become, in fact, even more limited.

The problems inherent in trying to predict the outcomes 10 or 20 years into the future (much less 100 years ahead) are revealed in a widely repeated story relating to early decisions made by billionaire Bill Gates, the founder of Microsoft. In the early 1980s, he set out to write a new operating system for personal computers, MS-DOS. At the outset, he had to answer the basic question of how many kilobytes of RAM (random access memory) would likely be required in personal computers in the foreseeable future. At the time, personal computers typically operated with 64 K of RAM. Gates predicted that future machines would not likely ever require more than ten times the RAM of 1984, or 640 K. Little did he know (even though he is, by all accounts, a genius in the computer business) that in a matter of a few years personal computer program developers would be seriously hampered by the 640 K RAM limitation. In 1984, Gates's imagination was grounded in his 1984 knowledge, so it is understandable that he could not imagine all that other programmers would eventually envision doing with "excess RAM," making their programs ever more powerful in response to technical advances and consumer demand. Even Gates could not anticipate that this book would be written in part on a laptop computer with fifty times the RAM limitation of MS-DOS.

Many modern predictions about technological advances have come true much earlier than expected. As late as 1980, little credibility was given to the idea that by the mid-1990s millions of people would be walking the streets carrying laptop computers (some weighing less than 4 pounds with the computing power of 1970s, if not 1980s, mainframes) that also include cellular phone and fax capabilities. Today, some prognosticators predict that laptop computers will have the power of supercomputers by the turn of the twenty-first century. This might reasonably occur sooner still, if someone can find one good reason to use that much computing power on the road (and someone probably will). What is certain is that people will find many new and unheard-of things that can be done with the computing power at hand.

Perhaps we should do what several of the seventy-four commentators did: concede that the future is likely to be far better than we can imagine today. Embedded in our own ignorance of what people will do in pursuit of their own dreams are grounds for optimism.

A lesson in the predictions made in the 1890s is that long-run predictions of economic progress—even unimaginable advances—are a safe bet, if people have the freedom to do their own thing and to adjust to the ever-changing conditions they confront. In the economic sphere (as distinct from the political sphere), people will not likely seek to undercut advancements; they are likely to be motivated to solve problems that emerge, not worsen them. However, predictions of the *exact content* of the progress (or exactly how people will live and what material things they will have) are not very good bets. No one knows enough about people's current plans, much less about people's willingness and abilities to adjust in the future to changing conditions, to be very good at envisioning people's living standards long into the future. As one of the commentators recognized, "Of all these forecasts, one thing may be said with tolerable certainty: Not one of them will be verified in its essential details."[47]

47. J. H. Beadle, quoted in *Will Man Fly?* p. 128.

Concluding Comments

The most misguided predictions of the 1890 commentators related to how they believed mankind's basic nature would be perfected by the 1990s. Humankind did not improve one iota over the last 100 years, as it probably has not changed (for the good) to any measurable degree over the recorded history of human existence. Material progress has not been, nor will it be, humankind's saving grace, as the seventy-four thought it would be. Seeing this point teaches us an important lesson: Technical and economic progress can be made in spite of people's worst tendencies to be concerned with self, to take from others, and to avoid contributing to the betterment of their communities and countries. We must all work toward constructing social and economic institutions that will corral people's worst tendencies by increasing the costs of doing wrong and by enhancing the benefits from contributing to the well-being of others.

We must proceed with caution, however, because the country's bright future could easily be dimmed. Unwittingly, we could make the same fatal mistake so many have made in the past; that is, we could make the mistake of assuming that the contents of a prosperous future can be designed by a few people working in government bureaus. The fate of the country would be held hostage to the ignorance of the few in power, who could not possibly know how to make the unfathomable number and array of adjustments that a brighter future will require. The lesson is simple: For the broad sweep of social and economic problems, we must not substitute the intelligence of the few for the intelligence of the masses. Such a substitution would ensure that more dreams are busted. We must use the intelligence of the few as if it were a precious resource, which it is, for solving the narrow, well identified and specified, and justified problems of the truly unfortunate.

The former Soviet Union made that mistake. We need not follow their example, but to avoid repeating their mistake we must understand the importance of knowledge, how broadly it's dispersed, and how little of it we each can hold. We also need to understand that progress in the United States has not been abated in recent times, the central concern of chapter 3.

3

THE UNHERALDED GAINS

> Rip Van Winkle wakes to a bright spring day in 1994 and, rubbing his eyes, quickly realizes the world around him has changed. He discovers almost 25 years have flown by since the start of his big sleep. . . . The contrast between American life then [1970] and now is astounding. Rip surveys the changes and concludes Americans have never had it so good. He is puzzled, though, that so few people share his sense of wonderment. People seem glum about the U.S. economy of the 1990s and look back to the time Rip went to sleep—the late 1960s and the early 1970s—as the apex of American prosperity. People reflect on that time as "the good old days" from which the U.S. standard of living has ebbed.
>
> Michael Cox and Richard Alm,
> *These Are the Good Old Days*

BAD NEWS sells—or so it seems from the stream of depressing books and newspaper and television reports on American life. Television producers in the Los Angeles area (and probably many other major metropolitan TV markets) are reputed to follow a simple programming rule: "If it bleeds, it leads." So, southern Californians are treated nightly to a familiar menu of ghastly crime scenes, car wrecks, and fires. The greater the number of shots fired, the better. The greater the pileup on the freeways, the more likely the deaths and injuries will make the nightly news "teasers," supposedly *news* worth staying tuned for. The bigger the fire, the better the ratings, and so forth. The fires, floods, riots, and earthquakes that bedevil California are not tragedies, per se, in newsrooms; they are the foundations of great headlines and good programming.

Many Americans seem to relish death and destruction, as judged by what they watch and read. Good news is, for the most part, no news, not sufficiently compelling to make leads and front pages, certainly not as often as bad news. The same can be said of good and bad economic news; the balance is missing, with the focus on the bad. In a search of a computerized media database, covering 2,500 media outlets for a sixteen-month period in the first half of the 1990s, plant closing were the subject of 19,109 news stories, whereas only 5,693 stories on plant openings were found. You might think that the production base was shrinking, but all the while it was expanding.[1] The country's industrial production index stood at an all-time high when the search was made.[2]

Job losses were the subject of 38,555 news stories, whereas job gains were mentioned in 11,395 stories. No wonder readers may be surprised to learn that during the period covered by the news reports, the economy's job base actually grew, *on balance* (after the losses and gains had been netted out), by more than 2.5 million. No wonder many Americans have a depressed outlook.

Scholars have also found value in dismal assessments of where the economy has been heading and where it might now head unless their policy advice is heeded. They, of course, concede the economic progress made over the past two centuries, but they staunchly underplay, and often refuse to recognize, the progress made over the past two decades. The past two decades were ones of economic retrogression of major proportions, or so it is widely argued.

I dare not even try to recount here all of the dismal academic tales of economic despair. I've taken up that challenge in another work.[3] All I need do is remind the readers of Stanford economist Paul Krugman, who accepts the decline thesis and who worried in his 1990 book that the country had moved quietly into an "age of diminished expectations," in which people would be satisfied merely if the economic performance of

1. The database is DataTimes Information Network, which included at the time the full texts of more than 125 international, national, and major regional newspapers, plus magazines, newsletters, wire services, and television news programs. The search period covered from January 1, 1993, to April 30, 1994.

2. The computer searches were made on the DataTimes Information Network on April 30, 1994.

3. See McKenzie, *What Went Right in the 1980s* (San Francisco: Pacific Research Institute, 1994).

the economy no longer deteriorated.[4] Wallace Peterson, an economist at the University of Nebraska, is convinced he knows the source of diminished expectations: Over more than two decades, the country has, with little notice, moved through a "silent depression," not just an ordinary, run-of-the-mill recession, but a substantial drop-off in the standard of living for the vast majority of Americans. He claims that "the outlook is bleak: recession-like conditions of economic decline have been the norm for at least twenty years."[5] He writes that the depression is "*silent* because there is none of the sound and fury that come with a major crash such as the one in 1929; much of the public, the press, and people in the government sense that something has gone wrong, but they aren't exactly sure what it is."[6]

What is amazing is just how many times authors can claim that the recession, or depression, has gone unheralded or remains silent, out of the upper consciousness of the American polity. One has to wonder what planet such writers are living on. They must not be reading many newspapers or watching television. In the period January 1, 1993, to May 1, 1994, recession (or depression) was the subject of more than 315,000 news stories, as determined from a search of the computerized media database—and these reports were written two to three years *after* the recession of the early 1990s had been declared over. The scholars must also be avoiding reading one another's works, because they all tend to cite the same data, even most of the same sources, and repeat many of the same arguments concerning the country's supposed economic long-term decline, busted dreams, and unnoticed recessions or depressions.[7]

4. Paul Krugman, *The Age of Diminished Expectations: U.S. Economic Policy in the 1990s* (Cambridge, Mass.: MIT Press, 1990).

5. Wallace C. Peterson, *Silent Depression: The Fate of the American Dream* (New York: Norton, 1994), p. 17.

6. Ibid., p. 10.

7. For a small library of dreary assessments of the economy (in addition to works cited in this chapter), see Alan S. Blinder, *Hard Heads, Soft Hearts* (Reading, Mass.: Addison-Wesley, 1987); Barry Bluestone and Bennett Harrison, *The Deindustrialization of America* (New York: Basic Books, 1982); Stephen Cohen and John Zysman, *Manufacturing Matters* (New York: Basic Books, 1987); Benjamin M. Friedman, *Day of Reckoning* (New York: Random House, 1988); Bennett Harrison and Barry Bluestone, *The Great U-Turn* (New York: Basic Books, 1988); Joel Kurtzman, *The Decline and Crash of the American Economy* (New York: Norton, 1988); Robert Kuttner, *The Economic Illusion* (Boston: Houghton Mifflin, 1984); Katherine S. Newman, *Declining Fortunes* (New York: Basic Books, 1993); Kevin Phillips, *The Politics of the Rich and the Poor* (New York: Harper Perennial, 1990); Robert B. Reich, *The Next American Frontier* (New York: Times Books, 1983) and *The Work of Nations* (New York: Vintage Books, 1992); and Lester C. Thurow, *The Zero-Sum Society* (New York: Basic Books, 1980).

A favorite argument is that while the country has had a long history of progress, that progress was abruptly halted and then reversed for most Americans in the early 1970s. Of course, all economic hell broke loose in the 1980s, which accounts for the country's continuing economic problems in the 1990s.

Everyone seems to be despairing about the unnoticed plight of contemporary America. In his 1992 run for the White House, Bill Clinton made a political fetish of just how bad economic conditions over "the past twelve years" had been. The problem is that everyone seems to think he or she knows that times have been tougher than ever before, maybe not in recorded history but centainly for a generation. "Everyone" may not be *dead* wrong on *all* economic facts; but they are certainly *cold* on many of them, far off the mark of what economic conditions have been in the country. Nevertheless, the decline diagnosis gives them an easy out for explaining the country's sense of woe: "Times are tough" seems to be more a matter of wishful thinking than critical analysis.

Washington Post columnist Haynes Johnson has raised writing and selling bad economic news to the level of a new journalistic art form. In 1991, he penned a best-seller, *Sleepwalking Through History,* a none-too-gentle denunciation, based on bad economic news, of just about every economic policy move the Reagan administration made.[8] In that work, he warned his readers that the country would be paying for the policy miscues of the 1980s in the 1990s.

In his most recent book, he remains intent on validating his earlier assessments and predictions, and he finds new ground—"the frayed American fabric"—to despair about the country's future. That is to say, the country will continue to stray from the path of prosperity unless Bill Clinton saves the day by reactivating and reenergizing the federal government. "Nothing in my previous experience," writes Johnson, "of traveling across America prepared me for the depth of feelings—the fears, the doubt, the anger, the *rage*—I encountered everywhere. Strongest of all was a feeling of bewilderment, a troubling sense that the assurances of the old America were passing and that the uncertain new America emerging promises to be far more unsettling."[9]

As have so many others, Johnson then chants the litany of long-term, not just short-term, woes facing the country: the escalation of the government debt, the rising inequality of income, the deindustrialization of

8. Haynes Johnson, *Sleepwalking Through History* (New York: Norton, 1991).

9. Haynes Johnson, *Divided We Fall: Gambling with History in the Nineties* (New York: Norton, 1994), pp. 17–18.

the country, the decline of the country in the global marketplace, perverse 1980s tax policies that favored the rich at the expense of the poor, the downsizing of corporate America, political institutions calcified by the financial influence of special interests, the loss of good jobs, the inability of the expanding service sector to offer Americans the type of work they need, and so forth. He then concludes, with only a small ray of hope, that Americans will reform their government's ways: "Traditionally optimistic Americans, who believed in progress, in themselves, and in the American Dream, find themselves anxiously wondering if their old belief that tomorrow will always be better than today is still valid. To increasing numbers, it is not."[10]

In early 1996, reporters for the *New York Times* penned a seven-part series on, what else, "The Downsizing of America," lamenting the declining count in jobs and wages. They argue that the widespread job destruction has given rise to the "the most acute job insecurity since the Depression" that, in turn, "has produced an unrelenting angst that is shattering people's notions of work and self and the very promise of tomorrow." Ignoring their own data that shows that only 9 percent of the people polled felt that they were "very insecure" economically, the reporters maintain that "Many Americans have reacted [to all the negative trends in employment and wages] by downsizing their expectations of material comforts and the sweetness of the future. In a nation where it used to be a given that children would do better than their parents, half of those polled by the *Times* thought it unlikely that today's youth would attain higher standards of living than they have. What is striking is that this gloom may be even more emphatic among prosperous and well-educated Americans."[11]

A Contrarian Perspective

As suggested in the epigraph at the beginning of this chapter, Rip Van Winkle would surely be rubbing his eyes and shaking his head in confounded amazement if he had awoken in the mid-1990s from a twenty-five-year snooze. He would quickly observe a paradox that economic times were much better for ordinary Americans than they were when he went to sleep. At the same time, he would find many well-placed analysts and policymakers in a state of economic psychosis, in spite of all

10. Ibid., p. 32.

11. Louis Uchitelle and N. R. Kleinfield, "On the Battlefields of Business, Millions of Casualties," *New York Times*, March 3, 1996, p. 14.

the positive changes that had transpired. He would be further perplexed to learn that the vast majority of Americans are happy. If there is a trend at all evident in the polling data, it is upward. That is to say, Americans are not becoming more unhappy with time.

More to the point, Figure 1 shows how Americans have polled on "happiness," as reported by the National Opinion Research Center at the University of Chicago.[12] The two sets of broken, up and down line segments in the chart are for selected years between 1957 and 1994 (the poll was not given in all years). The two straight lines represent the trends for the respective sets of broken data points. The top line represents the percentage of Americans in national polls who indicated that, all things considered, they were either "very happy" or "pretty happy." The bottom line represents the percentage who indicated they were "not too happy."

In sharp contrast to the "doom and gloom" claims, far more Americans—between 83 percent and 92 percent for the years covered—said they were "very happy" or "pretty happy" (the top set of points), and the trend for the years covered in the chart was upward, albeit ever so slightly. Less than 17 percent in any year (with an average of 12 percent) say they were "not too happy," and the trend is downward, albeit, again, ever so slightly.

But in spite of continuing claims during the 1980s and 1990s that the American economy was deteriorating, the stock market, which is the best measure we have of future economic conditions, has bounded upward with the Dow over 5500 in early 1996 after being less than 900 in 1980. That much of a jump has never before been recorded in such a short period in the last half century.

Admittedly, there was a slight dip in the "happiness index" between 1990 and 1994 of three percentage points, but it was still higher in 1994 than it was in the supposedly halcyon days of the early 1960s. The index in 1994 was also five percentage points above the level recorded for 1973, supposedly the year before the so-called Great U-Turn in the American living standard began.

The dip in the happiness index for the 1990s can be partially explained by the recession of the early 1990s. *American Demographics* magazine's "index of well-being" (which combines nearly a dozen measures of eco-

12. Data points for 1957 through 1988 are from Richard G. Neimi, John Mueller, and Tom W. Smith, *Trends in Public Opinion: A Compendium of Survey Data* (New York: Greenwood Press, 1989), p. 290. Data points for 1989 through 1994 were obtained directly by phone from the National Opinion Research Center, University of Chicago (Fall 1995).

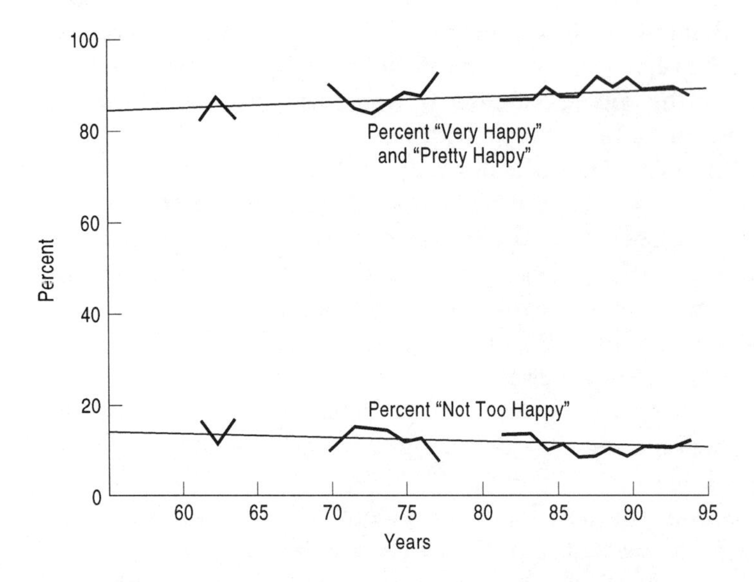

Figure 1. The happiness index. (From Richard G. Neimi, John Mueller, and Tom W. Smith, *Trends in Public Opinion* [New York: Greenwood Press, 1989], p. 290, and National Opinion Research Center, University of Chicago)

nomic and social health and has only been calculated since 1990) did drop between 1990 and the start of 1992, but the index has moved irregularly upward ever since.[13] At the very least, the pessimists must acknowledge, even grudgingly, that the evidence is mixed.

What Has Gone Right

One thing Haynes Johnson is right about is the sense of woe many Americans feel. What is remarkable to me is the conviction with which people—even well-off Americans—hold their assessments of the toughness of the times and their reluctance to accept the good news. Frankly, I have also been taken aback by reactions received to my earlier book *What Went Right in the 1980s.*[14] Those reactions are probably more instructive about the paradox of contemporary economic progress than the contents of the book itself.

Just after the book hit the bookstore shelves, I went into a Barnes and

13. Elia Kacapyr, "The Well-Being Index," *American Demographics*, February 1996, pp. 32–35 and 43.

14. McKenzie, *What Went Right in the 1980s* (San Francisco: Pacific Research Institute, 1994).

Noble bookstore in my hometown to see if copies of the book were available there. When I asked the manager (without telling him that I was the author) if he had my book, he confidently corrected me, "Oh, you mean *What Went* Wrong *in the 1980s,* don't you?" After correcting him, he found the right book on his computer, and I followed him on his search of several sections of the store in which the book might have been filed: current affairs, new releases, business, economics. No luck.

In some frustration, the manager then turned to me and asked quite seriously, *"What Went Right in the 1980s,* could that be a book of *humor?"* After assuring him that it wasn't, he persisted, "Fiction?" No, the book is neither humor nor fiction. It is a serious attempt to dispel a host of myths that have grown up about the 1980s, but the self-assigned task was more difficult than expected.

Probably the most widespread reaction by even those who should know better is that no one could possibly write a *whole* book on the things that went right during that momentous decade (especially not one that extends to 400 pages). Indeed, when a friend asked for the book at the counter of the local Brentanno's, a customer standing behind her muttered, "Short book, no doubt."

A telephone interview I had with a reporter from a major metropolitan newspaper was not atypical of many early media calls. The reporter started his interview as others had, "What *did* go right in the 1980s?" I could tell by the inflection of his voice that he could only imagine a short and inconsequential listing. I told him that, for starters, gross domestic product rose. I was surprised by his amazement that production had not fallen. Yet, during the 1980s national production rose in constant dollar terms by close to a third (or over a $1 trillion in 1990 prices), which is the equivalent of annexing the entire German economy (East and West) or adding once again to U.S. output the production of sixteen states (several of which are small: Maine, New Hampshire, Rhode Island, and Vermont; but the others are sizable: Connecticut, Iowa, Kansas, Massachusetts, Minnesota, Missouri, Nebraska, New Jersey, New York, North Dakota, Pennsylvania, and South Dakota). The economy would probably have expanded by hundreds of billions of dollars more for the decade if the Federal Reserve had not been forced to throttle the inflationary spiral of the 1960s and 1970s by radically curbing the growth in the money stock beginning in 1979.

The reporter was obviously taken aback, but he was also confident that all of the increase was in services (with, possibly, hamburger-flipping being the dominant new job) and that the country had definitely "deindustrialized." Not so. I assured him that the country's major gauge of industrial output, the Fed's industrial production index, had risen during the 1980s in line with the overall economy and stood at an all-time high for the decade in 1990, just prior to the advent of the 1990–1991 recession. The country's manufacturing output in real dollar terms rose faster than overall economic activity during the decade and, in 1989 (the year before a recession started), represented a higher percentage of national production (albeit slightly) than in 1980—or, for that matter, any year since the late 1940s. Moreover, in spite of the recession in the early 1990s and the painstakingly slow recovery thereafter, the industrial production index was 15 percent higher at the start of 1995 than in 1990.

Such data help explain why "hamburger-flipping" was not the only new job created in the decade, contrary to the exaggerated impressions left by critics. In the 1982–1989 recovery period, a third of the new jobs were in the "managerial/professional" category, a fifth was in "production," with the average wage in both categories above the overall national average for all new jobs. Jobs in "services," where many jobs are low wage (but where there are also many respectable jobs), accounted for less then 17 percent of new jobs, and the economy eliminated 4 percent of the farm sector's low-wage jobs.[15]

Of course, many believe that if there were income gains for most families, the gains resulted simply because more women joined the workforce. One part of that argument is definitely true: More women did go to work, and for good reason. The wages of female workers have tended to rise relative to the wages of male workers, with women earning 76 percent as much as men in the mid-1990s, up from 67 percent in the early 1980s. However, much of the remaining gap appears to be attributable to the undeniable fact that women have babies. Women in the twenty-seven to thirty-three age range who have never had babies earn practically the same as what men earn (98 percent).[16] It is also true that over the past several decades, two-earner households grew as a percentage of all households. In 1963, 78 percent of married white women and 71 percent of married black women between the ages of eighteen and forty-four were in households where the husband earned at least 70 percent of all family income. By 1990, 46 percent of young white women and 33 percent of young black women were in such house-

15. As reported in Edwin S. Rubenstein, ed., *The Right Data* (New York: National Review Books, 1994), p. 220.

16. See Danielle Crittenden, "Yes, Motherhood Lowers Pay," *Wall Street Journal*, August 22, 1995, p. A11; June O'Neill and Soloman Polachek, "Why the Gender Gap in Wages Narrowed in the 1980s," *Journal of Labor Economics*, January 1993, pp. 205–28; and June O'Neill, "Women & Wages," *The American Enterprise*, November–December 1990, pp. 24–33.

holds.[17] However, the Council of Economic Advisors figured in 1992 that only one-sixth of family income gains between 1970 and 1990 was attributable to the growth in two-income families.[18]

"Well, we may have grown absolutely, but didn't the country's production decline *relative* to the rest of the world?" is a favorite response. Nope, not in the 1980s. U.S. output as a percentage of the output of the rest of the world did decline in the 1960s and the first half of the 1970s (because of the relatively rapid expansion of other countries), but after the mid-1970s, the United States held its own vis-à-vis the total output of all other major industrial countries combined (with Japan being a notable exception). U.S. output as a percentage of the rest of the world's output (including Japan's) was the same in 1989 as it was in 1975. Of course, the U.S. economy grew relatively to the rest of the world into the mid-1990s, but mainly because of the sharp declines in the output of the former Soviet Union republics, not so much because the U.S. economy was pressing rapidly ahead.

With some obvious astonishment, the reporter, who should have known more of the facts than he did (in spite of the fact that he was from the metropolitan section), asked a concluding question, "Why then are so many people across the country convinced that the 1980s were a dreadful decade?" A tough question, no doubt, with no obvious single answer.

Clearly, a part of the answer is that, as noted, hardship sells a lot of newspapers and magazines. The media has perhaps had an economic incentive to play up the failures and losses of the decade and to ignore the successes, making for a distorted overall picture of economic life. A part of the answer may be that the country lost more than a million manufacturing jobs during the 1980s and another million since, but, then again, we probably would not have been a world-class industrial power at the end of the decade had those jobs not been destroyed largely through productivity increases.[19] The loss of manufacturing jobs was a

17. As reported by Alan L. Otten, "Two-Income Marriages Are Now the Norm," *Wall Street Journal,* June 13, 1994, p. B1.

18. As reported by Robert J. Samuelson, "Why Getting Ahead Feels Like Falling Back," *Los Angeles Times,* June 6, 1994, p. B11.

19. It is really not at all clear how many "manufacturing jobs" were lost in any given period for two reasons: First, there may now be a lot of "manufacturing" (in the sense that real goods are produced) by Americans that is not officially considered to be a part of the manufacturing sector. Second, manufacturing firms often outsource many of their services, for example, trucking. The displaced workers are counted as lost manufacturing workers. The workers in the firms where the manufacturing firms buy their services are often counted as a part of some other sector, for example, transportation.

worldwide phenomenon, the consequence of technological trends that were global in scope—and beyond the power of any country to abate (even if it wanted to do so, which, if the effort had been made, would have been foolish indeed).

Still, competition got tougher for many Americans, and the overwhelming majority responded by getting tougher themselves. The Ford Taurus would probably not have been the number-one selling automobile in the country in the mid-1990s, with quality to match its sales, had Ford not had to face the challenges it did in the 1980s. Automobile workers groaned at their difficult times in the early 1980s; they now freely admit that back then they simply were not producing the quality automobiles that consumers demanded. The late Joseph Schumpeter, Harvard economist, would probably be pleased with much that happened during the 1980s, for it was an era in which "creative destruction" blossomed (with as much or more emphasis on creativity than destruction).[20]

However, I'm now convinced that many people don't want to know the good news about that fateful decade or the times since, a point that has been driven home by encounters with university colleagues. Such knowledge blows political stances and forces a deeper and more taxing consideration of the issues involved and elements at work in the world that are beyond political repair.

Heady Assessments

At a weekly after-work gathering of staff and faculty at my university (which occurred while I was working on this book), an administrator came in waving a copy of the commentary section of a local newspaper that had carried a column of mine summarizing themes of my already published book on the 1980s, "I'm not believing a word in this," she proclaimed. Another administrator quickly snapped (only after hearing tidbits on what I wrote but before stopping to read the column), "Sounds like Stalinism to me." I could barely contain myself, but I did challenge him politely on how he could so quickly equate a recitation of many readily available facts (several of which were mentioned above) with the work of one of the most ruthless men in history? "Well, it's this revisionist history thing," he said, as if anyone who dares correct a mistaken view is necessarily seeking to distort reality. I suggested that he read the book, but knew full well that he would remain content in his quick assessment.

20. Joseph A. Schumpeter, *Capitalism, Socialism, and Democracy,* 3rd ed. (New York: Harper & Row, 1962).

What continues to be remarkable about people's reactions to the arguments in *What Went Right in the 1980s* is their inclination to find pat phrases to dismiss everything said. "Scientific fiction" is one such phrase used by someone who obviously wished that even the data on national production were not believable or that my figures had been fabricated. Is what happened to industrial production considered fiction, a fabrication? The doubters need to check out the data themselves, but, again, that might unsettle firmly implanted justifications for policy and political positions. The reactions to the book bring to mind Josh Billings's observation, "The trouble with most folks isn't so much their ignorance, as knowing so many things that ain't so."

In a more private conversation at the end of the happy-hour table, I was challenged politely on several fronts by a medical professor: "Surely the 1980s were a decade of greed?" No, greed was not invented in the 1980s. While greed is probably an underrated economic motivation even for the critics, there is literally no evidence, aside from a few anecdotes about Wall Street and S&L crooks, that greed was more unbounded in the 1980s than in earlier decades. And greed obviously did not end with the advent of the new Democratic administration in the 1990s, given that the President and Mrs. Clinton fared unbelievably well on her short-lived commodity trades in the late 1970s and that one of the new administration's strongest supporters, entertainer Barbra Streisand, was able to pull in a reported $20 million for a single concert. The critics, who have damned real-life entrepreneurs for their "princely incomes," appear to be willing to excuse such charges today in spite of the fact that the concert fee represents a rate of pay that must surely exceed the so-called excesses of most 1980s "paper entrepreneurs."

Furthermore, we can assess the claims of unchecked greed by looking at the charitable contributions of Americans during the decade. And charitable contributions in inflation-adjusted terms rose at a substantially faster pace in the 1980s than during the previous two and a half decades, even out-pacing consumer purchases on a host of goods and services that supposedly reflected the mood of the so-called "me-ism" decade (jewelry, meals eaten out, and membership in health clubs), as well as consumer debt. Even corporate giving as a percentage of corporate income rebounded in the 1980s. Charity fell off in the early 1990s, but that was to be predicted, given the recession and subsequent slow recovery.[21]

"Ah, but the rich got richer while everyone else got poorer." The data

21. See James Flannigan, "Feeling the Pinch," *Los Angeles Times,* March 15, 1995, p. D3.

is decidedly mixed. Yes, many rich people became much richer, but it is also true that many poor and middle-income American also got richer. Many people who were poor at the start of the decade were at the top of the income distribution at the end of the decade. Besides, the overwhelming majority of rich people made their fortunes in the good old-fashioned way: They earned them in much the same way that Wal-Mart's founder, the late Sam Walton, and Microsoft chairman Bill Gates earned theirs, by taking sizable risks and providing Americans with superior products on more favorable terms. They didn't steal their fortunes.

"But the rich made out like bandits when it came to taxes at the same time Reagan slashed welfare programs to the bone." Not so, again. Top income earners paid a higher percentage of federal taxes in 1990 than in 1980. Total real dollars spent on welfare programs for low-income families and children rose by close to a fifth during the Reagan years—at the same time that the number of poor people in the country actually fell by a small but nontrivial number (300,000). Furthermore, during the decade, a family of four at the poverty income line saw its real federal tax liability slashed by a whopping 75 percent.

"Surely the 1980s were a decade of debt." This was indeed true for government. However, it should be noted that one of the reasons (but not the only reason) debt rose so rapidly in real dollar terms, and as a percentage of national income in the 1980s, was that the government, with the cooperation of the Federal Reserve, stopped doing what it had previously been prone to do—inflate the federal debt away.

Moreover, it is patently wrong to assume the rise in private debt was largely unwarranted. Being richer, Americans could handle more debt, especially since financial markets continued to develop and innovate. A major unnoticed reason for the explosion of debt in the expanding 1980s was the collapse of American businesses' debt-to-asset ratios in the unstable, inflationary 1970s. Much of the assumption of private debt in the 1980s also went into real productive assets, which explains why Americans' real assets (not including their considerable human capital) rose by more than $7 trillion (in 1990 dollars) and their consolidated net worth rose by 14 percent, or by $2 trillion during the decade.

My friend was incredulous, but she was willing to confess what I had suspected: "You know, I just don't want to believe you are right."

Telling Reactions

Probably a more telling reaction came from a history professor friend (and an ardent critic of virtually everything Ronald Reagan ever did while in office). He indicated an interest in using my book in a graduate course that would also include readings from critics of the 1980s. He asked where he could get a copy because he wanted to read the book first, a reasonable point. I was flattered until he admitted, "I don't want to assign it if it is a good book." There was an obvious element of teasing in his voice (given his grin as he spoke), but there was also an element of truth. He had bought all of the myths about the decade; he was comfortable with a one-word explanation for what he believed to be hard times: Reagan. A "good" book would clearly make it tougher for him to insist that the only possible righteous way to economic prosperity is through the halls of Congress and the federal treasury.

My historian friend is convinced, as are virtually all critics, that the S&L disaster, which became painfully evident in the last half of the decade, revealed the intellectual and practical bankruptcy of Reagan's free-market policies. After all, the S&L industry was "deregulated" in the early 1980s. First, it must be noted that the actual deregulatory law was not Reagan's doing. The S&L deregulatory statute was actually proposed under Carter. Second, the S&L problems hardly reflect "free-market policies," under which people are fully accountable for the risks they take. On the contrary, the S&L debacle reflects a "national industrial (or, more accurately, a national financial) policy" gone awry.

The S&L debacle was an economic disaster in the making for five decades, given that the industry could not, by law, diversify its portfolio (it had to focus its loans narrowly on housing)—an obvious point of departure that causes critics of the 1980s to squirm. The industry was in deep financial difficulty in the early 1980s, primarily because of the inflationary spiral of the 1960s and 1970s that forced S&Ls, which had full portfolios of low-interest-rate, long-term loans, to pay escalating interest rates on their deposits. The failing industry, which was being drained of its capital by homeowners, needed a bailout, but Congress and the Carter administration did not want to infuse the industry directly with federal funds. In effect, Washington policymakers sought to orchestrate a bailout on the sly, by allowing the S&Ls to seek high-risk/high-rates-of-return investments and, at the same time, by assuring the S&Ls and the public that the added risks would be fully covered by more subsidized deposit insurance. Unwarranted risk taking and outright fraud became national pastimes for many S&L bankers, mainly because of the backdoor subsidies (through deposit insurance that took away incentives depositors would otherwise have to monitor their bankers).

Contrary to the critics' claims, the growing debacle proved that the flaws were in the government bailouts and industrial (financial) management, not in the free-market policies.[22] The S&L policy ploy is one that Ronald Reagan should have spurned with the same vehemence that he opposed the national industrial policy recommendations of Walter Mondale in the 1984 presidential campaign. While critics of the 1980s delight in having Reagan faulted for the S&L problems, they consistently seek to dismiss my reasoning not with effective counterarguments, but with a glib tag: "Twisted argument." Understandably, they want the weaknesses of the person, not the policy, to be at the center of disdain. The allure of industrial management from Washington is at stake. Regardless of how the S&L debacle is interpreted, we must understand that the real costs of the debacle were, for the most part, incurred in the past, when the mistaken investments were made. Those costs are completely sunk, and should be a dead issue because they can have no bearing on where we go from here, unless, of course, we refuse to heed the lessons of that part of our history.

Shifting Stands

At times, the critics have relented in their defense of unwarranted statistical claims about the 1980s, but all too often they concede no real ground. Instead, they seek to shift the terms of the debate, as they did throughout the 1980s. As the decade opened, the country was mired in a recession brought on, as noted, by the severe anti-inflationary policy of the Federal Reserve (inaugurated in October 1979). The critics were then confident that the country was caught in the "British disease," a long-term malaise because nothing seemed to be working very well (the late 1970s was a period of practically no growth in worker productivity).

When the recovery began, the argument shifted to the problem of economic decay and "deindustrialization." Once it became apparent in the mid-1980s that the economy was being transformed with a significantly more productive industrial base, the argument shifted to concern over long-term decline relative to other countries. After it became evident that this claim was way off the mark, the critics began to assert that the problem was one of a "great U-turn" in worker wages that was caused by unchecked greed.

With my book in hand and a lot of data to work with, any number of

22. For an extended discussion of this perspective on the S&L crisis, see William A. Niskanen, "Heads I Win, Tails You Lose," *National Review*, August 31, 1992, pp. 45–48.

critics have told me in so many words, "In spite of your evidence, we know better; the problem in the 1980s was the nasty attitude of those in power," which all too often translates to "Don't bother with trying to change my mind."

When I have insisted that some claims are worthy of checking, I can count on the critics seeking to hang the albatross of political intentions around my neck. Obviously, the book is the work of an apologist for Ronald Reagan, they say, which cannot be further from the truth. Although I supported many of Ronald Reagan's policy stands, I insist that I'm neither a Republican nor a Democrat (I voted for Bill Clinton, or, rather, against George Bush). In good humor, I submit that I'm something far worse, an academic economist who doesn't believe he has been able to tell the whole story of the 1980s, but who is convinced that he has sought to make a contribution, albeit minor, to balancing an important policy debate.

Warm-Hearted Support

The reaction has hardly been all negative. Not all Americans have bought into the economic mythology. I have been struck by the number of heartfelt thanks from people across the country for providing, if nothing else, an alternate view, one that more accurately described the America they knew in the 1980s. One radio talk-show host went so far as to suggest that the critics must have been living in "outer space," but I was especially struck by the comments of a woman from North Carolina who called while I was on the air to say with eloquence that cannot be captured here that she and her husband never made more than $23,000 a year during the 1980s, but they did improve their lot and were thankful for the chance to do their own thing and to have and educate their children. They now wanted "nothing from nobody." The attitude she displayed stood in sharp contrast with the prevailing sentiments of the time.

As should now be obvious, the 1980s have been variously described as a decade of *D*s: Decay, Decline, Deindustrialization, Debt, re-Distribution, and Despair. The facts make myths of those glib characterizations, but many of the critics don't seem to want to be bothered by the facts, possibly because they have a political and economic stake in keeping the eighties down and totally out. It appears to be no accident that critics of the 1980s accompany their sordid claims about the decade (or "the last twelve years," a phrase that has always flowed with unflinching ease from Bill Clinton's lips) with calls for "change"—that is, for reversal. A return to the "good old days" of the 1960s and 1970s of escalating government involvement in the economy—by way of health-care reform, managed international trade, expansive industrial policies, and labor mandates—requires, apparently, that the Reagan policies be trashed, and one of the best ways of doing that is to dump on the decade as a whole, to insist that the times were far tougher than they were and that the toughness of the times were all caused by Reagan (with no help from Congress).

Contrary to the claims of the decade's critics (as will be explained in some detail in chapter 6), Ronald Reagan and his political cohorts should probably be given far less credit or blame for what went right in the 1980s than they have been. After all, a Democratically controlled Congress was at work in the 1980s, and Ronald Reagan did not always get his way with Congress (and, according to his conservative critics, he should have pursued his domestic agenda with far more zeal). And it will be argued later that a return to the policy course of the 1960s and 1970s is not in the economic cards.

Moreover, Reagan's policies were nowhere near as "conservative" and "free-market oriented" as the critics would like to believe.[23] During the Reagan era, government continued to expand in real dollar and per capita terms. Federal government spending represented a higher percentage of national income during the Reagan administration than during the Carter administration.

Reagan's main contribution to conservative government, if it can be called that, is that he may have helped to cap the upward march of government spending as a percent of gross domestic product. I say "may" because government spending during the 1980s was being capped relative to national production in most other major industrial powers around the world with widely varying political philosophies, a fact that must make one wonder whether it could have been "all Reagan's fault (or credit)" and whether the capping of spending might not have been the consequence of global economic forces at work in the world on all governments' policies. Into the 1990s, those same global forces remain at work, causing the size of the U.S. government to fall relative to the national economy even under the activist Clinton administration. Total federal outlays averaged slightly more than 23 percent of gross domestic product under Ronald Reagan. By fiscal 1995, they had fallen to less than 22 percent under Bill Clinton (lower than any year under Reagan).

23. For a critique of Reagan's policy agenda and accomplishments, see William A. Niskanen, *Reaganomics: An Insider's Account of the Policies and People* (New York: Oxford University Press, 1988).

Upon finishing a presentation, I can count on critics persisting. They don't always deny the facts, which they tend to sidestep, but often start a new listing of problems that supposedly emerged in the 1980s. As one radio talk-show host suggested, "Aren't you simply presenting a warped case for the Reagan era by concentrating on a few favorable statistics?" She didn't seem to realize that the statistics I had presented on her show (and have quickly covered here) have been—or, at least, were—at the core of prior claims that the decade was an unmitigated disaster and that now come as a surprise to many. The strategy of critics appears to be one of keeping the decade in total disrepute by constantly changing the grounds for the debate and then claiming that defenders of the decade are considering irreleant issues, or worse yet, have not dealt with all issues, as if that were possible.

Nevertheless, progress is being made in rewriting history as it should be. Prior to 1994, Sylvia Nasar, a reporter for the *New York Times* who repeatedly purveyed dismal economic statistics on the 1980s as if they were undisputed truth and who has accordingly contributed in a nontrivial way to the decade's reputation, now admits that the defenders of the decade, who have been cast aside as apologists for the Reagan administration, are being proved right in the 1990s, given the turnaround in economic activity that is founded in the successes of the 1980s.[24]

It is clear that not everything went right during the 1980s. Competition got tougher for many worker groups, especially those Americans in previously protected (and unionized) markets and those with limited education (who could not or would not stay in school or go back to school). Some people's economic hardship was a product of bad choices. Crime continued to march upward. Divorce and teenage pregnancy boomed. Too many Americans suffered a lapse of civility, frugality, and diligence (critical points to which we will return in later chapters).

Nevertheless, much did go right in America in the 1980s, in spite of all the problems. That is the bottom line that too few Americans, Bill Clinton included, are willing to accept. However, Bill Clinton can thank his lucky political stars that his assessment of the "past twelve years" is largely wrong. In the considerable successes of the 1980s lie the seeds of prosperity for the rest of the 1990s and beyond.

24. Nasar writes, "The image of the United States as an economic winner, once associated with apologists for the Reagan era, is catching on. The French newspaper *Le Monde* and the Japanese newspaper *Yomiuri Shimbun* have each run long stories on the new U.S. Competitive Threat" (Sylvia Nasar, "The American Economy, Back on Top: Things Are Beginning to Turn Around for American Business and the Economy," *New York Times*, February 27, 1994, p. F1).

Beneath the Aggregate Statistics

If you have bought into the mythology of economic pessimism, and if the above broad-based income and output statistics don't impress you, you might be affected by more down-to-earth numbers. A report from the Federal Reserve Bank of Dallas paints a decidedly upbeat picture of the country's economic prowess during the past two decades, if not the past twelve years.[25] The report's writers, economists Michael Cox and Richard Alm, don't concentrate on arcane income statistics, which, admittedly, leave much room for misinterpretation and misuse. They go to the heart of America's living standard, what people have been buying with their incomes and doing with their time to enhance their quality of life.

Table 1 will, no doubt, make doubters run for political refutations. Data, especially data on consumer purchases, always has limitations, and that is certainly true of the data in Table 1. Individual statistics overplay progress in some ways and in just as many ways underplay it. At the same time, the overall picture painted by the data is compelling, revealing a sharp contrast between the rhetoric of commentaries and economic reality. If the American Dream has been busted, as claimed, we must wonder how the average size of new homes could have risen by a third over the last two decades, to over 2,000 square feet in 1990 from 1,500 square feet in 1970. Most of these new homes were far better equipped, as evident in the rise of homes with central air-conditioning to 76 percent in 1990 from 34 percent in 1970. And not all of the larger homes were bought by the "rich."

Granted, it is widely believed that today people can't afford to buy houses of any kind, much less the homes their parents did. Houses are expensive, with the median-priced home in the country in 1994 standing at more than $107,000. However, they became less expensive—more affordable (when not considering the tax advantages)—in the 1980s as mortgage interest rates fell.[26] In May 1994, the "affordability index" for houses stood at its highest level in more than two decades. In fact, in 1994, a family with median income, $38,310, had 141 percent of the income required to buy the median-priced home. Another way of saying the same thing is that the "median family" in the country could afford to buy a house worth $151,300 (or 41 percent above the median-priced house). No wonder the percent of households owning their own homes

25. Michael Cox and Richard Alm, *These Are the Good Old Days: A Report on U.S. Living Standards* (Dallas: Federal Reserve Bank of Dallas, 1994).

26. As reported in "Affordability of Homes Near 20-Year High," *Los Angeles Times*, May 11, 1994, p. D2.

Table 1. Measures of Living Standard

	1970	1990
Average size of a new home (square feet)	1,500	2,080
New homes with central air-conditioning	34 percent	76 percent
People using computers	<100,000	75.9 million
Households with color TV	33.9 percent	96.1 percent
Households with cable TV	4 million	55 million
Households with VCRs	0	67 million
Households with two or more vehicles	29.3 percent	54 percent
Median household net worth (real)	$24,217	$48,887
Housing units lacking complete plumbing	6.9 percent	1.1 percent
Homes lacking a telephone	13 percent	5.2 percent
Households owning a microwave oven	<1 percent	78.8 percent
Heart transplant procedures	<10	2,125*
Average workweek	37.1 hours	34.5 hours
Average daily time working in the home	3.9 hours	3.5 hours
Work time to buy gas for 100-mile trip	49 minutes	31 minutes*
Annual paid vacation and holidays	15.5 days	22.5 days
Number of people retired from work	13.3 million	25.3 million
Women in the workforce	31.5 percent	56.6 percent
Recreational boats owned	8.8 million	16 million
Manufacturers' shipments of RVs	30,300	226,500
Adult softball teams	29,000	188,000
Recreational golfers	11.2 million	27.8 million
Attendance at symphonies and orchestras	12.7 million	43.5 million
Americans finishing high school	51.9 percent	77.7 percent
Americans finishing four years of college	13.5 percent	24.4 percent
Employee benefits as a share of payroll	29.3 percent	40.2 percent†
Life expectancy at birth (years)	70.8	75.4
Death rate by accidental causes	714.3	520.2

*Figures are for 1991. †Figure is for 1992.

Source: Michael Cox and Richard Alm, *These Are the Good Old Days: A Report on U.S. Living Standards* (Dallas: Federal Reserve Bank of Dallas, 1994), p. 4.

held steady at about 65 percent from 1970 on, in spite of the fact that disinflation and the decreases in marginal tax rates in the 1980s worked to increase the after-tax cost of housing.[27]

27. The disinflation and the decreases in the marginal tax rates of the 1980s actually worked to increase the after-tax cost of housing. With inflation taken out of interest rates and with lower marginal tax rates, each dollar spent on housing meant a greater loss in after-tax purchasing power.

In addition, many critics charge that young people cannot "afford" to buy their parents' homes. That's true regarding the house the children were in immediately before they left home, but not true regarding the home their parents had when they started out in their marriage. The children can generally afford their parents' first home, but only if they would lower themselves to take it. Young people seem to want what their parents now have in the way of housing—which many young people are clearly unable to afford—not what the parents bought when they started out three or four decades ago. The problem is that they won't buy them; they aren't large enough and don't have the requisite add-ons, those things that are now "necessities" that not too long ago were considered outright "luxuries": dishwashers, garbage disposals, recessed lighting, ceramic tile floors, alarm systems, whirlpool baths, and so forth.

We've been told that practically everyone (aside for the rich) has been getting relentlessly poorer. However, the data in the table suggests much the opposite occurred. Households with color TVs rose to over 96 percent of all households in 1990 (meaning that color television reception was then a universal luxury in rich and poor American homes) from under 34 percent in 1970. Households with cable TV expanded nearly fourteenfold. No one had a VCR at home in 1970, mainly because VCRs were not commercially available at reasonable prices for home use, but 67 million American households, including millions of poor households, had VCRs in 1990. The percent of households with two or more cars also doubled during the 1970–1990 period. One of the problems that Americans had in buying homes was that the prices of luxuries like VCRs and computers were falling so precipitously, becoming so much more attractive relative to housing, that they were switching, quite rationally, from purchases of homes to the purchases of other goods and services. The Cox and Alm report adds,

> Three-quarters of U.S. homes had a clothes washer in 1990, up from less than two-thirds in 1970s. At the same time, ownership of dryers jumped from 45 percent of households to almost 70 percent. About 45 percent of households had dishwashers, up from 26 percent two decades ago. Between 1970 and 1990, the typical U.S. household gained 4.5 times more audio and video products, more than twice as much gear for sports and hobbies, 50 percent more in kitchen appliances and 30 percent more in furniture. In short, most Americans consume far more than previous generations.[28]

28. Cox and Alm, *These Are the Good Old Days*, p. 15.

How could this be? Americans simply got richer. Table 1 shows that median household net worth (which is assets minus debt) more than doubled in real, 1990 dollar terms during the same period. Notice that the data is for median household net worth, implying that 50 percent of households are below and above the figures given. The only way for the median to rise—in fact, double—is for households with low net worths to advance. If only the top 50 percent (or top 20 percent, 5 percent, or 1 percent) of households saw their net worths rise between 1970 and 1990, the average net worth would have risen, but then the median net worth, which is in the table, would not have risen at all. But the median rose!

Moreover, when Americans are grouped into broad household categories and the groups' growth in wealth is computed between 1983 and 1989 (the latest years of wealth data available from the Federal Reserve System), there is a surprising degree of broad-based growth.[29] The group of households with one of the lowest increases in wealth during the period was married couples with no children; their wealth grew by 12 percent in real (1989) dollars. Married couples with children, however, saw their wealth grow in the 1983–1989 period by a third. Single men, with or without children, had an increase in wealth of 41 percent, while the growth in the wealth of single women with no children at home grew by 14 percent. Only single women with children, as a group, experienced a decline in wealth, and the decline was a disquieting 12 percent. However, note that the wealth of whites grew by 24 percent, the wealth of blacks grew by 35 percent, and the wealth of Hispanics grew by 54 percent. Overall, average American household wealth grew in constant dollar terms by 20 percent.[30]

The growth in household wealth should only be surprising if the myth that Americans have not been saving very much is accepted as gospel. Careful analysis of American saving patterns reveals that, after appropriate but complicated adjustments are made, Americans have been saving at rates on par with the rates of saving found among the supposedly frugal Japanese.[31] The saving of Americans continues to rise at a healthy

29. As reported by John C. Weicher, "Getting Richer (At Different Rates)," *Wall Street Journal*, June 14, 1995, p. A16.

30. Ibid.

31. Official statistics have the Japanese saving rate at 16.6 percent in 1986, a year in which the U.S. saving rate was measured at 4.3 percent. However, if savings were computed on the same basis and by the same methods, the saving rates in the U.S. and Japan would both be in the 16 to 17 percent range [Kenichi Ohmae, *The End of the Nation State: The Rise of Regional Economies* (New York: Free Press, 1995), pp. 16–18].

clip (although there is certainly room for improvement in many American households). The total value of all American pension and retirement accounts (not including Social Security), as measured by the Washington-based Employee Benefit Research Institute, was $3.1 trillion in 1985 (in 1993 dollars), $5.1 trillion in 1991, and $5.8 trillion in 1993.[32] That's an increase of 87 percent in the retirement pool in real dollar terms in only eight years or 14 percent in two years.[33] As a nation, we probably should be more frugal, but we certainly have not been as profligate as widely claimed.

Just look through Table 1 and see if you don't want to ask at the end, "Who's been pulling my leg? Did the vast majority of Americans really retrogress or stagnate during the most recent two decades?" Again, not everything went right in the 1980s, much less the 1970s. Economic growth could have been higher, especially in the 1970s. More Americans could have advanced more rapidly, and fewer Americans could have fallen off the income ladder (which, no doubt, would have been the case if the Federal Reserve had not had to throttle in the 1980s the inflationary spiral of the 1960s and 1970s). Probably more Americans saw their incomes fall than was the case during previous decades; there was a great deal of churning in the economy during the most recent decades. The churning has continued into the 1990s with a growing vengeance in some sectors of the economy. Those decades have been decades of extraordinary technological progress and of economic challenges for many, union families especially, given that all former worker groups and firms with market power saw their power dissipate with the emergence of global competition. However, it is certainly true that the difference in the number of people who fell down the ladder is nowhere near as great as advertised. As evident in Table 1, many things obviously did go right over the past so-called decades of decline.

Other evidence exists demonstrating the improved lifestyle and economic status of the American people. Housing units lacking complete plumbing fell from being a small problem in 1970 to virtually a nonexis-

32. As reported by Robert J. Samuelson, "Whining about Boomers' Savings," *Washington Post National Weekly*, August 7–13, 1995, p. 5. The savings figures include contributions to pension plans, 401(b) plans, individual retirement accounts, and retirement savings other than Social Security.

33. The rich have always controlled a lion's share of the country's total material wealth, but their share appears to be contracting in the 1990s. The richest 1 percent held 30 percent of the total net worth in 1992, down from 37 percent in 1989. The bottom 90 percent of the population, with the least net worth, held 33 percent of net worth in 1992, up from 32 percent in 1989 (as reported in Richard W. Stevenson, "Rich Are Getting Richer, but Not the Very Rich," *New York Times*, March 13, 1996, p. C1).

tent problem in 1990. Homes without telephones fell by half. Less than 1 percent of American households had microwave ovens in 1970. By 1990, nearly four-fifths of American households had them. During the same period, as noted earlier, Americans also renewed their beneficence, giving away their income and time to charitable causes at unprecedented post–World War II rates.

Progress also came in many noneconomic forms after 1970. Heart transplants rose dramatically in the 1970–1990 period, although the number remained relatively low in 1990 (2,125). Accidental deaths at home and work fell. Health-care costs have continued to rise, but so has the overall healthiness of the population, as Americans themselves assess their health and as data reveals:

> Surveys by the U.S. Department of Health and Human Services show a steady drop in the proportion of Americans who rate their health as "fair or poor," from 12.2 percent in 1975 to 9.3 percent in 1991. Infant mortality rates fell from 20 deaths per 1,000 live births in 1970 to less than 9 in 1991. The death rate from natural causes fell by 27 percent from 1970 to 1990, with the most progress coming in diseases of the heart. Cancer death rates are up slightly, but modern medical science provides treatment that prolongs life. The portion of the adult population with high cholesterol fell sharply over the past two decades. What once was fatal can in many cases now be treated. Heart, liver and lung transplants, almost unheard of in the early 1970s, are common today.[34]

Even the index of air quality in the country improved, a fact that is clearly evident in Figure 2(a). That does not mean the country and world is not without environmental problems. Most are aware of serious problems that extend from overpaving the terrain to global warming, but it is equally clear that the environmental gains have gone unheralded: "Levels of such major pollutants as particulate matter, sulfur oxides, volatile organic compounds, carbon monoxide and lead were their highest in 1970 or before. Levels of nitrogen oxides peaked in 1980. Overall, air quality is better now than at any time since data collection began in 1940. Water quality has improved since 1960, when authorities banned fishing in Lake Erie and fires erupted on the polluted Cuyahoga near Cleveland. The U.S. Geological Survey, examining trends since 1980, found that fecal coliform bacteria and phosphorous have decreased substantially in many parts of the country. Other traditional indicators of water quality—dissolved oxygen dissolved solids, nitrate and suspended sediments—have shown little change."[35]

34. Cox and Alm, *These Are the Good Old Days,* p. 19.
35. Ibid.

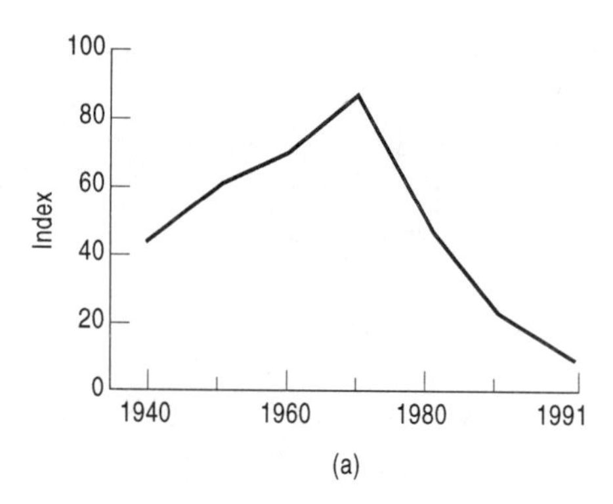

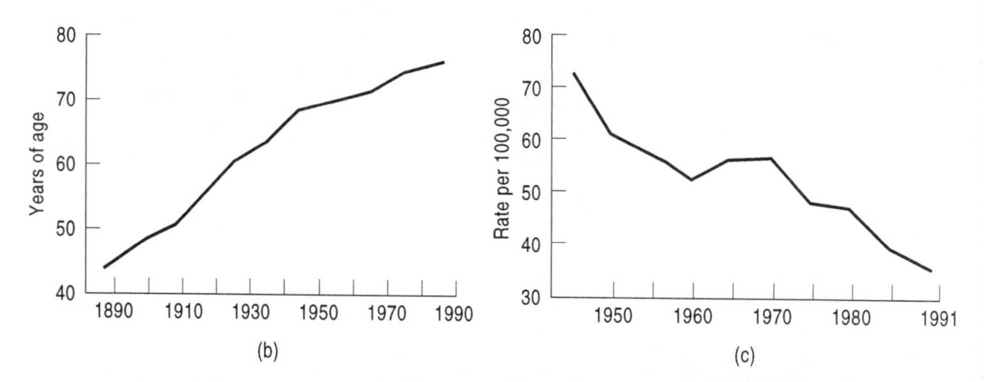

Figure 2. Measures of quality of life: (a) air pollution; (b) longevity; (c) accidential death. (From Michael Cox and Richard Alm, *These Are the Good Old Days: A Report on U.S. Living Standards* [1993 annual report] [Dallas: Federal Reserve Bank of Dallas, 1994], p. 16)

All the while in the 1970–1990 period, national production expanded by nearly three-quarters. The country was simply producing more with less, especially less energy (per unit of output) from both natural and human sources. The average workweek fell by 7 percent between 1970 and 1990, while the time spent working in the home dropped by 10 percent. Indeed, the Cox and Alm report reveals (a fact not included in Table 1) that working Americans labored 181 fewer hours in 1990 than they did in 1973, partly because the average number of vacation days and holidays rose by 45 percent, to over 22 days in 1990 from 15.5 days in 1970. Employee benefits as a percent of payroll reached 40 percent in 1990, up from 29 percent in 1970, a finding that partially explains the measured (and widely reported) decline in some workers' money wages.

The number of retired people doubled, as workers retired earlier. The percentage of women in the workforce also doubled, a change that has been praised (because women now have more economic opportunities) and damned (because children are not getting the motherly care and time that they once did). As evidence of greater relaxation for many Americans, we can point to the fact that the number of adult softball teams expanded by more than sixfold at the same time that the count of recreational golfers more than doubled. Even the number of Americans attending symphonic concerts more than tripled (and no telling how many more young Americans were attending concerts of their favorite singers).

There were no compact disks sold in 1970 or, for that matter, in 1980. There were only 23 million sold in 1985, but more than 333 million were sold in 1991, an increase of fourteenfold in a mere six years. Overall, Americans raised their recreational expenditures from 5 percent of total personal consumption in 1970 to 8 percent in 1991 (the same period when Americans' real-dollar total consumption expenditures rose by 80 percent).

One of the disheartening facts of the past two decades has been the lack of progress in student performance on standardized tests. The heartening side of the record (and a side worthy of note because of the improvement, not the absolute level of the statistics) is that the percentage of American high school students receiving their diplomas rose to nearly 78 percent in 1990 from under 52 percent in 1970. The percentage of Americans completing college rose to over 24 percent in 1990 from under 14 percent in 1970. The number of books sold in the expanding discount-book store business expanded by 20 percent between 1982 and 1991.

Finally, Americans' life expectancy at birth rose at a slightly lower pace in the 1970s and 1980s than in earlier decades [Figure 2(b)]. However, it still rose by more than 6 percent, to over seventy-five years in 1990 from under seventy-one years in 1970—partly because, as evident in Figure 2(c), the rate of accidental deaths per 100,000 residents dropped from about 55 in 1970 to 35 in 1991. The facts simply show that, when adjusted for population changes, fewer people are dying on the job, at home, and in automobiles and airplanes now than at any time in the recent past.

Much has been made of the supposedly "overworked American."[36]

36. See Juliet B. Schor, *The Overworked American: The Unexpected Decline of Leisure* (New York: Basic Books, 1991).

However, Americans can expect to spend over 17,000 fewer hours at work on the job and at home over the course of their lives than they could have expected in 1973. Because of that fact and their longer life spans, Americans could expect in 1990 to have on average 42,000 more hours of "waking leisure" time over the course of their lives than they could have expected in 1970 (and more than three times as much waking leisure, or 209,000 hours, than Americans averaged in 1870).[37]

The picture offered here is, admittedly, distorted; more good things happened during the 1970s and 1980s than can possibly be presented here. All the reader needs to do to verify that fact is look around the home and office or peruse the many home-shopping catalogues that fill the mailboxes to see the many things that are now available but that were unavailable just a few years back. Table 2 provides a short working list of improved products and medical advances since 1970, not the least of which are camcorders, voice mail, pagers, home exercise equipment, airbags, CAT scans, and soft contact lenses. Many things that were available in earlier years have been greatly improved. Audiosystems rival live concerts. Tires last longer and no longer blow out as frequently, with the cost per mile, measured in workers' time, reduced by nearly 40 percent over two decades. New cars almost never need a tune-up. Computers can do many more things faster, the color on color television sets is more vibrant, and carpets are easier to clean than ever before. When people can buy a wristwatch that includes not only a battery of features from a stopwatch to a calendar to an alarm, but also a four-function calculator and built-in remote control for television and audiosystem, all for less than $100 when first introduced in the mid-1990s (which means its will eventually sell for much less), somehow you've got to believe that the core economic problems of the country are only tangentially related to what Americans are able and willing to buy. (If you think that such a watch is too frivolous, consider the watch that sounds out the time for the visually impaired or the one that doubles as a Dick Tracy–style pager.) There is simply more "stuff" everywhere. If that were not the case, we wouldn't face the trash problem that we do.

The irony of progress when based on quality improvements is that official statistics can understate, if not totally miss, the realized economic gains. The quality improvements can raise production costs and prices, but even when the improvements are worth more than their costs, official statistics can portray declining real income, defined as so much money adjusted for inflation but not for quality.

37. See the calculations made by Cox and Alm, *These Are the Good Old Days*, p. 8.

Table 2. New and Improved Products and Medical Advances Since 1970

New or Greatly Improved Products Since 1970		
microwave oven	electronic date book	small-screen TVs
camcorder	electric knives	CDs and CD players
voice mail	in-line roller skates	remote controls
cellular phone	miniature radios	sound systems
ultrasound	exercise equipment	digital/LED displays
home security systems	all-terrain vehicles	videogames
synthesizers	videocassette recorder	food processors
pagers	laser printers	aspartame
quartz/digital watches	cordless phone	interactive toys
fax machines	personal computer	cable TV
coffee makers	answering machine	airbags
Medical Advances Since 1970		
cosmetics (Retin-A)	biosynthesized drugs	soft contact lenses
organ transplants	(recombinant DNA techniques)	cornea transplants
artifical pancreas	antidepressants	decongestants
painkillers	CAT scan	antiallergenics
(acetaminophen, ibuprofen)	radial kerotonomy	home pregnancy tests
cosmetic surgery	monoclonal antibodies	antiulcer drugs
(facelifts, implants, liposuction)	in vitro fertilization	

Source: Michael Cox and Richard Alm, *These Are the Good Old Days: A Report on U.S. Living Standards* (Dallas: Federal Reserve Bank of Dallas, 1994), p. 12.

The impact of the miscalculation of inflation and benefits is best seen in the computed changes in worker incomes. Without taking into account the changes in fringe benefits and by using an out-of-date consumer price index to compute real wages, critics of the American economy can show a great U-turn in worker wages between the early 1970s and the early 1990s.[38] Real average worker wages declined by 13 percent between 1973 and 1994. However, when the corrected consumer price index is used and worker benefits are added, worker wages may have actually grown by more than 10 percent, slow by historical standards, but growth nonetheless.[39] Moreover, growth in real hourly compensation and worker productivity remain closely tied in the 1990s, as

38. See Harrison and Bluestone, *Great U-Turn.*
39. See McKenzie, *What Went Right in the 1980s,* chap. 4.

was true in earlier decades.[40] The country's basic problem may be in the growth in productivity, but even productivity growth is probably a mirage of statistics gathering.

Federal Reserve chairman Alan Greenspan estimates that because of inadequate adjustments for quality improvements, the consumer price index may have overstated inflation in 1994 by as little as a half of a percentage point to over a full percentage point when the inflation rate was officially measured at under 3 percent, for a possible overstatement in the rate of between 19 and 52 percent for the year.[41] Although we can't be certain of the exact effects of quality improvements over long stretches of time, we can surmise that the growing emphasis on the quality of goods and services over the last two decades may have substantially understated the real-income growth over the last couple of decades, perhaps by several tens of percentage points.[42]

Even without pairing back the consumer price index, the income gains of the overwhelming majority of Americans have been unheralded. A great deal of attention has been paid to the *distribution* of income as represented by the mean or median income of families and households distributed over five groups or quintiles. I found that the mean income of every quintile rose modestly during the 1980s, although the highest income group had almost twice the percentage growth of the lowest quintile.[43] However, such evidence can be misleading, given that anyone in the bottom quintile whose income improves substantially can be catapulted to higher quintiles while anyone in the top bracket whose income goes up has nowhere to go. Hence, narrow focus on the income distribution by quintiles can hide substantial changes in the incomes of individuals who have moved *among* the quintiles.

40. From 1950 until 1995, total real compensation of workers rose 144.2 percent; productivity rose 144.9 percent during the same period. The close connection between compensation and productivity was only lost during the 1970s and first few years of the 1980s, and the divergence between the series was slight (see Herbert Stein, "A Primer on Pay and Productivity," *Wall Street Journal*, August 23, 1995, p. A10).

41. As reported in Kenneth N. Gilpin, "Changing an Inflation Gauge Is Tougher Than It Sounds," *New York Times*, February 22, 1995, p. C1.

42. For a discussion of the serious difficulties in estimating the size of the potential biases in the consumer price index, see Mark A. Wynne and Flona D. Sigalla, "The Consumer Price Index," *Economics Review* (Federal Reserve Bank of Dallas: Second Quarter 1994), pp. 1–23.

43. I found that between 1983 and 1996, the mean real income of households in the bottom quintile rose by 11 percent, while the mean income of households in the top quintile rose by 18 percent. See McKenzie, *What Went Right in the 1980s*, chap. 4.

Michael Cox and Richard Alm have clarified critical points in the debate.[44] They identified 3,725 individuals in the University of Michigan's Panel Survey on Income Dynamics whose annual earnings were recorded for all years between 1975 and 1991. Table 3 reports their basic findings. Contrary to all the talk about the "rich getting richer and the poor, poorer," they found the earnings gains of the "poor" (those in the lowest quintile) to be far greater in absolute and percentage terms than the gains of the "rich" (those in the top quintiles). Measured in 1993 dollars, the mean income of the lowest quintile was $1,153 in 1975 and $26,475 in 1991, an increase of $25,322, or nearly 2200 percent. The mean of the highest quintile was $45,704 in 1975 and $49,678 in 1991, an increase of $3,974, or less than 9 percent.[45]

An obvious explanation for the relatively faster income growth rates at the bottom of the income distribution is that those people tended to be young and unemployed, with the first condition always temporary and the second condition usually temporary. However, with their methods, Cox and Alm find far more upward income mobility than the critics have ever imagined, much less admitted. More than three-quarters of those in the bottom of the income distribution in 1975 made it all the way to the top 40 percent by 1991. Seventy percent of those in the second from the bottom quintile in 1975 had moved up at least one bracket by 1991. A meager 5 percent of those in the bottom quintile in 1975 were still in the bottom quintile in 1991. And a scant 1/2 percent were in the bottom quintile for all seventeen years covered by their study. Cox and Alm also found relatively rapid rises in individual incomes, mainly because of education. Workers who finished college saw their mean income increase by fivefold during the 1975–1991 period. Those who finished high school saw their mean income double. Even high school dropouts made significant gains, according to Cox and Alm.[46] They insist, understandably, that the American Dream remains achievable. All Americans need to do is follow a few simple and obvious rules: get educated, get a job,

44. W. Michael Cox and Richard Alm, *By Our Own Bootstraps: Economic Opportunity & the Dynamics of Income Distribution* (Dallas: Federal Reserve Bank of Dallas, 1996).

45. Ibid., p. 8. Cox and Alm's general conclusions are supported by the work of Isabell V. Sawhill and Mark Condon, "Is U.S. Income Inequality Really Growing? Sorting Out the Fairness Question," *Policy Bites* (Washington, D.C.: Urban Institute, June 1992) and the work of the U.S. Department of the Treasury, Internal Revenue Service, SOI Bulletin, Publication 1136 (Rev. 10-95), Fall 1995 and Office of Tax Analysis, "Household Income Changes Over Time: Some Basic Questions and Facts," *Tax Notes*, August 24, 1992.

46. Cox and Alm, *By Our Own Bootstraps*, pp. 8–10.

Table 3. The Poor Are Getting Richer Faster

Income Quintile in 1975	Average Income in 1975	Average Income in 1991	Absolute Gain	Percentage Gain
Fifth (highest)	$45,704	$49,678	$ 3,974	9
Fourth	$22,423	$31,292	$ 8,869	40
Third (middle)	$13,030	$22,304	$ 9,274	71
Second	$ 6,291	$28,373	$22,082	351
First (lowest)	$ 1,153	$26,475	$25,322	2196

Source: W. Michael Cox and Richard Alm, *By Our Own Bootstraps: Economic Opportunity & the Dynamics of Income Distribution* (Dallas: Federal Reserve Bank of Dallas, 1996), p. 8.

work hard, retrain, save, form a family, move occasionally, and stay the course.[47]

Indeed, the income data suggests we haven't become a "nation of hamburger-flippers" as critics contend. Clearly, the service sector of the economy has risen absolutely and relatively. Just as clearly, employment in fast-food restaurants has expanded rapidly over the past several decades, rising from under 10,000 in 1948 to 2.9 million in 1994. However, fast-food workers still represented only 2.4 percent of all employed American workers in 1994 (up from .01 percent in 1948). But the growth in the service economy has reflected terrific gains in agricultural and manufacturing productivity, as well as an increase in the demand for a variety of services, most of which involve jobs that are far removed in terms of wages and sophistication from hamburger-flipping. I am squarely in the service economy; most readers will be involved in the production of services that have grown rapidly over recent decades and who earn incomes some indefinite multiples of the wages of the lowest-paid, if not the most highly paid, assembly-line jobs in manufacturing. Even the critics who point to the erosion of worker wages in the 1990s can't deny that their own measure of the "quality" of jobs—called, appropriately, the "job quality index" (JQI)—has been on the rise since the mid-1980s. The Center for National Policy, a Washington-based think tank with a decidedly liberal political agenda, has found that while worker compensation declined by less than 3 percent between 1985 and the end of 1994, the JQI rose by 15 percent (which doesn't account for the quality biases in the measure of inflation mentioned earlier).[48] The rise of

47. Ibid., p. 15.

48. As reported in "1994 Saw Strong Gains in National Compensation with Jobs Up Sharply, But Worker Pay Still Lagging" (Washington: Center for National Policy, news release, January 11, 1995).

the service economy has simply not been the bane to the American economy that it has been made out to be. Indeed, the growth in the service economy has been an unheralded source of the growth in the productivity in the manufacturing economy.[49] No wonder the Switzerland-based World Economic Forum and Institute for Management Development rated the U.S. economy in the mid-1990s as "No. 1" in its ranking of the competitiveness of major industrial economies.[50]

Again, I understand that not everything is better now than in past years. Some things are worse. Problems abound, but there were problems 100 years ago, and 20 years ago. There will always be problems. People simply have a knack of extending themselves until they create problems that must be solved. The difference that distinguishes the ages is probably more in the attitude that people have when they face their problems. The point that needs to be stressed time and again is the positive aspects of our time, mainly because the positive side of economic progress has tended to get short shrift in the give and take of the country's political and economic debate.

Contrary to critical claims, the economy, per se, is not the basket case that it has been made out to be. As opposed to having less, the overwhelming majority of Americans, not just a tiny subset of those who are well off, have more of just about everything—or they could have had more, if they had not cut back on the time spent on the job! The goods and services are there; opportunities exist. And the future *can be* as bright as the past.

The Downsized Economy

Some of the angst Americans feel is clearly attributable to the fact (as well as constant news reports) of corporate "downsizing," or the elimination of literally thousands, if not tens of thousands, of jobs within single firms. The rate of job destruction has, understandably, moved up and down with the business cycle, but the trend appears to be upward. During the 1980s, one in every twenty-five American jobs

49. For more details on all of these arguments, see Michael Cox and Richard Alm, "The Rise of the Service Sector: Give It Some Respect," *Federal Reserve Bank of Dallas: 1994 Annual Report* (Dallas: Federal Reserve Bank of Dallas, 1995).

50. The rankings are based on a complex formula involving 378 criteria, ranging from attitude to management quality. According to the report, the United States was, in 1995, 5 percent more "competitive" than the second-ranked country, Singapore; 23 percent more competitive than fourth-ranked Japan; and 43 percent more competitive than fifteenth-ranked Sweden.

were destroyed; during the 1990s, one in every twenty jobs were destroyed.[51]

Large firms, many of whom were thought by retired Harvard economist John Kenneth Galbraith to be a fixed part of the "new industrial state" thirty years ago, have been using the ax with particular force. Table 4 lists twenty-five of the largest layoff announcements between 1991 and first-quarter 1994. IBM had announced plans to cut its staff by an astounding 85,000 workers, including many middle- and upper-management positions. AT&T had announced layoffs totaling 83,500. The smallest layoff on the list of 9,000 workers was announced by two firms, Honeywell and U S West. The recession had long been over since the first quarter of 1991, but the layoffs were continuing into the mid-1990s (probably with no letup as this book appeared). The layoffs listed in Table 4 total 627,750.

These widely publicized layoffs represent, however, only a minor fraction of the total number of job losses, given that many mass layoffs occur at much smaller companies all across the country, and the trend of job losses has been upward. The count of destroyed jobs was 1.2 million workers in 1979, rising to 3 million in 1983, and falling back to 2 million by 1989. By 1992, the count of jobs destroyed was back up to 3.4 million. The Labor Department estimates that 3.3 million jobs were destroyed in 1995. All told, between 1979 and 1995, more than 43 million American jobs were eliminated (nearly 25 million were in blue-collar occupations and nearly 19 million were in white-collar occupations). The cuts were not apparently caused by lagging corporate profits; profits were running at record levels, according to reports by DRI/McGraw Hill, an economic consulting firm.[52]

What are we to make of all of this "bad" news? No one should overlook the economic distress and emotional pain that many laid-off workers and their families feel. Job losses can create dire troubles for the affected workers, not the least of which may be lost houses and marriages, and even thoughts of suicide for some. Many have dwelled on that dark side of layoffs—without noting the brighter side. Changes in the economy must be evaluated with an eye to both sides of the economic ledger, the dark and the bright.

Even critics must recognize that not all layoffs make the laid-off workers worse off. An untold number of workers, mainly at large private

51. Louis Uchitelle and N. R. Kleinfield, "On the Battlefields of Business, Millions of Casualties," *New York Times*, March 3, 1996, pp. A1 and A15.

52. Matt Murray, "Amid Record Profits, Companies Continue to Lay Off Workers," *Wall Street Journal*, May 4, 1995, p. A1.

Table 4. Job Death: Twenty-five Large Downsizings, 1991–May 1994

Company	Staff cutbacks
IBM	85,000
AT&T	83,500
General Motors	74,000
U.S. Postal Service	55,000
Sears	50,000
Boeing	30,000
NYNEX	22,000
Hughes Aircraft	21,000
GTE	17,000
Martin-Marietta	15,000
DuPont	14,800
Eastman Kodak	14,000
Philip Morris	14,000
Procter & Gamble	13,000
Phar Mor	13,000
Bank of America	12,000
Aetna	11,800
GE Aircraft Engines	10,250
McDonnell Douglas	10,200
BellSouth	10,200
Ford Motors	10,000
Xerox	10,000
Pacific Telesis	10,000
Honeywell	9,000
U S West	9,000
Total	627,750

Source: People Trends, as cited by John A. Byrne, "The Pain of Downsizing," *Business Week,* May 9, 1994, p. 61.

firms and public institutions, are "bought" out of their jobs with cash payments and higher-than-planned-for retirement incomes and benefits. For example, in its efforts to downsize, the University of California system has offered older, long-term employees eight additional years of credit for computing their retirement benefits, plus full coverage of medical insurance for life.[53] IBM and AT&T, to name just two, made

53. Many of the "retired" professors have returned to work in their same offices with retirement incomes equal to their previous academic salaries, plus 50 percent pay for supposedly half-time work. They have, in effect, achieved a substantial increase in their lifetime pay.

similar offers in order to reduce their ranks. Workers have taken their "buyouts" with the intent of going to work elsewhere in the economy. The ones who are then "laid off" or "retired" (pick your choice of words) change their economic status voluntarily and must construe their new economic circumstances superior to what they would have had if they had stayed on.

In addition, we should not overlook the fact that many of the fired workers have, serendipitously, found diamonds in the rough—that is, the tough, perhaps unexpected times they have encountered. They report, of course, the terrible frustrating first days and weeks of unemployment, but many often freely add that a lost job provides a "time out" in a career: "When you're on the job, you don't get a chance to discover about yourself. This was a process of self-discovery" (an assessment from a fired 41-year-old engineer).[54] Another"victim" of a downsizing computer firm was able to reflect, once she had another job, "For me, it was a very positive experience. Looking back, I found what I really wanted to do in life." Another displaced worker reports that he found a new sense of freedom: "You're in control of your own future. For many people, this chance to take control is the first time in their lives. It was a neat feeling."[55]

These people's reflections are apparently not all that atypical. An employment counselor reports that 90 to 95 percent of the 150 or so displaced professional workers he had advised over the previous five years "would say that losing a job was a step forward in their lives."[56] Again, we can acknowledge the pain. The news account that contained the above reaction led with the case of a depressed, displaced woman who took her life after being displaced. Nevertheless, we must not use the pain to excuse oversight of the positive things that happen to many others who lose their jobs.

Critics might like to think that virtually all corporate efforts to downsize are the consequence of managers losing their economic marbles or of sheer unadulterated greed being the only motivating force. Greed has surely been a powerful force throughout history, for good and bad purposes. Managers sometimes lose touch with economic reality, just as their workers do. They are spurred to action by managerial fads. "Reengineering the corporation," including efforts to downsize, does appear

54. As reported in John Balzar, "Job Loss Sets 4 on Path to Self-discovery," *Los Angeles Times,* October 20, 1993, p. A26.

55. Ibid.

56. Ibid.

to have become something of a contemporary fad among managers interested in boosting the bottom lines of their companies. Having conceded those points, however, I rush to stress that the downsizing efforts of firms are often pressed by what are more powerful forces, such as competition, firm survival, and efficiency improvements.

Most firms downsize because owners and managers often recognize at some point the waste in their organizations. NYNEX announced plans to lay off 15,000 to 25,000 workers from its payrolls in 1994 partly because it needed to reduce its costs to remain competitive in the rapidly changing communication market and partly because internal investigations revealed gross inefficiencies. For example, NYNEX's Executive Vice President Robert Thrasher was astounded to learn that the company "bought 83 brands of personal computers a year; that dozens of New York Telephone employees spent their time repainting newly purchased trucks a different shade of white at a cost of $500 a truck; that NYNEX spent $4.5 million to find and bill only $900,000 in previously unbillable telephone calls."[57] All told, the firm was able to identify 300 specific changes in the way the company did business that would save the company $1.5 to $1.7 billion by 1997, or one-quarter of its current operating expenses.

NYNEX could of course expect to benefit from its cost-saving efforts—but so could its customers and remaining workers. The firm's efforts to downsize increased the work burden on the remaining employees, but at the same time, the efforts may have saved their jobs. The proper perspective to evaluate layoffs is not the number of jobs lost, per se, but how many jobs are cut in comparison with how many jobs a firm may have been left with if it had not made explicit efforts to cut employment. Failure to trim jobs purposefully can give rise to job losses by default. The reality of the American (and global) workplace is that job cuts have practically become mandatory, a point recognized with full clarity in 1993 by Edwin Artzt, chairman of Procter & Gamble, who announced job cuts of 13,000 from a workforce of 106,000: "We must slim down to stay competitive. The consumer wants value. Our competitors are getting leaner and quicker, and we are simply going to have to run faster to stay ahead."[58] In the main, workers can fret about the competitive forces that are beyond their control but yet affect their livelihoods, but there is not much they can do about them, aside from helping their companies go with the global flow and compete aggressively, taking their lumps in the process.

57. John A. Byrne, "The Pain of Downsizing," *Business Week,* May 9, 1994, p. 63.
58. Murray, "Amid Record Profits, Companies Continue to Lay Off Workers," p. A1.

For years IBM went its merry way, expanding its product lines and jobs. It sought to avoid job cuts, and it even created a corporate culture that essentially made saving jobs, even at sizable costs to the firm, a corporate mantra. It eventually found itself losing market share and was forced to cut its workforce. One can only imagine how many workers would now have been working for IBM if it had, along the way, made a more directed effort to keep its job and cost growth under control.

Moreover, it is important to recognize that much downsizing occurs, as in the IBM case, because of job growth elsewhere in the economy. IBM was having to reduce its workforce in part because Gateway Computers, operating out of North Sioux City, North Dakota, was producing more cost-effective personal computers and was, accordingly, expanding its workforce.

Textile firms in the Carolinas lost tens of thousands of jobs over the past ten or twenty years because other textile firms were expanding (because they were more competitive). Also, other industries in the Carolinas were expanding, drawing in labor at the same time that they were pushing up worker wage rates, causing some textile firms to close or contract because they could no longer afford the labor. The BMW plant that went into operation in the Spartanburg, South Carolina, area in 1994 no doubt will destroy any number of jobs in that area. Some firms will simply not be able to compete with BMW for labor.[59]

There is, in other words, a bright but unheralded side to the downsizing announcements, but the linkages are often obscured by distances in time and space between the reports of job gains and job losses. Of course, it is natural to think of the job cuts as "losses"; that's how most people describe them. However, it is probably far more accurate to think of the cuts as "gains" for the economy, mainly because the workers who will no longer be working for IBM or NYNEX or Bellsouth or U S West can go to work elsewhere in the economy. Even after it cut its workforce, NYNEX expanded its output—an accomplishment that it should not deny, but brag about. It was doing more with less! Moreover, there were former NYNEX workers that could then be put to work elsewhere in the economy, to rebuild their incomes and provide more goods and services to Americans, to make dreams come true.

The economic failures and problems of some are clearly net gains to the economy as a whole. The question is whether the gains are sufficiently widespread to make them tolerably acceptable by the polity. The

59. Many of these issues are dealt with more extensively in Richard B. McKenzie, *The American Job Machine* (New York: Universe Books, 1988).

critics often recant that those who are unemployed by announced job terminations are virtually always net losers, but are they? The anecdotes reported above should cause one to pause. Also, the displaced workers certainly lose in the instance of their own job losses. However, they gain when other firms and workers, spurred by competition, improve their goods and services and lower their prices through productivity increases and job cutbacks. The workers who suffer their losses are simply parts of a historical process—one that has been both creative and destructive at the same time—under which jobs have been created and destroyed through the centuries, all building to the prosperous economic state that is now the fate of this country. Workers are where they are in their economic lives because others have suffered through time as they now suffer. Their task is to pick themselves up and move on, reentering the workforce where possible.[60]

The creative and destructive economic process over the last century is revealed in Table 5, which lists the country's top thirty jobs at different points in this century: 1900, 1960, and 1991. Farmers and their laborers constituted the largest group of workers at the turn of the century; they didn't make the cut in 1960. Professors were not on the list as late as 1960, but they made the cut in 1991. You can go up and down the lists and detect major changes in the occupational rankings with a host of entrants and exits.

Tables 6 and 7 carry the analysis further. The top half of Table 6 shows the jobs destroyed in various industries by comparing their job counts today with some previous year. For example, the number of railway workers fell from over 2 million in 1920 to approximately one-tenth that level in 1993. The bottom half of the table shows the job gains in various industries by comparing the employment levels in various occupations today and in some year in the past. Naturally, no one was a commercial pilot in 1900, as planes had not yet been invented; but there were almost a quarter million pilots in 1993.

These tables are useful and informative, but misleading in that they underplay the employment change in the economy. They give the impression that just because job categories remain on the lists from one period to another that the jobs actually remain more or less the same. The job of being a farmer was radically different in the 1990s than it was at the turn of the century. Technology has made farming a far more

60. The linkages of economic success to economic failure, and the positive attributes of failures to the economy, are discussed in Dwight R. Lee and Richard B. McKenzie, *Failure and Progress: The Bright Side of the Dismal Science* (Washington: Cato Institute, 1993).

Table 5. America's Top Thirty Jobs Since 1900

1900		1960		1991	
Farmers	5,674,875	Retail salespersons and managers	4,351,867	Retail salespersons	6,200,000
Agricultural laborers	4,410,877	Farmers and farm managers	2,525,907	Teachers	4,029,000
General laborers	2,577,951	Teachers	1,683,667	Secretaries	3,791,000
Servants	1,453,677	Truck and tractor drivers	1,662,723	Truck drivers	2,666,000
Merchants	790,886	Secretaries	1,492,964	Farmers and farm managers	2,368,000
Clerks	630,127	Private household workers	1,281,740	Janitors and cleaners	2,126,000
Salespeople	611,139	Farm laborers	1,244,276	Bookkeepers	1,912,000
Carpenters	600,252	Manufacturing laborers	960,998	Engineers	1,846,000
Railroad workers	582,150	Bookkeepers	936,270	Cooks	1,779,000
Miners	563,406	Carpenters	923,837	Vehicle mechanics and repairers	1,778,000
Teamsters/coachmen	538,933	Waiters and waitresses	896,273	Nurses	1,712,000
Teachers	438,861	Engineers	871,582	Freight and stock handlers	1,688,000
Launderers	385,965	Vehicle mechanics and repairers	862,363	Police and guards	1,669,000
Dressmakers	346,884	Apparel and textile workers	808,378	Financial salespersons	1,612,000
Iron and steel workers	290,538	Construction workers	751,085	Wholesale commodities brokers	1,601,000
Machinists	283,145	Assemblers	686,754	Nursing aides, orderlies, attendants	1,506,000
Painters	277,541	Janitors and sextons	621,027	Accountants and auditors	1,446,000
Bookkeepers	254,880	Sewers and stitchers	617,029	Health technologists and technicians	1,379,000
Cotton mill workers	246,391	Cooks	597,056	Waiters and waitresses	1,355,000

Tailors	229,649	Typists	543,801	Computer programmers and operators	1,287,000
Blacksmiths	226,477	Machinists	515,532	Carpenters	1,277,000
Firefighters	223,495	Mfg. checkers, examiners, inspectors	514,135	Precision production supervisors	1,227,000
Shoemakers	208,903	Policemen and guards	513,200	Assemblers	1,119,000
Sawyers	161,624	Cashiers	491,906	Heavy equipment operators	1,022,000
Masons	160,805	Packers and wrappers	491,695	Child care workers	972,000
Housekeepers	155,153	Accountants and auditors	476,826	Engineering technologists and technicians	947,000
Printers	155,147	Deliverymen and routemen	438,002	Mathematical and computer scientists	923,000
Seamstresses	150,942	Painters	416,040	Postal clerks, mail carriers, messengers	923,000
Physicians	132,002	Launderers and dry cleaners	412,042	Groundskeepers and gardeners	890,000
Tobacco factory workers	131,452	Attendants (hospital, nursing home)	408,587	Professors	773,000
Total of top 30 jobs (78.7 percent of employment)	22,894,100	Total of top 30 jobs (42.6 percent of employment)	28,998,562	Total of top 30 jobs (46.1 percent of employment)	53,823,000
Total employment	29,073,233	Total employment	67,990,073	Total employment	116,877,000

Note: The changing composition of America's top thirty jobs over the past century affirms that jobs lost in one field are replaced by jobs in emerging occupations. Between 1900 and 1991, for example, sawyers, masons, and miners disappeared from the list. In their places came professors, engineers, mathematical and computer scientists, and others, which illustrates the increasing importance of education in today's workplace.

Source: U.S. Bureau of the Census as reported by Michael Cox and Richard Alm, "The Churn: The Paradox of Progress" (Dallas: Federal Reserve Bank of Dallas, 1992 Annual Report, May 1993), p. 9.

Table 6. Creative (Job) Destruction over the Past Century

	People Employed		
	Today	Yesterday	
Destruction			
railroad workers	231,000	2,076,000	1920
carriage and harness makers	*	109,000	1900
telegraph operators	8,000	75,000	1920
boilermakers	*	74,000	1920
milliners	*	100,000	1910
cobblers	25,000	102,000	1900
blacksmiths	*	238,000	1910
watchmakers	*	101,000	1970
switchboard operators	213,000	421,000	1970
Farmworkers	851,000	11,533,000	1910
Creation			
airline pilots and mechanics	232,000	0	1900
medical technicians	1,379,000	0	1910
engineers	1,846,000	18,000	1900
computer programmers/operators	1,287,000	*	1960
fax machine workers	699,000	0	1980
auto mechanics	864,000	0	1900
truck, bus, and taxi drivers	3,328,000	0	1900
professional athletes	77,000	*	1920
TV and radio announcers	60,000	*	1920
electricians/electronic repairers	711,000	51,000	1900
optometrists	62,000	*	1910

*Fewer than 5,000

Source: U.S. Bureau of the Census as reported by Michael Cox and Richard Alm, "The Churn: The Paradox of Progress," (Dallas: Federal Reserve Bank of Dallas, 1992 Annual Report, May 1993), p. 11.

sophisticated and complicated occupation. The same could be said of being a pilot or a professor or a secretary. Secretaries used to take shorthand. Only a small percentage still do. Most secretaries now manage computers and programs from their desks that are more sophisticated and powerful than the ones that computer center directors managed maybe one or two and, certainly, three decades ago. The simple fact is that jobs are remade constantly even when they are kept, and the faster the technological development—or "creative destruction"—the faster the pace of remaking jobs.

We often talk about "managers destroying jobs," but in reality they

Table 7. Out of the Home and Into the Market

Home Activity	Business or Industry	Home Activity	Business or Industry
Yardwork	*Yardwork*	*Household Maintenance* (*cont.*)	*Household Maintenance* (*cont.*)
Mow the lawn	Lawn Mowing	Design the home	Architects
Prune trees	Tree service	Decorate the home	Interior decorators
Trim bushes	Yard Maintenance	Exterminate pests	Pest control, exterminator
Weed and fertilize	Lawn and garden care	*Family Finances*	*Family Finances*
Install sprinklers	Yard service	Fill out tax forms	Accountants, tax preparers
Clothing	*Clothing*	Establish a financial plan	Financial planners
Wash and dry clothes	Maid, dry cleaning	Manage investments	Brokerages
Iron, starch, and fold clothes	Laundry, dry cleaning	Prepare will, legal documents	Lawyers
Sew, knit, and tailor garments	Clothing makers, tailors	*Personal care*	*Personal care*
Food	*Food*	Cut and set hair	Barber, beauty salon
Grow fruit and vegetables	Farming	Groom (manicures, facials)	Beauty shops
Raise livestock	Ranching	Educate Children	Schools, colleges
Preserve fruits and vegetables	Canning, packaging	Babysit	Child-care centers
Slaughter and cure meat	Butchery	Administer health or medical needs	Doctors, hospital
Cook and serve meals	Restaurant, catering	Care for the elderly	Nursing home
Clean the dishes	Restaurant	Exercise (jogging, calisthenics)	Health and fitness centers
Household Maintenance	*Household Maintenance*	*Automobiles*	*Automobiles*
Clean house	Maids	Maintain vehicles (change oil)	Auto service station
Wash windows	Window cleaning	Wash and vacuum vehicles	Car wash
Shampoo rugs	Carpet and rug cleaners	Repair vehicles	Auto repair
Clean drapes	Drapery cleaners	*Miscellaneous*	*Miscellaneous*
Make minor repairs	Plumber, electrician	Make gifts	Gift and craft shops
Repair appliances	Appliance repair	Care for pets	Kennel, veterinarian
Paint the house	House painting	Cut and split wood	Firewood, central heating
Make or restore furniture	Furniture, upholsterers	Repair mowers, bikes	Machine shops
Build homes or additions	Home building, construction		

Note: As U.S. living standards have risen, and especially as more women have entered the workforce, chores once done by family members have become services provided by the marketplace.

are, for the most part, only responding to technological and economic forces afoot in the domestic and world economy. Table 7 shows how various inventions have destroyed and created various jobs (at the same time they have remade the jobs that remained). For example, the automobile industry has been a major creator of jobs in this century for assemblers, designers, road builders, petrochemists, mechanics, and truck drivers. Cars replaced horse-drawn carriages, trains, and boats, causing the elimination of jobs for blacksmiths, wainwrights, drovers, teamsters, railroad workers, and canalmen. Again, most of the jobs that now exist in the automobile industry are a far cry from what they were (in terms of how work is done and what is required of people holding the jobs) not too many years ago.

Clearly, the pace of job change has speeded up. At the same time, we must be careful to not exaggerate what the actual pace has been. For most Americans, the pace appears to have been manageable, in spite of the insecurities created. A 1991 Labor Department survey found that half of all workers forty-five to fifty-four years of age had been at their jobs for at least 10 years. In 1983, half of all workers had been at their jobs for only a little longer, 10.3 years. According to columnist Robert Samuelson, "In 1991, about 10 percent of workers shifted occupations—not much different from 1978 (12 percent) or 1966 (9 percent). One-third of this shift occurs among young workers under 25; another third occurs among those under 35. Less than 5 percent of those over 45 change. New technologies (computers) may alter job content, but people adapt."[61]

We can expect the process of "creative destruction" to continue apace well into the future, given the current rate of technological development. We may fret about it, we can heed to it, but, frankly speaking, we can't stop it. This ongoing process is worldwide in scope and power. Americans must continue to change, and to change more than they ever have in the past. That is our generation's burden, but the ongoing change is also the foundation of vast opportunities. Dealing with both the burdens and the opportunities seems as doable for the vast majority of Americans as it has been in the past.

What Can Be Done

Still, the problems some face in job losses cannot be rubbed from the consciousness. We can read about them in the papers, and we can't

61. Robert J. Samuelson, "Life Is Shakier, But Not Shattered," *Los Angeles Times*, December 29, 1993, p. B11.

avoid them on television programs. What can be done? What should be done? Those questions are easier to pose than to answer. The quick answer is "Have the government fix everything." But, what? How? And how much? These are the taxing questions.

We might concede, for the sake of argument, as was done in chapter 1, the question of what governments can and should do for Americans who are in dreadful states because they have always been at the bottom of the income ladder: A helping hand, with recognized limitations on the amount of help, is needed. The government should always look for opportunities to improve its delivery of help to the truly disadvantaged. At the same time, we must recognize the prospects that some help can have perverse consequences for the targeted workers. Their plight in life can be perpetuated by the very programs designed to relieve their burden.

So much of the concern over the churn in the economy extends far beyond the ranks of the disadvantaged into the ranks of advantaged, lower- (but not lowest), middle-, and upper-income Americans. What about them? Here the country needs a healthy dose of realism. The government is and will always be a limited resource for doing good, and its scarcity must be recognized by those who have problems and who are concerned about the plight of those who are harmed by the economic "churn" or "creative destruction." As evident in the fiscal problems governments face and the constant flow of reports on what they do wrong when trying to do right, governments apparently already have more problems on their political plates than they can handle.

Do we want to extend the arm of government further? That's not as easy a question as it might seem, even to antimarket liberals, mainly because of the inevitable trade-offs that are implied. Even antimarket liberals must hesitate with their reactions, primarily because when the government seeks to extend its reach in one direction, it can't extend it elsewhere. It might even be forced to retract its reach in one direction or another. The problem is especially difficult in times when government resources are tight, when all sorts of other claims are being made on those limited resources. Efforts to raise taxes can only compound the economic difficulties of the country, given that higher taxes on those who are successful can dampen the incentives people have to save, invest, and create the replacement jobs that Americans want.

In addition, the political process has a way of translating the best of policy intentions—including when help is intended to serve deserving social or economic ends—into so much political pork, designed to pad the pockets of politically powerful interest groups. Besides, we must worry that government cannot possibly help more than a small subset of those deemed deserving, a fact that does not necessarily mean that the government should not help anyone, but only that the benefits may not be broadly distributed.

The fact remains that government simply cannot afford to help more than a small fraction of those who might lose their jobs in a period of broad-based churning in the economy. For the most part, American workers must help themselves.

The current policy fad is for government to be responsible for creating "good jobs." President Bill Clinton and Labor Secretary Robert Reich have made "good jobs" the administration's Holy (policy) Grail. To disapprove of the federal government's pursuit of "good jobs" is tantamount to advocating lower living standards for American workers. Why? Because "good jobs" raise worker earnings and "bad jobs" don't. Hence, "bad jobs" are necessarily bad for people and the country.

But are they really? Even if we accept the fact that America is overburdened with "bad jobs" (which I don't), a little reflection will prove otherwise. Those who favor government providing "good jobs" have a fairly clear working definition of them: jobs that require high skills and are highly paid. The critics mistakenly presume that the growth in low-wage jobs has not improved worker welfare.

In this regard, the critics (Clinton and Reich included) make the same analytical mistake a North Carolina state legislator made a number of years ago when he proposed that the state raise the average wages of North Carolina workers by encouraging only those firms with above-average wages to move into the state. Having firms with below-average wages move in would lower average wages—or so he thought. The legislator failed to see that an increase in the number of low-wage jobs would increase the demand for low-wage workers and therefore their wages and fringe benefits. Indeed, higher wages paid for those holding bad jobs would certainly raise the state's average wage, and it might even do more to relieve the state's social and economic problems than might higher wages for those already holding good jobs.

Note the emphasis placed on "skilled jobs." There are two problems with this myopic policy focus: First, it presumes that officials in Washington, or even state capitals, can devise a variety of programs to produce the types of skilled workers the country needs. In the increasingly complex and technologically sophisticated world that politicians recognize as a part of the jobs problem, the ability of government officials to orchestrate cost-effective good jobs programs has become increasingly lame. They simply do not have the requisite knowledge about the great variety of employment conditions and the trade-offs employers and employees are willing to make to plan for the jobs of more than a handful (or minor fraction) of American workers. All the Washington-based talk about "skilled jobs," or even "good jobs," is something of a policy smokescreen, the pretense of knowledge of the details of employment conditions that can be known only by the people who make the jobs happen, that is, employers and employees.

Second, the critics' myopic policy focus is guided by the fundamental fallacy that tens of millions of American workers don't want "bad jobs." Certainly, everyone wants to be paid more for what they do and to acquire greater skills at no cost to themselves. More is always preferred to less, but that does not mean they should be paid more, and neither would they necessarily be willing to incur the costs associated with raising their pay, including the acquisition of higher skills and the assumption of risks. Nor does it mean that they would be happier.

The plain fact is that millions of Americans believe that their "bad jobs" are a better economic bargain than the "good jobs" the critics have in mind. Why? Few Americans seek poverty, but it is patently obvious that many Americans prefer what others consider "low pay" if earning it means that they exert little effort, suffer little risk, accept little or no responsibility, and avoid dedication to their jobs and firms. In short, many Americans have chosen their "bad jobs." They don't believe the jobs of so-called "symbolic analysts" (Robert Reich's favorite term) are, on balance, all that good, given what has to be done to get those types of jobs.

Concluding Comments

One observation is obvious: Not all Americans did well over recent decades. In times of progress and associated change, hardship can abound. That said, the critics of the past twelve years or past two decades need to make an even greater concession: Those years were far more prosperous than they have claimed. With the concessions, we all can get on with the business of choosing policies that fit economic reality, not what seems to be wishful rhetoric of retrogression. Haynes Johnson found lots of depressed people on his trip through America who tended to look at a half-full glass of water and think, "Half empty." Accordingly, he was able to paint a dismal picture of the economic world beyond the Washington Beltway.

The evidence suggests that I could take a similar trip across the country and find many people who have prospered, even in spite of difficult circumstances, who don't share Johnson's dismal assessment of the country's future, who share the optimism that pervades these pages. I say that simply because I've heard from such people.

During many radio interviews and talk shows around the country, I have heard from a number of callers who took issue with everything I've said, all the facts presented, although they almost always refused to follow my admonition to look up the facts themselves. However, I've been struck by the disproportionate number of people who have been living in another America, who frequently profess to having limited incomes, and who call in to say in so many words, "It's about time someone looked at the glass and thought, 'Half full.' No, 'Overflowing.'" But, then, that may be a part of the emotional malaise the country is going through. As suggested by Yale University computer scientist David Gelernter in his analysis of American life since the late 1930s, when the New York World's Fair hawked the technological glories of the future to come, as a country we just might be suffering from having to achieve the promised glories. "When you live in utopia you can't yearn for utopia anymore, and the community of faith is dead."[62]

The history of progress has been one of people looking at the world that way and taking advantage of the opportunities at hand. A century ago, many opportunities existed in the West. Chapters 4 and 5 show that the closing of the West has not meant that opportunities have been diminished. If anything, contrary to popular wisdom, the exact opposite has been the case. What we need to do is rethink our past and recognize that there is still reason and time to resuscitate the "community of faith." Much depends on seeing our problems from a new perspective.

62. David Gelernter, *1939: The Lost World of the Fair* (New York: Free Press, 1995), p. 72.

4

THE CLOSING OF THE WEST

> Behind institutions, behind constitutional forms and modifications, lie the vital forces that call these organs into life and shape them to meet changing conditions. The peculiarity of American institutions is the fact that they have been compelled to adapt themselves to the changes of an expanding people—to the changes involved in crossing a continent, in winning a wilderness, and in developing at each area of this progress out of the primitive economic and political conditions of the frontier into the complexity of city life.
>
> Frederick Jackson Turner,
> "The Significance of the Frontier in American History"

WHEN—in the mid-nineteenth century—distinguished journalist Horace Greeley, founder and editor of the *New Yorker* and the New York *Tribune,* admonished young men to "go West" and "grow up with the country," he was actually paraphrasing the thoughts of social commentator John Babsone Lane Soule.[1] Moreover, Greeley was not advising his readers to trek across the entire continent; to him, Ohio, Indiana, Illinois, and Michigan comprised the West.[2]

Nevertheless, the optimistic sentiments that "Go West Greeley" expressed (in practically every issue of the *New Yorker* in the late 1830s)

1. As quoted in Suzanne Schulze, *Horace Greeley: A Biography* (New York: Greenwood Press, 1992), p. 13.
2. Ibid.

were shared by succeeding generations of Americans. For the first 100 years or so of this country's history, the West was wide open to anyone who dared to move there and settle.

Obviously, part of what the West represented at that time was just so much untamed and unclaimed territory, but the lands beyond the reaches of the settled East were alluring for another important reason: They symbolized unbounded opportunities for hard-working, determined people to prosper or, as Greeley put the matter,

> The one great point of superiority enjoyed by our countrymen over their cousins in western Europe is the facility wherewith every American who is honest, industrious and sober may acquire, if he does not already possess, a homestead of his own; not a leasehold from some great capitalist or feudal baron, but a spot of earth of which no man may rightfully dispossess him so long as he shall shun evil courses and live within his means.[3]

The West, being on the same continent, became a relatively convenient escape hatch when times got tough in the East. By the late 1830s, the country was caught in a depression that lasted until 1842. According to American historian Ray Allen Billington, by late 1837, numerous banks had closed because of runs on them. As a consequence, "half of the Northeast's business concerns were closed, beggars roamed the streets of every city, and unemployed workers fought for meager fare doled out by soup kitchens."[4] Nevertheless, Greeley could exhort his readers, "Fly, scatter through the country, go to the Great West, anything rather than remain here,"[5] and, on another occasion, add, "If you have no family or friends to aid, and no prospect [for work or going into business] open to you, turn your face to the great West, and there build up a home and fortune."[6]

The moral was none too subtle: Americans need not remain mired in unfortunate circumstances. If they but chose, they could break out and go west, leaving their past and misfortunes behind them. The West was, for generations of Americans, a metaphor for a fresh start—perhaps even a second or third chance for some who had failed in the East or others who wished to literally leave their pasts behind them. The West

3. As quoted in Robert V. Hine, *The American West: An Interpreted History* (Boston: Little, Brown, 1973), p. 320.

4. Ray Allen Billington, *Westward Expansion: A History of the American Frontier* (New York: Macmillan, 1967), p. 372.

5. As quoted in Billington, *Westward Expansion,* p. 372.

6. As quoted in James Parton, *The Life of Horace Greeley* (New York: Arno Press and the New York Times, 1970), p. 414.

was the stuff of which American dreams were made, and often it was there that they were realized, in spite of the dire difficulties that were often endured.

What American schoolchild has not—upon reading of the explorations of Lewis and Clark, the adventures of Daniel Boone, or the scramble of those who rushed to find gold in the hills of California—concocted romantic dreams of what life would have been like "back then," free and filled with the hopes and aspirations of a very exciting life? By the same token, what schoolchild spends much time thinking about the work required and the hardships endured by those earlier settlers who did "go west" to follow their dreams?

Certainly, the West no longer stands for such hope. The West is no longer the metaphor for open-ended opportunity that it was 100 years ago. It is now closed to homesteading (which commenced in the 1850s). Land can no longer be taken legally from anyone without payment (as it once was from Native Americans). In that sense, it is no longer free. Few contemporary Americans would take Greeley's admonition seriously if it were repeated today. But then, they might have weighed Greeley's advice alongside the advice of others to go in many different directions.

But does that mean that the sentiments Greeley expressed cannot be meaningfully reinterpreted for contemporary Americans? Is there nothing, no place similar to the West, that inspires Americans to think thoughts and have aspirations similar to those of the pioneers and settlers when they contemplated the homes and fortunes they would build?

Many contemporary commentators furnish a transparent answer: The West no longer exists, in reality or metaphorically—period. They argue that Americans once lived in a world of superabundance, a continental Shangri-La, so to speak, in which resources were not a terribly important binding constraint. People of the past were, indeed, *free* to prosper, because they could tap the array of free (or low-cost) resources.

By way of contrast, critics lament that we now live in a world of progressively binding constraints. Scarcity extracts a terrific toll on the fate of humanity by stealing away the ability to dream new dreams of an even more prosperous future. Young Americans today face a future of economic retrogression because the country's resources are dipping dangerously low, or so we are told. Energy is scarce, and supplies are diminishing rapidly; in the not-too-distant future, they will run out. "Good jobs" are as scarce as energy, and they, too, will dry up. The country, the critics chant, is up to its proverbial neck in the trash that continues relentlessly to pile up because we have run out of places to dump it. Environmental resources have been abused and overused. Fertile soil is built upon, paved over, or allowed to wash into the seas at alarming rates. Fisheries are either being seined clean of fish or poisoned by waste. The rain forests, on which the protective ozone layer depends, are being cut and burned to the ground. The rate at which a growing array of species are disappearing threatens to destabilize the world's supposedly delicate ecological balance and portends an implosion of life-giving forces. Growth in the world's human population continues to impose an ever-tightening grip on people's dreams, given that they face a reality in which resources are rapidly being used up.

Face it, the critics charge, many Americans will be forced to remain bogged down in unfortunate circumstances that will only get worse, and they would be unrealistic to dream as they once did.

But is such a dismal outlook actually warranted? On reflection, we can see that while the geographical West has indeed been closed, the metaphorical West has always been open and has actually begun to open wider than ever before. Paradoxically, it is the opening of a *new* West—not the closing of the *old* West—that has created so much unease and made dreaming of a more prosperous future so difficult.

Nevertheless, strange as it may seem, it is the uneasiness people feel right now that will ensure a more prosperous future for the generations of Americans to come. This current concern, or alarm, will ensure that Americans in the future can reach for their wildest dreams (or nightmares, as the case may be). But such a view is not shared by many noted scholars who remain mired in the dominant material world of the past and see as meaningful only those resources that came, in one way or another, from the good earth. Many historians reason that the "closing of the West" a hundred years or so ago represented an ominous turning point in the country's institutional development. Before we can cope with—and challenge—that daring point, we must understand the so-called frontier thesis.

The rest of this chapter is devoted to the frontier thesis, as developed by Frederick Jackson Turner, because his thesis continues to fortify contemporary pessimism and because two points need to be made very clearly in order to understand the optimistic tenor of this book: First, Turner and his followers were correct to argue that the concept of untapped opportunities, "escape hatches," are important to the economic, if not emotional, health of individuals and the country as a whole. Such escape hatches have both liberating and, paradoxically, constraining effects on what people and their governments do.

Second, Turner and his followers were wrong to think "geography" would continue to carry the importance that it did a century ago. That fact suggests that Turner and his followers were wrong to deduce that American opportunities, and the benefits that spring from them, would collapse once the West was closed. As shown in the following chapters, opportunities for discovery have just begun to mount. In the not-too-distant future, opportunities may, for all practical purposes, be unbounded. The problem Americans will then face, as they are beginning to face today, is sorting through the myriad opportunities. Before we can make those points, we need to carefully examine Turner's thesis with an eye toward understanding where he went right *and* wrong.

The Closing of the Frontier

Frederick Jackson Turner was a remarkable American historian. He wrote about American history, and at the same time, he changed the way generations of historians have thought about American history and institutional development. Contemporary Americans' pessimism may have been fueled by Turner's analysis handed down by historians who have stressed its continuing import to American conditions.

Turner wrote the words in this chapter's epigraph in 1893 when he was only 32 years old, and he spoke them while giving a paper at one of America's more memorable conventions of historians. He was the last of five presenters at what must have been a long session, but by all accounts he left the dedicated scholars who had remained in the audience in awe. Volumes of supportive and critical scholarly articles have since been written on the "Turner thesis." According to one American historian, who probably speaks for many others, Turner's seminal article "has become the most widely known essay in American history, [and has] revolutionized historical thought in the United States."[7]

What did he say? Simply stated, Turner's analysis of the impact of the West on American economic development began with an agreeable claim that behind the existing political institutions under which we all live and work had to be what he called "vital forces" that ultimately give rise to and fortify those institutions. Institutions are, in other words, conditioned by their time and place and must adjust to changing circumstances—a premise that, when stated in general terms, is easily accepted.

The West—defined, in Turner's mind, by the area of the continent beyond the advancing frontier along which life was constantly returning

7. George Rogers Taylor, "Introduction," *The Turner Thesis: Concerning the Role of the Frontier in American History* (Boston: Heath, 1949), p. v.

to "primitive conditions"—was one of the more prominent and powerful of the multitude of forces that shaped American institutions and gave them their unique character. Clearly, the country's European heritage played a role in the selection of political institutions, as almost all historians had previously stressed. After all, the Founding Fathers were generally well versed in European political history and theory, which turned them toward representative democracy. However, historians before Turner had stressed the supreme importance of European influences. Turner found such discussions not so much wrong, as incomplete and myopic. European forces did not, could not, wholly explain the uniqueness of American political institutions and economic attitudes that Turner believed emerged because the country was born with uncharted and unclaimed territory stretching literally from coast to coast.

Moreover, the West had one obviously profound attribute: The land was "free" to anyone willing to take it from the Native Americans. The offerings of free land led inevitably to a constantly advancing frontier, which Turner also described as the "meeting point between savagery and civilization."[8] The West was settled in what Turner characterized as waves, first of explorers, then of pioneers, and finally of the settlers, farmers, merchants, and manufacturers. The very existence of the West, coupled with the manner in which it was developed, had a profound impact on the national character and psyche of the American people and, in turn, on the political institutions they chose. In Turner's words (again written in 1893), "American social development has been continually beginning over again on the frontier. This perennial rebirth, this fluidity of American life, this expansion westward with its new opportunities, its continuous touch with the simplicity of primitive society, furnish the forces dominating American character."[9]

At first, the American frontier was the Atlantic coast, which is to say that the Atlantic coast initially was Europe's frontier. But as time passed and as settlers moved into the interior of the country, the force of European influences faded and the frontier became progressively more American. When the first pilgrims landed, the frontier immediately became the unknown area beyond the perimeter of their settlements. During the seventeenth century, the frontier became the fall line in the eastern colonies, as the tidewaters became the settled areas. By the time of the Revolution, the frontier had been pushed into what are now the

8. Frederick Jackson Turner, "The Significance of the Frontier in American History," in *The Frontier in American History* (Tucson: University of Arizona Press, 1986), p. 3.

9. Ibid., pp. 2–3.

states of Kentucky and Tennessee. By the first quarter of the nineteenth century, the frontier had moved to the Great Lakes, the Mississippi River and into Florida. At the midpoint of the nineteenth century, Minnesota and Wisconsin still bore frontier traits, but the real frontier, where civilization stood shoulder-to-shoulder with primitive conditions, had advanced all the way to California.

By the time Turner gave his paper at the meeting of historians in 1893, the frontier movement had, for all practical purposes, ended—or so he argued (with the support of the U.S. Census Bureau that had, in 1890, maintained that it could no longer identify a "frontier"). The West had, by then, been closed, and land was no longer free for the taking. Native Americans had been put in their places, and Turner's frontier thesis would not have attracted the attention it did had it been simply a way of describing the means by which the West was won. The real importance of his thesis lay in his contention that the West and the advancing frontier provided distinctly American answers to important questions.

Turner believed the answer to why the country was unified and not a collection of independent states lay not in the civilizing European principles of government, but in the unifying forces of the indigenous people's opposition to the advancing frontier. (Europe had remained a group of warring nations throughout the nineteenth century and first half of the twentieth century.) Native Americans were an ever-present danger that had to be thwarted by cooperative action among the colonies. According to Turner, "It is evident that the unifying tendencies of the Revolutionary period were facilitated by the previous cooperation in the regulation of the frontier."[10] Communication and transportation systems followed the settlers west and sustained and fortified the interdependence of people in the East and those out West, increasing the ability of the settlers to advance the frontier further and reducing the dependence of East Coast residents on Europe. As Turner argued,

> [T]he wilderness has been interpenetrated by lines of civilization growing ever more numerous. It is like the steady growth of a complex nervous system for the originally simple, inert continent. If one would understand why we are to-day one nation, rather than a collection of isolated states, he must study this economic and social consolidation of the country. In the progress from savage conditions lie topics for the evolutionist.[11]

10. Ibid., p. 15.
11. Ibid., pp. 14–15.

Why was the country built on principles of individualism, not of collectivism? The independent frontiersmen are much to blame (or credit). People on the frontier, Turner reasoned, frequently did not comply with decisions made by the distant government, and few tax collectors or regulators in the East could even find pioneers and settlers in the West, much less exact enough taxes to cover the cost of their collection. "As has been indicated," Turner mused, "the frontier is productive of individualism. The tendency is anti-social. It produces antipathy to control, and particularly to any direct control. The tax gatherer is viewed as a representative of oppression."[12] Contrary to what it had anticipated, the federal government was unable to use the western territories as a source of revenue, mainly because the settlers could move beyond the reach of the government. Turner agreed with John Quincy Adams and quoted him approvingly, "My own system of administration, which was to make the national domain the inexhaustible fund for progressive and unceasing internal improvement, has failed."[13]

The West effectively gave rise to a special brand of democratic order in the United States that ultimately imposed a serious check on the power of the federal government to regulate and tax businesses and the individuals that ran them. In so doing, the West encouraged free enterprise—that is, reliance on markets and individual inventiveness—and the can-do (must-do) spirit that has characterized Americans. How? First, people could escape the taxing and regulatory authority of eastern governments by going further west, taking their assets and income capabilities to places so remote that taxes could not be collected efficiently or regulations effectively enforced. Frontier people could, in effect, take their enterprises beyond the reach of eastern government where they could, indeed, operate freely.

Second, and perhaps more important, governments in the East had to worry that onerous taxing and regulatory policies would cause residents to move west. Hence, eastern governments had to temper their enthusiasm for collectivist solutions to social problems. The powers of collective decision making under democracy were surely circumscribed by constitutional checks and even by competition for human and physical capital among the established states; but they were also tempered by a force that had not been fully appreciated at the time of the signing of the Constitution (a little more than 100 years prior to Turner's talk).

According to Turner, the West tempered the country's enthusiasm for

12. Ibid., p. 30.
13. Ibid., p. 126.

collectivist solutions in a more indirect but perhaps more powerful way: It moderated the tendency of workers (whom Turner viewed as often oppressed) to seek remedies for what they perceived to be oppression by governments and businesses. Workers who felt oppressed could escape to the West; thus the West provided a safety valve that relieved the pressure of worker discontent and, at the same time, checked somewhat the power of businesses (which Turner thought were becoming progressively more monopolized) to exploit their workers:

> Whenever social conditions tended to crystallize in the East, whenever capital tended to press upon labor or political restraints to impede the freedom of the mass, there was this gate of escape to the free conditions of the frontier. These free lands promoted individualism, freedom to rise, democracy. Men would not accept inferior wages and a permanent position of social subordination when this promised land of freedom and equality was theirs for the taking. Who would rest content under oppressive legislative conditions when with slight effort he might reach a land wherein to become a co-worker in the building of free cities and free States on the lines of his own ideal? In a word, then, free land meant free opportunities. Their existence has differentiated the American democracy from the democracies which have preceded it, because ever, as democracy in the East took the form of highly specialized and complicated industrial societies, in the West it kept in touch with primitive conditions, and by action and reaction these two forces shaped our history.[14]

In Turner's mind, the West was a liberating force. It offered Americans (and Europeans, many of whom moved to the country in search of "free land") an opportunity to move away from all forms of oppression, private and public. To that extent, the oppressors' powers were checked perhaps more assuredly by geography than by constitutional precepts written on paper. The powers of the oppressors to control those who remained behind were accordingly also checked.

The governments of the East had to consider that if they clamped down too much, the oppressed would move west, thus they had an economic incentive to thwart the advance of the frontier. Indeed, if it had had its way, the English government would have "checked settlement at the headwaters of the Atlantic tributaries."[15] Closing off the escape hatch would have expanded the economic and political powers of the British by making it easier for them to impose and collect higher taxes.

14. Frederick Jackson Turner, "Contributions of the West to American Democracy," in *The Frontier in American History,* pp. 259–60.

15. Turner, "Significance of the Frontier in American History," p. 133.

In many regards, Turner shared, albeit implicitly, a vision of government held by the founders, especially James Madison.[16] Madison wrote eloquently about the need for formal constitutional checks on the power of government (for example, first amendment rights and majority vote requirements in the two houses of Congress with the President holding the right of veto), but he also recognized the importance of "auxiliary" checks, most notably the competition that would likely emerge among states for the country's human and physical capital. Such competition among state governments would restrain each somewhat from raising taxes, just as competition among businesses restrains them from imposing higher prices on their customers (although not necessarily to the same extent).[17] Turner simply added (by way of inference from his commentary) that the vast territory of the West was another, and more serious, source of competition *and* restraint.

Although they did not use the vernacular of modern economics, both the founders and Turner (and his followers) envisioned people having a demand for living in any given governmental jurisdiction (formally modeled by modern economic theorists[18]) and that their demand would be responsive to the price paid. The price would include not only the cost of provisions but also the taxes to be paid, the regulations imposed, and the toll in terms of suppressed wages and oppressive working conditions. The higher the "price" charged in any given jurisdiction, the fewer the number of people who would live there. Turner argued that the "free land" in the West that could be reached "with a slight effort" increased, in effect, the responsiveness of people to all forms of oppression. Their heightened sensitivity and the fact that they could escape imposed a nontrivial check on the powers of eastern governments to tax and regulate their citizens and the capacity of private trusts to oppress their workers.

The Realization of Dreams

How is is that the West enabled generations of early Americans to dream, to accomplish their dreams, and even to succeed beyond their

16. See Alexander Hamilton, John Jay, and James Madison, *The Federalist: A Commentary on the Constitution of the United States* (New York: Modern Library, 1937).

17. See Vincent Ostrom, "The Political Theory of a Compound Republic: A Reconstruction of the Theory of American Democracy as Presented in *The Federalist*" (Evansville, Ind., manuscript copy, n.d.).

18. See Geoffrey Brennan and James M. Buchanan, *The Power to Tax: Analytical Foundations of a Fiscal Constitution* (New York: Cambridge University Press, 1980).

wildest dreams? There are probably many answers. Obviously, some who went west fortuitously struck gold, and others grubbed it out. A force more obscure than luck and fortitude was at work, however, and its effects proved far more profound, if Turner's thesis is to be taken seriously (which it is here).

Economists have long argued that free enterprise and free markets promote the accumulation of wealth and incomes like no other economic system known to man. However, since the days of Adam Smith, economists have also argued that those who work within a largely free economic system may not understand why the system performs as well as it does. Adam Smith spoke of the "invisible hand" of markets that can lead an individual participant in the market "to promote an end [greater wealth and well-being for the larger society] which was no part of his intentions."[19] Although market participants may understand only their own actions, even actions driven by self-interest often can produce good results, those that are important to overall societal well-being, apart from the improvement of individual well-being, though the actors may not appreciate or understand their contributions. In fact, their individual contributions to the well-being of all others may be so small that the contributors can miss their contributions altogether. Nonetheless, something important does happen; the process of the market generates measurable societal improvements that appear somewhat mysteriously—as if by an invisible hand—given that no one believes his or her own actions have a material impact.

Some scholars have made a fetish of focusing on the driving force of *self-interest* in Smith's (and his followers') theoretical framework and in real-world markets, often with the intent of damning both. After all, good results can be expected to arise only from good intentions, they reason, and pursuit of self-interest is usually perceived as a character flaw. Thus some scholars have missed the true importance of Smith's invisible hand. What Smith was trying to say is that individuals may not know enough about the "social good" to pursue it directly, and they only have limited resources and knowledge at their own disposal about how those resources can be used. However, Smith was saying, in effect, that if people are given the right to pursue their self-interest in open and free markets, then they can be expected to deploy the resources they have at their disposal in their most highly valued uses—that is, in the most economical way (with, of course, allowance for errors, given the

19. Adam Smith, *An Inquiry into the Nature and Causes of the Wealth of Nations* (New York: Modern Library, 1937), p. 423.

prevalence of risks and uncertainties). This process will give rise to competition, which will, in turn, force people to find the most cost-effective methods of production and to set prices at competitive levels. The end result, though perhaps inadvertent, will be a level of prosperity above what anyone anticipated. Indeed, it might be said that the prosperity will exceed everyone's anticipations—and dreams.

What did the West do? By promoting competition among private firms, as Turner argued, the West made markets work more effectively, because without the West there may have been more opportunities for monopolies to form and warp the allocation of resources away from their most valued uses. By promoting competition among governments, the West helped check and restrict (at least for a time) the willingness and ability of the federal and state governments to impose taxes and to regulate markets. Thus more resources were available for private deployment, and there were fewer restrictions on the extent to which private market participants could deploy their resources for their self-interests, which were indeed the most productive uses.

The West effectively promoted the market system, albeit indirectly and perhaps even inadvertently. It facilitated the work of Smith's "invisible hand." The West brought about freer, more progressive markets than Americans would have allowed otherwise. The wonder is that this market improved the well-being of Americans in ways that were wholly unanticipated. As individuals worked hard and smart in pursuit of their own privately conceived goals (with profit being only one possible goal), they were encouraged or pressured by the competition they faced. They benefited not only from their own labors but also from the more efficient use of resources by many other Americans who were working harder and smarter because of the competition they too faced.

Clearly, the resources the West provided helped Americans build a world-class economy, but there must have been more to the story. Many countries in the world have an abundance of resources but never prosper (consider twentieth-century Russia). Some countries, like postwar Japan, have few natural resources but prosper in spite of what they don't have. If we consider Turner to be correct in his assessment that the West provided Americans with opportunities to escape from public and private (political *and* economic) oppression, the mere existence of the West fostered investment (because governments' powers to appropriate the investments were impaired), competition (because of varied opportunities for production), and reliance on markets (because governments could not extend their regulatory intrusions into the hinterlands). If the insights Smith offered are correct, American markets fostered wealth accumulation to an extent that few would have dreamed, which naturally fed many Americans' optimism. Moreover, those Americans who kept their economic efforts closely focused on their own economic (self-) interests—who most likely didn't ponder the philosophical, social-welfare arguments for markets—probably believed, with good reason, that their own prosperity resulted from personal "good fortune," on par with stumbling on a gold mine, rather than necessarily from the collective consequence of their private intentions, but which could not be attributable to no one's actions.

Few modern-day scholars understand the extent to which the prevalence and forces of market institutions depend on forces as elusive as competition among governments—or on the mere existence of escape hatches. It is unrealistic to expect many Americans to fully appreciate the competitive/institutional/historical foundations of their own prosperity or lack thereof. To most, their economic status comes as something of a "surprise" and is not fully explainable by their own efforts. No wonder so many Americans before Turner lived to prosper beyond their wildest dreams. They could not possibly have imagined the many direct and indirect consequences of the West on their own lives.

Turner's Critics

For forty years after Turner presented his frontier thesis, historians and social scientists alike adopted it without serious criticism. The basic assumptions seemed reasonable. After all, institutions don't spring from a social, geographical, and political vacuum. "Vital forces" are bound to matter, and changes in those forces are likely to give rise to changes in political and social institutions. Although the West had been closed, for all practical purposes, by the time Turner spoke in 1893, he grounded his thesis in an old and honorable political theory dating at least to the days of the Founding Fathers. Turner simply applied the founders' theory that safety valves do matter to what was, at the time, an unrecognized condition—the West. Turner's students and followers took up the master's challenge and began exploring how the frontier could have affected the details of democracy in the United States and how the closing of the West might change social and political institutions.

Many supporters extended the safety-valve component of Tuner's argument, arguing that free land should be understood to include not only the surface area but also the many other natural resources that lay on and beneath the surface. They observed, as did Turner, that the closing of the West would likely increase political and private oppression, social unrest, and the collectivist leanings of American politics, as well as international interventionism by the federal government. In effect, oppressed Americans, no longer able to escape to the West, would have to stand and fight, so to speak. Misfits, no longer able to find solitude in remote areas of the country, would be forced to find ways of fitting in and, in the process, create tensions. No longer free to take land from Native Americans, criminals would most likely start taking property from their fellow countrymen, and the federal government might want to use the military powers to expand its influence to other parts of the hemisphere.

Turner's theory became popular because many of his predictions came true early in the nineteenth century. American historian Robert Hine notes, "Within a decade [of Turner's original talk], he was proved right [in international adventures] as America annexed Hawaii, challenged the disintegrating Spanish empire, took economic dominion over Cuba, and annexed outright the Philippine Islands, Puerto Rico, and Guam."[20] Furthermore, labor unrest—measured by union membership, strikes, and episodes of strike-related violence—did mount after the turn of the century, and the United States did wait until the Great Depression to enact a significant, government-sponsored welfare safety net, long after European governments had done so. Such facts, combined with the focus of the Turner thesis on heroic Americans who made their own way in the world without the aid of Europeans, gave Turner a receptive audience.

In the 1930s, however, historians again began to scrutinize the Turner thesis and spotted serious weaknesses, which they belabored. One of the more caustic critics was historian Louis Hacker, who in 1933 decided, "Turner and his followers were fabricators of a tradition which is not only fictitious but also to a very large extent positively harmful."[21] Hacker faulted Turner for having turned the attention of historians inward at a time when their attention should have been focused on the growing role of the United States in world events. Tuner also exhibited "a complete disregard of the basic antagonisms in American history; and profound ignorance of the steps by which monopolistic capitalism and imperialism were being developed in the country."[22]

Historian George Wilson Pierson criticized Turner for skipping over the perverse, not-so-positive consequences of western expansion (for instance, "antisocial" behavior and "crudity" supposedly were given

20. Hine, *American West*, p. 108.

21. Louis M. Hacker, "Sections—Or Classes?" *Nation*, July 26, 1933, in *Turner Thesis*, ed. George Rogers Taylor, p. 61.

22. Ibid., p. 63.

greater license in the West). Pierson also charged that Turner inadvertently postulated a theory of economic development founded on "geographic or environmental determinism," suggesting that the distinctly American components of the country's political institutions were the product of people responding mindlessly to geographic and environmental conditions.[23] Pierson maintained that American institutions were products of intentional design, to a degree not admitted by Turner, because Europeans who came to this country wanted to leave many of the old ways behind.[24] Dixon Ryan Fox, president of Union College, protested in the early 1940s that the Turner thesis introduced unwarranted defeatism into the American historical psyche, given that economic opportunity in the Turner theory was predicated heavily on the existence of free arable land that no longer existed.[25]

In 1945, American historian Fred Shannon argued that Turner's 1893 safety-valve thesis was not particularly novel, given that its essence had been part of the country's folklore at least since 1844 when the *Working Man's Advocate* noted,

> In those regions [of the East] thousands, and tens of thousands, who are now languishing in hopeless poverty, will find a certain and a speedy independence [in the West]. The labor market will be thus eased of the present distressing competition; and those who remain, as well as those who emigrate, will have the opportunity of realizing a confortable living.[26]

Shannon also maintained that the thesis should have been declared dead long before Turner gave his paper and that it would have been had Turner or his predecessors or supporters made the slightest effort to test the thesis. Shannon argued that the flow of people moving West was hardly sufficient to have had the consequences Turner and his predecessors imagined. People were not always escaping to the West for reasons Turner surmised.[27]

23. George Wilson Pierson, "The Frontier and American Institutions: A Criticism of the Turner Theory," *New England Quarterly* (June 1942), in *Turner Thesis,* ed. Taylor, p. 68.

24. Ibid., p. 69.

25. As reported by Pierson, "Frontier and American Institutions," p. 65 (note 1).

26. As found in John R. Commons et al., eds., *A Documented History of American Industrial Society,* quoted in Fred A. Shannon, "A Post Mortem on the Labor-Safety-Valve Theory," in *Turner Thesis,* ed. Taylor, p. 51.

27. Shannon maintained, "No responsible person has ever tried to deny that at all times in America some few of the more fortunate laborers could and did take up land. But the seepage of the stream which went on almost constantly did not prevent the

Turner and his supporters had failed to address an important question: Was the flow of humanity through the supposed safety valve sufficient to justify their conclusions, which were that economic and political institutions were shaped by the West's existence and would continue to be shaped by its closing? Shannon maintained, based on available statistics, that the flow was fairly meager, though there was a net flow toward farming on free western lands. Based on those same statistics, one could argue that the emerging industrial sector provided a safety valve for people who sought refuge from depressed working conditions on farms.

From 1860 to 1890, the farm population expanded from 19 million to 28 million, or by an average compounded annual rate of 1.3 percent. However, the country's nonfarm population grew at the much steeper compounded annual rate of 4.7 percent; that is, from 12 million in 1860 to 48 million in 1900. The number of farmworkers actually grew very slowly compared to the increased number of non-farmworkers. Furthermore, the overwhelming majority of farms (86 percent) were run by tenants, not by resident owners, and most of the resident-owned and managed farms were east of the Mississippi.[28] Finally, Shannon notes that in 1890 at least twenty farmers moved to urban areas for every urban worker who moved to a farm, and "ten sons of farmers went to the city for each one who became the owner of a new farm anywhere in the Nation."[29] These facts caused Shannon to conclude that the "safety valve that actually existed worked in entirely the opposite direction from the one so often extolled."[30]

---

pressure from rising when too much fuel was put under the boiler, and the seepage almost stopped entirely whenever the pressure got dangerously high. It was not until the 1830s, when the factory system in America began to bloom and the labor gangs were recruited for the building of canals and railroads, that any situation arose which would cause for a safety valve. The shoemaker or carpenter of colonial days who turned to farming did not do so as a release from the ironclad wage system, as millions between 1830 and 1890 would have liked to do if they could. It was an era of slipshod economy and easy readjustment, where no great obstacle was put in the way of misfits. Even if one admits that a scarcity of free labor for hire was one of the minor reasons for the late development of a factory system, and that the choice of close and cheap land kept down the supply, yet a far greater reason was the scarcity of manufacturing capital. When the factory system began, it was easy to import shiploads of immigrant laborers" ("Post Mortem on the Labor-Safety-Valve Theory," p. 53).

28. Ibid., pp. 54–55.
29. Ibid., p. 55.
30. Ibid., p. 59.

Reconciling Some Differences

Turner's frontier thesis is certainly open to debate, because it was not carefully crafted when he delivered his fateful paper. The paper was designed to be a speech and, as such, was intended to keep the attention of the audience. It was not a journal article intended to precisely model the ways the West affected institutional development in the country. Turner's purpose, it would seem, was to provide the broad outlines of a research program guided by a central point: *The West—not just Europe—matters.* He probably did overgeneralize from his thesis. After all, the West was not the only "vital force" operating in the first 100 years of the country's existence. Turner's students were probably awestruck by the simplicity of their master's thesis, and history no doubt would have been better served had they been more critical of his methods.

Acknowledging these caveats by critics should not destroy the broader notion at the heart of the Turner thesis: *"Vital forces" do count.* The crucial problems lie in identifying the forces and in assessing their relative consequences. It may be true that Turner turned the attention of historians inward, but given the circumstances of the time, that judgment call may have been reasonable. Turner employed a form of geographical Darwinism into historical discussions, and he focused on the consequences of the "West" as a place. At the same time, one could be more generous and conclude that what Turner actually had in mind was discussing how people's opportunities were altered by the existence of a place called the West and how people responded to the set of opportunities at their disposal.

The data clearly shows that not as many people ventured West during the nineteenth century as the Turner thesis might lead one to expect. But critics—Shannon, in particular—do not seem to appreciate an important distinction between the *actual* number who moved West and the *potential* number who could have moved, and he certainly was apparently unable to comprehend the relevance of the distinction. Turner focused on the number of *actual* movers, and the effects they might have on the American character and American institutions, and since the number may not have been all that large, Turner can be faulted. Nevertheless, the great number of *potential* movers could have been an added "vital force" that exerted pressure with effects similar to those of actual movers. Eastern governments and private firms had to be concerned about those who *could* move as well as those who *did* move. Responses by both public and private institutions to the combined pressures generated by the actual *and* potential movers may have had much the same effect of curbing taxes and controls somewhat and inspiring a more market-oriented and prosperous economy.

Turner can perhaps also be chastised for having succumbed intellectually to the romance of the frontier and not recognizing that it represented "the edge of the unused," to use Dixon Ryan Fox's turn of words.[31] If Turner had thought in terms of the "unused," he might have seen that the vision he was expounding could be applied to one degree or another to various other conditions—that there were *edges* of the unused, or unexploited opportunities, all around him and other Americans, whether they were on the western frontier or the urban frontier or the technological frontier.

Had Turner shifted his perspective just a bit, he might have realized that many Americans were living on multiple frontiers outside his analytical purview but no less important to the development of the American character and American institutions. Seeing the world in terms of multiple frontiers (defined only by that which was "unused" and perhaps unimagined) might have made Turner and his followers more optimistic about the prospects for the future. Though the West was already closed, other frontiers were opening wider than ever before. Had that not been the case, we as a nation and as individuals most likely would not have continued to rapidly develop economically, technologically, and scientifically well into the twentieth century.

Turner expounded his thesis in overly simplistic terms: Land was "free" and movement west could be managed with "slight effort." Accordingly, opportunities were "free" (or virtually so) prior to the closing of the West. Those words certainly colored the debate, because they implied that the closing of the West meant that opportunities would no longer be "free." Whatever opportunities remained would rapidly become too expensive for most Americans to achieve, and there would probably be fewer viable opportunities. However, labeling something "free" does not make it free, even if no price tag is attached. Given the unsophisticated modes of transportation available in the early nineteenth century—mainly horses, wagons, and boats—just getting to the supposedly "free" land was an arduous task. Trips overland often took months of risk-filled and uncertain travel. The first overland trip to California by sixty-nine settlers, drawn to their goal by exaggerated stories of the good life on the country's West Coast, began in Platte County, Missouri (close to halfway across the country), in May 1841.[32] The trip ended

31. As quoted in Pierson, "Frontier and American Institutions," p. 65.

32. According to reports, "No Mountain Men or experienced western travelers were present to serve as an antidote to the geographical ignorance of the group.

in November 1841, six months after it began. Subsequent trips became shorter and less arduous, but by today's standards, they remained lengthy—running into weeks—*and* they were costly. The settlers' lost wages while on the westward trips inevitably imputed a price to the land. Clearing the land and making it productive added to the cost. Taking the risks associated with trying to wrestle a living from land belonging to hostile Native Americans and being far removed from even rudimentary medical services compounded the total price of moving west. Many people understandably chose not to move and to wait until the land was more settled and the communication and transportation lines were better developed—or until the imputed price of the land had fallen.

Land in the West was never "free," nor could it ever be acquired with "slight effort," as Turner so glibly claimed. When Greeley urged young men to go west, he did not intend that they dream of "getting suddenly rich by speculation"; rather, he was challenging them to be

> neither afraid nor ashamed of honest industry; and if you catch yourself fancying *anything* more than this be ashamed of it to the last day of your life. Or, if you find yourself shaking more cordially the hand of your cousin the congressman than of your uncle the blacksmith, *as such,* write yourself down [as] an enemy to the principles of our institutions, and a traitor to the dignity of Humanity.[33]

Concluding Comments

Frederick Jackson Turner remains an important historian because he did, in the main, what noted academic historians do: He not only reported facts of history, but changed the way his colleagues have thought ever since about the facts. The shift has had good and bad effects. The posi-

---

. . . A further complication resulted from the presence of a number of women and children. . . . With nothing to guide them save the admonition to bear due west from Salt Lake they plunged into the unknown, abandoning wagons in favor of pack animals to gain time. . . . With their supply of beef exhausted and surrounded by 'naked mountains whose summits still retained the snows of perhaps a thousand years' they struggled until October 29, when they despaired of reaching California. But the following day they discovered a westward flowing river, the Stanislaus, which they followed to the site of Sonora. So exhausted were they when they arrived in the San Joaquin Valley that they could not believe they were in the promised land itself. California, some thought, must be five hundred miles away" (Billington, *Westward Expansion,* pp. 565–66).

33. As quoted in Parton, *Life of Horace Greeley,* p. 414.

tive effect is enduring: He foucsed the attention of scholars and ordinary citizens on a powerful force in American institutional development, the West.

On the flip side of the token, his theory was overly simplistic and myopic (probably as it had to be, given that complicated theories obscure important contributions), leading to pessimistic assessments of the future. Far too many scholars and ordinary citizens bought his assumption that the closing of the West meant a major watershed in the development of the American psyche, primarily because the closing of the West meant future generations of Americans could no longer dream the dreams of their forebears. Still viewing the closing of the geographical West as a watershed even in American social history, all too many academics continue to teach and, regrettably, inspire pessimism. Turner (and too many modern-day commentators) completely overlooked other social and political escape hatches that should have been blatantly obvious. In a sense, by claiming that land was free, Turner rigged (inadvertently) the debate by implying that moving west was a frontier unto itself, economically far more attractive than other non–land-based frontiers, for example, those in scientific spheres.

Clearly, it was right that Turner should stress how the West represented an unexploited opportunity for generations of Americans. At the same time, many, many Americans found other opportunities closer to home and exploited them at lower costs than they would have incurred had they made a westward trek. The closing of the West at the turn of the twentieth century did not close all doors of opportunity. Scientific and technological developments, coupled with the growth in competition among emerging and expanding industries, gave rise to greater national incomes that, in turn, led to expanded educational opportunities, to increases in physical and human capital, to greater concern for environmental amenities, and to broader vistas—to more dreams to dream.

The economic and social escape valves that remained after the closing of the West were simply less obvious, but they functioned the same way. Today, a whole new West that Turner could never have imagined—a whole new economic and social escape valve—is emerging and being populated by modern-day pioneers, settlers, and merchants (even in the type of "waves" Turner discussed). This frontier goes by many names, with Cyberspace being one of the more common if not overused tags. For millions of Americans it is a productive technological playground. They think of "place" as where the mind is, not as a piece of geography, as Turner thought. As I show in chapter 5, the great endearing and enduring aspect about this new West, Cyberspace, is that its exploitation does not use up the resources but increases the uses that can be made of it. In this new thoroughly modern West, Fox's comments are as relevant as ever: "Failure now . . . would not be a failure of opportunity; it would be a failure of nerve."[34]

34. As quoted in Pierson, "Frontier and American Institutions," p. 65.

5

THE OPENING OF THE VIRTUAL ECONOMY

> The central event of the twentieth century is the overthrow of matter . . . [W]ealth in the form of physical resources is steadily declining in value and significance. The powers of mind are everywhere ascended over the brute force of things.
>
> George Gilder, *Microcosm*

BY WAY of Disney's animated film version of the *Arabian Nights* story "Aladdin and the Wonderful Lamp," audiences around the globe are taken on a magic carpet ride into a fantasy world of erupting volcanoes, raging lions, and ghastly snakes. Aladdin always narrowly escapes brutal annihilation. He is basically a good young man in spite of the fact that he is, as described by his pursuers, a "street rat," one who apparently lives by thievery, the justification for which is simple: He's broke and hungry. By way of sharp contrast, the other lead character, Jasmine, is a princess, inundated in royal splendor, whose only complaint in life is that she is not free to make her own choices, especially when it comes to the person she will marry.

Jasmine and Aladdin meet and fall in love, virtually at first sight. On the magic carpet ride the two take over the kingdom, Aladdin shows Jasmine a "whole new world" from "a new fantastic point of view." The two, however, must forsake their newfound love and go their separate ways because she is royalty and he is not.

The story continues as an epic battle between the forces of good (Aladdin and Jasmine, who seek eternal love) and evil (Jaffar, who seeks control of the empire). Jaffar succumbs to his own fatal conceit, the desire to become all-powerful, and that wish damns him to eternal captivity inside the lamp. Aladdin and Jasmine eventually marry and, of course, live happily ever after. The film ends with Aladdin and Jasmine riding their magic carpet over the clouds and into the sunset.

A very nice story, but there's more to the film than that if modern theatergoers wish to reflect on prospects for the future. Most certainly realize that the roles in the film represent pipe dreams; the plot is as old and familiar as the ageless fairy tales, and the total bliss Jasmine and Aladdin experience remains as unattainable today as it was a millennium ago. Much can be learned, nevertheless, by examining the technology used to make viewing the film an other-world experience. The future for most Americans may not match the world of *Aladdin,* but it's a sure bet that the future will be as far removed from current experience as today's world stands apart from the experience of our great-grandparents.

A Whole New World

The story line of *Aladdin* adds an important perspective to any discussion of economic dreaming not so much because the film is about a whole new fantasy world, which it is, but because it is an example of a whole new modern world of visual and technological wizardry that could not have been imagined, much less experienced, 100 years ago when the West was being closed to further homesteading.[1]

Granted, 100 years ago children could read the story, and maybe they let their imaginations roam freely over how the story line was played out. Children today still have that option, but they have an additional option, the film, filled with scenes that, because they were created by way of computer-generated animation, extend the potential powers of the mind. The film represents the flow of what can come from the new West, appropriately dubbed the "virtual economy." At the same time, the film must be viewed as a metaphor for the vast array of new ways of doing things, mainly with technology, on a global scale.

Through arduous wagon travel, the pioneers of more than 100 years ago made their way into a whole new world where they could work, play, and add value to their own and other people's lives. The Disney artists cannot move west as their ancestors did (they are already there!), but their ability to travel, so to speak, has not been closed. Through computer animation, the artists were able to translate their own fantasy worlds into a form that others can appreciate and enjoy,

1. For a discussion of how *Aladdin* was produced by way of computer-generated imagery, see Gary Pfitzer, "Ancient Tale, Modern Impact," *Computer Graphics World,* November 1992, pp. 46–51.

and then to travel through the fantasy world they created, the movie *Aladdin*.

For the couple of hours they are in the theater, viewers are treated, as was Jasmine, to a whole new fantastic point of view of the world—a vision of the age-old struggle between good and evil—embellished with kaleidoscopic colors and sounds that are, in a manner of speaking, hallucinogenic. This new West where the animators and viewers meet is unlike the western plains in many regards. The look and feel of the two Wests are obviously different; one is real and the other is pure fantasy (although what is real and what is fantasy is not, upon careful reflection, easily distinguished, given romantic images carefully cultivated about the real West). Nevertheless, the virtual economy of the new West has many of the essential characteristics of the West that Frederick Jackson Turner (whose work was the focus of chapter 4) had in mind.

Like the old West, the new West has a frontier that is constantly being pushed back as artists and technicians explore new vistas, new technologies and techniques. Their purpose is not merely to find out what is around the next bend in the road, but to determine where or how the sensory receptors can be excited in some new way and what new dimension can be added to animated action. Travel through the old and new Wests was and is as much a discovery as a production process. The pioneers of yesterday "opened up" the old West, making it habitable for themselves and others who followed in their footsteps. They discovered soil so black and rich in the Midwest that you can, as Midwesterners say, spit on it and something will grow. They also discovered passages through mountains that must have, from a distance, seemed impassable.

Upon reaching a crest at the entrance of Yosemite Valley, the western travelers must have been awestruck, as tourists are today. Miners, of course, discovered gold and a host of other usable minerals, all extending the productive capabilities of the American economy. The pioneers of yesterday learned to live with and use what they found or, as often was the case, suffer the not-so-pleasant consequences. When practical, people in the old West specialized, thereby increasing the efficiency with which the many required goods and services they wanted were produced, but their specialization meant that they had to rely more extensively on markets. They created communities, new social networks that added meaning and value to their lives. Not everyone played by the rules, of course. Some—the "bad guys"—held up banks and stage coaches and rustled cattle, as the old western B-movies have perhaps exaggerated.

The pioneers of today have opened up—and continue to open up—the new West to habitation by others, who may be less skilled and less venturesome than the new pioneers themselves who dare to take the risks. One of the more important first modern ventures came in the form of the first personal computer sold to the general public, the Altair 8800, in 1974. The machine was a clumsy collection of wires and lights, came with no software, and required fifty commands, accomplished by flipping switches, just to get started![2] The computer pioneers who followed—computer hardware developers, programmers, and hackers—have discovered, partially through specialization of their efforts, what powerful and creative things can be done with integrated circuitry, microprocessors, and hard drives. Although the developers of the components of modern computers, programmers, and the hackers never intended to search for vast acreage of fertile land, new reservoirs of oil, and deposits of iron (as well as a host of other basic minerals), they discovered them anyway, as serendipities, on their journeys to do things to and with computers. They found the new reserves and deposits in the most unlikely of places: sand. Silicon, a foundation of computer chips, is the second most abundant element of the earth's crust; it occurs in compound form in silicates, which are commonly found in sand.

By refining computer technology, modern computer pioneers dramatically increased the productivity of computers, enabling them to be downsized and miniaturized to the point that futurists now talk not about laptop or palmtop computers, but about computers on a ring (which necessarily will take commands and give results by voice). Pioneers have permitted teleconferencing, not only dramatically decreasing the need for travel (which uses up oil reserves) but also speeding up product development by as much as 30 percent as times have been cut by 20 to 30 percent.[3] They also enabled computers to be fitted into a variety of instruments and machines—from combines and reapers to flight instruments and robots—allowing these tools to be downsized, if not miniaturized, and used on farms and in factories that also have been reduced in size (as measured by acres plowed in the case of farms and by square feet covered in the case of factories). Output has continued to rise with the growth in computer power, with the speed of available personal computers increasing by a factor of five or six during the time this book was to be turned from manuscript to printed pages. The downsized production processes, all requiring progressively less energy

2. As reported by Evan Ramstad, "PCs Evolving into Information Furnaces," *Los Angeles Times*, June 30, 1994, p. D7.

3. Rochelle Sharpe, "Work Week: Lights, Camera, Meeting," *Wall Street Journal*, February 21, 1995, p. A1.

and material inputs, including iron and oil, have effectively freed up land and known oil reserves and iron deposits for doing things other than expanding farms and building larger factories, pieces of machinery, and mainframe computers. In a meaningful sense, computers have become modern oil derricks; everywhere they go, they seem to make strikes.

The Nets in the New West

Rolling Stone magazine had good reason to suggest that computer hackers, among others, are the true modern pioneers, "traversing packet-switched networks, outdials and trunks all over the physical world."[4] Hackers have penetrated the computer monitor as if it were the gateway to a whole new territory in which they can make new discoveries about the outside world they live in and about the inside world they enter for purposes of computations, composition, design, entertainment, and even a sense of community—with an estimated 80 percent of the users looking for companionship in a community, albeit a virtual one.[5] In a meaningful sense, modern-day pioneers go to work *in* their computers in much the same way, and with similar effect, that pioneers of old went to work in their cornfields. A major difference is that yesterday's pioneers had to have both body and soul exactly where they worked. Modern-day pioneers, on the other hand, are not simply at work *on* or *in* their computers; they are at work wherever their transmissions are sent. They can be, in effect, many places simultaneously, which means that they can be vastly more productive at the same time that their efforts can be, measured by raw physical exertion, less strenuous.

The inhabitants who work and play in the virtual economy of the new West have—in much the same spirit but not in the same form as the pioneers of old—linked up to form an exploding number (well over 50,000 in the mid-1990s) of electronic communities in the form of bulletin board systems (BBSs). Here they engage in what can be endless coversations with people from around the community or the globe whom they have never met and, in most instances, will never meet, except on communication networks. Nevertheless, the inhabitants of the "nets" offer many of the same benefits achieved in real communities: commercial

4. As quoted by Jon Katz, "Bulletin Boards: News from Cyberspace," *Rolling Stone*, April 15, 1993, p. 35.

5. As reported in Jill Smolowe, "Intimate Strangers," *Time*, Spring 1995 (special edition), p. 20.

trade, conversation, sense of identity, counsel, praise, condolence, criticism, and entertainment.

On the net, there are bulletin boards for people who just want to chat about the topic of the moment, ranging from the President's latest policy move to when or whether women younger than fifty should get mammograms. There are "adult" bulletin boards where participants may engage in forms of "cyber-sex" (arms-length titillating chat on par with porno phone services). Medieval historians from around the world have a net, as do technical support staffs at colleges and universities, where they can solve mutual problems and reduce duplication of efforts. Global Marketplace provides participants who seek information about company products and services with referrals to information sources. Nets even exist for helping people navigate other global nets. There are nets for teens and college students, high-tech computer wonks, artists, and political partisans (conservatives or liberals). There's a net that brings together Keyboards for Christ, and nets dedicated solely to gays, lesbians, and bisexuals, as well as to senior citizens, all of whom have special problems, perspectives, and needs to ponder or resolve. Self-described "Digital Queers" use net technology to discuss the host of practical and emotional problems associated with "coming out" at home or office and to advance their political cause of nondiscriminatory treatment in the country's workplaces.[6] When this book was begun in 1992, nets were novel; when it went to press, they were "old hat."

What has remained constant is the impact of technology. The current elderly generation's range of experience has been unique in human history, because of how much change they have observed, including the reconstitution of the senior community via a net. The lives of today's seniors have been an ever-advancing and unfolding frontier: "We have gone from sitting by the radio for fireside chats to seeing a war start while watching CNN one evening, from hearing about the invasion of Poland a day later on the radio to watching the butchery in the former Yugoslavia nightly, from the agony of plucking and cleaning chickens to the joy of buying them bare-bottom clean. . . ."[7] On other nets, "plains-state farmers trade weather, price and livestock information on agriculture boards; graphic artists trade computer-animation programs; psychologists alert one another to new research and treatment techniques; parents look for summer camps. There's a conference on wildlife

6. Martha Groves, "Advocates of Gay Rights Look to Technology to Further the Cause," *Los Angeles Times*, October 19, 1993, p. D1.

7. S. R. Shannon, "Conversing On Line with Older Americans," *New York Times*, October 19, 1993, p. B7.

and dozens for those who want to trade information about virtual reality and other computer technology."[8] Even economists have set aside many of their statistical tables to prowl the net for professional colleagues with anecdotal news that might help them understand the policy direction the Federal Reserve might take, given that lots of money can ride on correct predictions of interest rates.[9] Then there are the "newsgroups," which represent a whole new category of "narrowcasting in the extreme: [news] content created by consumers for consumers. While cable-TV executives still dream of hundreds of channels, Usenet [for newsgroups] has thousands."[10] And, yes, there are the "bad guys" who break into other people's property, stealing credit-card records and small fortunes in software, and hate groups, such as the wanna-be techno-Nazis, who pass around their social venom about outsiders with insiders.[11]

The creation of network communities within the virtual economy of the new West is in many ways like the creation of communities in the old West. People must establish some rules by which they can conduct their conversations and business, but net communities have special problems and opportunities (which may explain the existence of the *Journal of Virtual Culture*). Given the dependency on typed words, protocols have had to be created for showing feelings and emotions (displeasure or pleasure, hostility or acceptance). For example, a means of "shouting" (by using all capital letters) had to be developed.

Net participants remain at a distance, behind the veil of pixels and electronic impulses. Accordingly, they have an opportunity to present themselves as they are or to redefine their personas. For that matter, they can define several personas, revealing different ones on different nets or on the same net at different times or to different people. Students who might otherwise be shy about speaking up in class frequently are able to pour out their thoughts when linked with their teachers by nets. Renowned experts who appear unapproachable in person are often readily available when they join the net, partly because the professional halo is not always known (hidden behind passwords and netnames). Some who would not dare be critical to another person about his or her work are able to find bluntness and incisiveness in the anonymity of the

8. Ibid., p. B36.

9. Fred R. Bleakley, "Economists Turn to Chats, Internet, Informal Polls to Get Jump on Fed," *Wall Street Journal*, January 1, 1995, p. A2.

10. Philip Elmer-DeWitt, "Welcome to Cyberspace," *Time*, Spring 1995 (special edition), p. 10.

11. Jared Sandberg, "Immorality Play: Acclaiming Hackers As Heroes," *Wall Street Journal*, February 27, 1995, p. B1.

nets. Nets come about as close as any institution can to being "equal opportunity employers," with age, sex, disability, appearance, and gender being less of a basis for judgment than in other institutions.

Trust is one such problem in building any community, but it is, as can be imagined without face-to-face contact, a special problem for people on nets. Some people can never be quite sure how much of themselves they can reveal to others, because they can never be sure who the others are, whether they are who they say they are or not. A teenage girl or boy, for example, may never know whether the people with whom they are conversing are close to their age or several times their age. For that matter, they may not know whether they are the sex they profess to be—or have the education and credentials they profess to have. But then education and credentials are often irrelevant. Nets are highly egalitarian, which is why many people join them.

Being able to make credible commitments on nets will, however, likely remain an enduring problem. But the problems of working out relationships may at times be easier on nets than in real life. Many couples have found that nets provide them with an opportunity to return to arms-length Victorian dating, given that they can't touch but can work through many aspects of their relationship before they see one another.

By way of contrast, an academic netter tells the story of another netter named Julie who worked the net primarily because she was disabled, only able to push the keys with a headstick. But "on the net, Julie's disability was invisible and irrelevant. Her standard greeting was a big, expansive 'HI!!!!!!' Her heart was as big as her greeting, and in the intimate electronic companionship that can develop during on-line conferencing between people who may never physically meet, Julie's women friends shared their deepest troubles, and she offered them advice—advice that changed their lives. Trapped inside her ruined body, Julie herself was sharp and perceptive, thoughtful and caring."[12]

The interchanges between Julie and her net friends continued until one of the women decided to locate Julie in real life, which she did, only to discover that she was not what she proclaimed; Julie was a middle-aged male psychiatrist who, when caught, confessed, "I was stunned at the conversation mode. I hadn't known that women talked among themselves that way. There was so much more vulnerability, so much more depth and complexity. Men's conversations on the nets were much more

12. Allucquere Rosanne Stone, "Will the Real Body Please Stand Up? Boundary Stories about Virtual Cultures," *Cyberspace: The First Steps* (Cambridge, Mass.: MIT Press, 1991), pp. 82–83.

guarded and superficial, even among intimates. It was fascinating, and I wanted more."[13] The damage done? More than might be thought. Julie's net friends confessed, on learning of her disguise, of feeling "violated," even "raped."[14] Again, working the nets is more like real life than all the high-tech facilities might suggest. The medium might be different, but most of the people seem to be the same.

The Endless Frontier Within Cyberspace

"Virtual reality"? Admittedly, the term is faddish, but its use here cannot be avoided. It is a place or state of mind, depending upon your perspective, that defies exact definition. This is because virtual reality is bounded only by what people can conceive of and translate into computer-based images in something called cyberspace. William Gibson, author of the pace-setting science fiction novel *Neuromancer* (1984) in which the term was first used, envisions cyberspace as a condition under which people live much of their sordid lives in their machines and are controlled by them. In Gibson's novel, cyberspace was "consensual hallucination" or a "neologic spasm: the primal act of pop poetics . . . awaiting received meaning."[15]

Others, however, perceive cyberspace more favorably, in terms that necessarily have a poetic quality. Cyberspace is a

> [n]ew universe, a parallel universe created and sustained by the world's computers and communication lines. A world in which the global traffic of knowledge, secrets, measurements, indicators, entertainments, and alter-human agency takes on form: sights, sounds, presences never seen on the surface of the earth blossoming in a vast electronic night. . . . The tablet become a page become a screen become a world, a virtual world. Everywhere and nowhere, a place where nothing is forgotten and yet everything changes.[16]

Cyberspace does not exist in one sense—after all, it is the multidimensional space that the hacker sees as he or she stares at the flat face of a computer monitor. At the same time, it is no less real than mathematics, law, art, religion, and philosophy. It is a place where something can be

13. As quoted in Stone, "Will the Real Body Please Stand Up?" p. 83.
14. Ibid.
15. As quoted by Peter Anders, "Young Architects," *Progressive Architecture*, July 1993, p. 24; and Sydney Pokorny, "Things That Go Bleep," *Artform*, April 1993, p. 14.
16. Michael Benedikt, "Introduction," *Cyberspace: First Steps* (Cambridge, Mass.: MIT, 1991), p. 1.

made from virtually nothing, where nonmaterial forms, although grounded in data, are the essence of what exists.

Cyberspace is best visualized in terms of computer screens with altered artistic forms of lines and shapes and figures in contorted pictures (one of which is used on the cover of this book), but cyberspace need not be limited by the visible dots in a computer picture. Each dot on the screen is a potential doorway to subspaces upon subspaces filled with new shapes, lines, sounds, and videos contained, in a manner of speaking, within the surface dots. Cyberspace pioneers and settlers can literally navigate through an infinite array of subspaces, never quite sure what may come next:

> Cyberspace has a geography, a physics, a nature, and a rule of human law. In cyberspace the common man and the information worker—cowboy or infocrat—can search, manipulate, create or control information directly; he can be entertained or trained, seek solitude or company, win or lose power . . . indeed, can "live" or "die" as he will.[17]

Cyberspace is the all-encompassing new West, where *Aladdin* was conceived and brought to term and, at the same time, where audiences traveled while in theaters. As in the old West, there are pioneers in the new West who are constantly advancing the frontier, dividing what has been tried and been proven true from that which is not. A major difference between the old and new pioneers is that the frontier work of the new pioneers may be more accurately described as *creation*, not just *discovery*. The new West is the product of the imagination, meaning it would never have existed had not someone *willed* it. Moreover, the pioneers of yesterday were constrained by the laws of physics; the new pioneers are not so constrained, at least in some ways, as evidenced by the fact that Jasmine and Aladdin rode their carpet, which was capable of showing emotion as well as motion, anywhere they liked.

The overriding difference between the old West and the new is that the former pioneers laboriously and gradually traversed the western territories until they reached the Pacific, at which point the old West could be considered closed, even fully peopled, because of the defined limits of that West. Not so much so for the technologically grounded new West. Its exploration and settlement does the exact opposite—expands its scope. There is no obvious end to the advancement of the frontier in the new West, because there are no known limits to the dimensions of

17. Michael Benedikt, "Cyberspace: Some Proposals," in *Cyberspace*, ed. Benedikt, p. 123.

the cyberspace, per se—because cyberspace has no dimensions aside from those that the users define for their particular purposes, which need not conflict with the defined limits of others.

In cyberspace, exploration and exploitation expand the space and what can be done with and in the space. More can be explored and exploited because the exploration and exploitation itself so often leads to more previously unseen or unimagined dimensions. If limits are ever found to cyberspace, they are likely to be mental, that is, defined by what the individual mind can conceive and manage, even with the help of more microprocessors and RAM. There are, for example, *possible* limits to how many computer programs people are able or willing to learn (or just icons they are able and willing to identify). Nevertheless, the evolving networks are a means by which the mental limitations are being surmounted.

Individuals in the nets might be the counterparts of computer chips. By themselves, they have narrowly defined capabilities. A stand-alone computer chip can be as "dumb" as the sand at its foundation. With the aid of other components in the computers, the capabilities of the chips begin to come alive. When the chips are linked by electrical impulses, their power begins to mount synergetically. The communications that move in all directions over nets can, so to speak, enable the system of individuals to do far more than the sum of their total. People, appropriately linked, become parallel processors, with the work being divided among them to make it manageable by individuals. In addition, modern technology offers the prospects of far more people linking up than ever before. Recognition of that fact is important because it means that the economy of the future will be able to draw on the particular knowledge of far more diverse people in widely diverse circumstances. Yet, the results can be expected to supersede what they all could have accomplished without the linkages, or even could have imagined.

In a special regard, the virtual world of cyberspace is much like knowledge. As what is known expands, there is more to discover, more questions to answer, and more to know. Why? Answering that question is not easy, but think in terms of knowledge as both the nodes in a web and their actual or potential connections to each other. As the number of nodes expands, the number of potential linkages explodes. With one node, there are no linkages. With two, there is one. With three, there are six. With ten, interestingly, there are close to a million. With a million nodes, don't even try to count. There is simply more to know—more linkages—the more we know. There is going to be more "space" in cyberspace, the more it is settled. In this regard, cyberspace is itself an expanding universe, not a static one, the limits of which are more a matter of philosophy than practice.

Unlike Turner's West, there will be no fading frontier and no closing of the new West, or so it seems for now and the foreseeable future. What is crucial to understand is that all the talk about technology does not mean that there is only one new West or only one new frontier, that described by computer power and hookups. Molecular biology means that the body can be explored in heretofore untold ways with all the adventure, and possible payoff, of the Gold Rush. The cosmos is being opened for exploration. Even our past represents a new frontier that historians, paleontologists, and archaeologists are exploring with new insights and new methods and new tools. The "global economy" is no longer a figment of pipe dreams; it represents unexplored opportunities to do productive things with literally hundreds of millions of people who not too long ago had to do their own thing with people close at hand.

Virtual "Farming"

This whole new technology-based world, only a minor part of which was exploited by the Disney animators or can be described here, is literally a world apart from the one central to Turner's (and so many of our forebears') conception of the world in which "vital forces" that ultimately shape institutional design were at work. Turner focused on the *West* because his world was one in which, to a large extent, geography in the large, on the scale of the western United States, was the foundation of much national economic activity and political pride. Earth—or so many acres of land—was crucial to economic value in that earlier world. People needed land to farm in order that they could feed themselves and their families, and they spent much of their daily efforts and incomes working the soil.

In 1893, half the country's population worked in agriculture. Manufacturing also was, in Turner's world, involved in producing *real* things, for example, horse harnesses and buggies and dresses. It was a world of *material* dominance, in which running out of the stuff of production could be a real concern, and was. Abstractions were of less value then because they were difficult to present in understandable terms to ordinary people, and ordinary people had little patience with abstractions because they could not be eaten or worn or used for shelter.

The world of today is dramatically different. Land still carries some weight, but only some. Less than 3 percent of the country's population live and work on farms. Material objects are still consumed, but the relative value of the material contained therein is diminishing with the growing importance of the nonmaterial, as noted, with whole new worlds that are created on celluloid or, better yet, imagined inside computers and networks. The world represented on the screen (in a theater or computer monitor) is probably every bit as meaningful to modern Americans as the West was to Americans who crossed the plains and the western mountains.

As in the case of Turner's real frontier, the American psyche is constantly being reshaped by discoveries made at the new frontier. Box-office reports clearly indicate that the animators at Disney did something very productive, even though the economic value of what they did was contained largely in an abstraction—the concept of doing the movie the way they did—and not in the material content of their creation, which was so much celluloid. After all, what the animators did amounted to no more than electrical impulses (which are as close to nothing as one can get) that formed lines and colors on computer screens that, eventually, became frames on film, which, in turn, gave a form of surreal life to the lines and colors. As evident by the number of children (and many of their parents) who want to dress up as Jasmine and Aladdin for Halloween and other times, the children (and adults) who went to the movie got something of value that was equally abstract, a source of inspiration to be someone good, nice, and attractive.

The Disney animators worked as hard in their virtual economy as did settlers in their fields. The animators, effectively, "farmed" their "West"—productively.

As early as 1983, McGraw-Hill, Inc., a textbook and magazine publisher with $2 billion in revenues in 1992, realized that eventually much of the printed word would be transmitted electronically, and it has learned to "farm" the computer and telecommunication technology that has emerged over the last decade or so. It now offers a number of electronic data services that were once available only on paper. Given that much of the data relates to securities markets (for example, its Standard and Poor's stock service), the data is more timely and more valuable to the users and less costly for McGraw-Hll to provide. In addition, McGraw-Hill now publishes textbooks that are printed according to which chapters individual professors select (from a list of available chapters) for inclusion. Once more, the individualized textbooks can be made available for classroom use within twenty-four hours after the orders are received—and the books can even be sent to college bookstores or students electronically.[18]

18. As reported in James Flanigan, "To Find Riches in Information, Ignore the Hoopla," *Los Angeles Times*, October 27, 1993, p. D1.

Clearly, the American psyche has been shaped, to a degree, by the daily newspaper, before and after Turner. News coverage of political candidates and policy issues can make or break the candidates and policy proposals. Graphic news stories and nightly television pictures of the dead and dying soldiers during the Vietnam War affected the course of that war, and, maybe to a degree, the course of human history. Television pictures of precision bombing in the brief 1991 Gulf War had, perhaps, a similar effect. Opportunities are, in effect, giving rise to themselves.

There are commentators and analysts, even futurists, no doubt, who believe that Americans are too wedded to the printed page to take their morning news electronically, that is, through some form other than two-minute news drills on television news programs. However, Rodger Fidler, founder of Knight-Ridder Tribune Graphics, a firm that provides digital graphics for newspapers and video animation for television stations, believes that Americans can be enticed away from their newspapers and television sets into a blended news/information medium: the "newspanels," flat-panel hand-held computer screens (much like those on laptop computers), with laser-quality resolutions, that can be used to provide what might be called "virtual news."[19] If the newspanels can be improved (or, perhaps more optimistically, *when they are improved*), Fidler believes that the computer will substantially increase the value of news people receive, partly because of the embedded search capabilities of computers and partly because of the sound and video components that will be appended to electronically printed news stories. As social commentator George Gilder notes,

> What the Model T was to the industrial era—the teenage training board, the tinkerer's love and laboratory, the technological epitome—the PC is to the Information Age. Just as people who rode the wave of automobile technology—from tiremakers to fast-food franchisers—prevailed in the industrial era, so the firms that prey on the passion and feed on the force of the computer community will predominate in the information age.[20]

They will do so because they can provide the core product in the information age: lots of information at what seem now to be unbelievable speeds.

Once the technology has sufficiently evolved, the morning newspaper companies will no longer be the gatekeepers on information flows for

19. As reported by George Gilder, "Telecosm: Digital Darkhorse—Newspapers," *Forbes ASAP* [technology supplement to *Forbes*], 1993, pp. 139–49.
20. Ibid., p. 149.

mass audiences. Their control is fading as fast, if not faster, than their circulations are falling and the number of news outlets is rising. Readers will be able to pick and choose the news they actually receive on their panels. Scott Sassa, head of the Turner Entertainment Group, muses,

> In the future, when we have expanded distribution and total interactivity, the consumer won't need to subscribe to a 24-hour channel. He or she will just get it on demand. The future won't be 500 channels—it will be one channel, *your* channel. So instead of subscribing to some a la carte, 24-hour channel, you'll just get the show you want on demand, whatever, wherever, and whenever you want it.[21]

The new technology will fundamentally change the relationship between the provider and receiver of the news. The "smart" providers will no longer determine what the "dumb" receiver will get in the way of news. The providers will far more frequently broadcast whatever stories are submitted, leaving it to the receivers' computers to pull in stories that are of interest to the receivers. What stories are actually received and read will then depend far more on the intelligence of the receivers than the providers. How much news (or any other form of information) can be distributed electronically for selection by readers? We really do not know, because we do not know the carrying capacity of a single fiber optic the size of a human hair. As Nicholas Negroponte, founding director of MIT's Media Lab and author of *Being Digital,* has noted, research shows that close to a trillion, and maybe more, bits of information can be delivered in a single second on a single fiber. This means that such a fiber has the ability to "deliver every issue ever made of the *Wall Street Journal* in less than a second," and more information—more news, television channels, more programs, and more sound—can be sent by simply adding more fibers.[22]

As in other uses of cyberspace, readers will navigate their way through the flood of information being created throughout the world. If they want more than sketchy news accounts presented on the "front page," they can simply point and click here or there on the screen to obtain more details on particular parts of the news that are of interest to them. To this extent, readers will be further empowered to choose their own routes to informed opinions by determining what they, the readers—not editors—find to be worthy of print. Again, opportunities are literally opening before people's eyes.

21. As quoted in "Notable & Quotable," *Wall Street Journal,* February 16, 1995, p. A16.

22. Nicholas Negroponte, *Being Digital* (New York: Knopf, 1995), p. 23.

The empowerment of news-hungry readers is nothing particularly new to inhabitants of the new West. A growing number of Americans get their news through electronic networks. An exploding number of Americans and Canadians (in 1995, 24 million Americans[23]) get their news the way they want, as much as they want, through electronic wire services, or they just pass the stories, from distant or local sources, through the nets at speeds that the gossip networks of yesterday would find breathtaking. These Americans are also engaged in modern virtual "farming," a means of creating opportunities that is likely to bear greater fruit in the future as computer and telecommunication hardware and software improve and the number of people joining nets increases.

A teacher in Plainboro, New Jersey, heard that forty Russian students contaminated by the Chernobyl nuclear power plant explosion were visiting England. She had her students send get-well messages over Internet, the closest thing the world has to a electronic superhighway. She sent all fifty messages in less than thirty seconds to England on a Tuesday morning, only to receive a thank-you reply from the Russian teachers the next day. "They [the Russian teachers] were amazed," the American teacher reported, "that U.S. children knew and cared about the plight of their students. History, science and language arts blended to make a personal sense of current events tangible to our students in a way otherwise impossible."[24] The extent to which the teachers and students "farmed" the net for educational purposes is obvious. But could it be that teachers have not yet broken the surface of what is educationally possible?

Education as we know it might be a thing of the past in the not too distant future. Publishers like McGraw-Hill and HarperCollins may go on-line with their books and add audio and video lectures that students can use and "attend" at their convenience, even getting degrees in the process, not from traditional high schools, colleges, and universities, but from the publishers themselves.

Financial analysts and brokers, especially those who work for large institutional investment houses, can easily be overwhelmed by too much data on the stocks they are following. At TIAA-CREF, where money managers handle $106 billion of pension funds for college professors, a partial solution has been found in cyberspace. A *Forbes* reporter described how the money managers watch their Pacific Rim investments:

23. As reported by Peter H. Lewis, "Technology: On the Net," *New York Times*, October 10, 1995, p. C3.

24. As reported in "Stories from 'The Net,'" *Scientific American*, August 1993, p. 105.

"Picture this. You are sitting at your computer screen, looking down at a football field, as if you're sitting in the press box. But you are not stuck there. With your Spaceball control you can fly into the screen—cyberspace—and swoop down over, down to, and even through the field below," with the gridiron covered not with people but with different shapes (that rectangle, chips) that represent different stocks on a number of the world's stock exchanges (Tokyo, Hong Kong, Thailand, etc.) and that change colors, depending on whether prices are going up or down. With your Spaceball, you can choose to close in on any shape to get more details on how the stock is doing.[25]

A full range of additional information on identified stocks can be obtained instantly with a clock on the chips. Indeed, the 3-D graphics and the flights of financial fancy enable the money managers at TIAA-CREF to absorb and act on more information than could possibly be managed in conventional tabular or graphical form. They use cyberspace terrain to more effectively handle money, which means resources outside of cyberspace, in the real world, are freed up to be used in other ventures. To that extent, cyberspace terrain can have real effects on the outside world that are potentially no less profound than those effects the country's West had on the East. Both Wests can be major escape valves.

In the past, in order to use libraries, Americans had to live near them. In order to buy houses, they had to actually look inside. In order to buy stocks, they had to be in New York or work through a local broker. In order to practice the art of doing business while in MBA programs, they had to sign up for courses and work through case studies as presented in written words. Before they operated, surgeons had to cut and explore the dimensions of the problems as they were uncovered.

Not so any more. People can tap libraries around the country and world from their homes or offices with computers outfitted with $50 modems. In fact, in the mid-1990s, they can have whole libraries—over 2,000 books or 200,000 news articles from an untold number of news outlets—in their homes on one CD disk (with the expectation that the disk library could be extended to 20,000 books in the not-too-distant future, given that techniques had by the mid-1990s been developed for increasing the storage capacity of CDs by tenfold[26]). But even the enormous capacity of CDs pales by comparison with what the future may

25. William G. Flanagan, "Cyberspace Meets Wall Street," *Forbes*, June 22, 1992, pp. 164–65.

26. John Markoff, "New I.B.M. Laser Method Stacks Data on Disks," *New York Times*, May 13, 1994, p. C1.

store on yet-to-be-developed storage devices. According to IBM CEO Lou Gerstner, IBM labs have a project underway that may lead to storage devices that can hold all 26 million volumes in the Library of Congress on a disk the size of a penny.[27] Of course, the worldwide web is simply exploding on a daily basis, and this means that the research resources are multiplying with new home pages and papers and books that people are making available for free or for a fee.

People can take "walk-throughs" of houses they wish to build or buy without ever leaving the real estate office. With three-dimensional animation, they can go down halls and into every room with clicks on a mouse. For that matter, they can walk into surreal yards with the planned landscaping to see how the yards might look when the plants are planted and what they might look like once they have grown for a period of years.

Surgeons can even get three-dimensional visual representations of the parts of the body they intend to operate on, and actually practice their surgical maneuvers prior to ever cutting their patients with "virtual lasers" and "virtual scalpels."[28] People can just as easily buy stocks from a mountaintop as they can from the stock exchange floors. Case studies in business schools now come on CDs, complete with videos of board and stockholder meetings, plus discussions by financial experts of the various dimensions of the case.

Washington is perennially one of the most visited cities in the world. The White House is a favorite site. Hordes of tourists still walk the street there and go through rooms at 1600 Pennsylvania Avenue, but a growing number "visit" the city by way of their computers. In the first six months after the White House went on-line, it was "visited" 1.3 million times, with the "visitors" downloading a total of 18 million files, including pictures and the latest budget information. By the time this book reaches print, the frequency of visits to the White House and all other government net locations will, by the standards at this writing, be some unbelievable multiple of the initial frequency of visits. Should it be any wonder that hordes of companies are setting up their own net storefronts to tap into the commercial potential of the surfing shoppers or that other companies are establishing net "malls" or specialized agencies that deal in every service or product line from travel to books or that pro-

27. As reported by Sebastian Rupley and Carol Levin, "The Next 'Next Big Thing,'" *PC Magazine,* January 23, 1996, p. 31.

28. Lee Dye, "Virtual Applications Expand," *Los Angeles Times,* February 22, 1995, p. D4.

fessors, like myself, are establishing their own home pages to make available their latest research papers for other surfing researchers?

To say that a whole new world is upon the current generation is an understatement. There's more than one. As stressed, the frontiers seem to be everywhere, and it has just begun to move. To where? We couldn't possibly imagine. No one is smart enough to do that, simply because no one is able to imagine what everyone else is able to imagine and how the multitudes of people will be reacting to one another, virtually endlessly. In that fact lies a great deal of the hope and promise that this book is founded on.

Back to the Future West

The Turner thesis had an impact because it did two things. First, Turner explained how and why the American West affected the character and psyche of the American people and the unique features of American political institutions. The American West was, for example, responsible for the high allegiance to individualism and free enterprise. Second, he predicted that the closing of the West would have identified effects. For instance, it would lead to a greater tendency toward international imperialism, labor strife, and socialistic domestic policies.

All the modern criticisms notwithstanding, Turner was right, albeit to a more limited degree than he thought, both in the development of his conceptual model of competitive markets and governments and in the consequences. The old West was an escape valve of sorts for millions of Americans, which expanded the array of potential opportunities facing American workers, entrepreneurs, and politicians. As explained in the previous chapters, the force of competition is dependent upon the existence of options, and the West surely presented a multitude of options. Employers had to consider the prospect that their actions could send their workers packing. Governments had to consider the prospect that, similarly, their actions on taxes and regulations could send their taxpayers fleeing to the one still great and expansive tax haven, the West, which, no doubt, as expected by the Founding Fathers and modern political theorists, tempered governments' willingness to impose additional taxes and regulations. The closing of the West was very likely one of several "vital forces" that in the first half of this century sent American workers to seek company in unions and enabled Congress and state legislatures to pile on progressively higher taxes and regulations.

If Turner was correct—or, rather, to the extent that he was—the opening of the new technology-based West should have many of the same effects, but in reverse. The new West should be an added safety valve through which new generations of Americans can escape to their own multidimensional worlds in which they seek new forms of community, goods and services, identities, freedoms, and relationships—new terrains that can be "farmed" for their own individually conceived productive ends, out of reach of those who might be inclined to oppress, whether public or private. Those who would be inclined to oppress might, understandably, embrace the emergence of the new West unenthusiastically because it, too, can be a "vital force" for reshaping Americans' character and psyche and their institutions, just as the old West did but in reverse. The competitive pressures felt should, following reversed Turnerian reasoning, be unrelenting in their growing intensity, for so long as the new frontier expands forever outward, constantly redefining where the new West is or what it is.

What are the expected results? Growing reliance on markets will be a consequence, given that nets reduce the cost of communications and market transactions. Growing competitiveness in both product and worker markets is clearly expected, given the greater ease with which people from far and near can enter the growing array of markets. Growing competitiveness among governments who face ever-tightening fiscal constraints should also be expected. Growing individualism, with more emphasis on voluntary solutions to social problems and less emphasis on forced governmental solutions to social problems, would also be likely.

Which of these has not been observed in the world during the very era that the virtual reality of cyberspace has developed? Clearly, other "vital forces" have been at work, a point that I have made clear at length elsewhere, but such a concession should not deny the vitality of the cyberspace force and so many other frontiers that are ill-defined and extend at least to the corners of the globe, and maybe far beyond.[29]

Electronic Immigration: The New Way the World Works

The world today works differently. Nowhere is this more apparent than in modern immigration debates. Both the opponents and proponents of open immigration in the United States (as well as all other countries)

29. For an extended discussion of the growing impact of capital mobility on the fiscal and regulatory powers of governments, see Richard B. McKenzie and Dwight R. Lee, *Quicksilver Capital: How the Rapid Movement of Wealth Has Changed the World* (New York: Free Press, 1991).

have missed an obvious fact: The American borders are wide open and cannot be closed to hordes of modern-day immigrants—mainly because the opportunities to immigrate, to move about the globe in all directions, have been vastly improved by technology. The early settlers had to take boats to get here; the new settlers don't even have to move to be here, or any other place.

The half million or so aliens who annually steal across the United States' southern borders in the dark of night are a mere trickle of the flow of undocumented immigrants who make thier way into the American economy. Literally millions of other undocumented immigrants enter each day with impunity from immigration laws. A few enter in the dark of night, but most come across in broad daylight, slipping past the guards, uncounted, in the blink of an eye. Most are welcomed with outstretched American checkbooks. Few rouse any concern, mainly because even if they could be stopped, no one would want to.

How do they come in? They do it in the new-fashioned way—that is, electronically, along rapidly expanding communication networks that extend to the far corners of the globe. Many come by way of phone calls, others by way of faxes. The largest portion probably enter the U.S. market via personal computers. No one knows for sure how many "electronic immigrants" there are, but the count must be at least 5 million *each day* (because there are at least that many international phones calls on a daily basis).

The partisans to the immigration debate are still captured by the mind-set of bygone centuries during which a person actually had to move body and soul into another country to work there. Little do they know that times have changed—drastically.

Unnoticed is the fact that brainpower, the crucial factor of modern production, can now go practically anyplace in the world, at any time, and at low cost. When American employers hire workers in Ireland or Barbados to do computer work that is sent to them electronically, those workers enter, *de facto*, the American labor force. Similarly, a German or Japanese engineer who calls contacts in the United States to solve a problem or to plot strategy for a new computer chip or factory has slipped by America's border guards. These workers may not have a corporal presence in the economy, but their brains certainly do. They mix and mingle with American resources for productive ends, just as surely as they would have had they updated their passports, acquired green cards, and flown in.

The electronic immigrants have many of the same effects on the American economy as do the "physical immigrants" (those who come by foot). Frequently, they accept lower pay than their American counterparts, and they draw on and redirect American resources. The big difference between the two groups of undocumented immigrants—the electronic and physical ones—is that the former enter when they are wanted, draw on the American economy only so long as they contribute more than they earn, and can make no claims on American taxpayers. Physical immigrants are far more problematic, because current laws give them, in effect, keys to the country's public treasuries.

The country's political leaders in Washington are still encumbered, apparently, with an outdated view of how human resources move about the world. They seem wedded to the belief that a person's economic value is a matter of corporal presence, thus it can neither move in nor slip away unless workers physically get up and move.

Admirably, a number of policymakers—most notably President Bill Clinton and Secretary of Labor Robert Reich—have recognized the importance of capital, even human capital, to the global economy and the country's future prosperity. They recognize the mobility of physical capital, namely plant and equipment, and have accordingly reasoned that government subsidies should not be given to corporations. They can too easily move themselves and take the subsidies with them. People, they say, are different: They can't move nearly so easily internationally. Hence, they have deduced that higher taxes, especially on the rich, can be levied on people because they cannot physically move across borders with ease.[30]

These policymakers appear unaware of the hordes of electronic immigrants who are already here, or the even greater hordes that could be here. Certainly, they do not acknowledge that higher tax rates and more onerous mandates and regulations will cause foreign electronic immigrants to be even more attractive to American employers, reducing job opportunities in this economy and inducing Americans to employ their brainpower elsewhere in the world by means of modern electronics.

Granted, when Americans use their brainpower elsewhere, they will earn an income that can then be taxed. At the same time, their electronic migration will mean less brainpower will be driving the American economy.

As never before, brainpower—not brawn—now makes the heart of the value-added economy go round. Policymakers must recognize that the American economy will continue to drag so long as policies fail to consider the ease with which people can migrate electronically. Growing

30. See Robert B. Reich, *The Work of Nations* (New York: Random House, 1991).

reliance on markets will also be a consequence, given that nets reduce the cost of communications and finalizing market transactions.

The Ability of People to Enter the New West

But some people can't move into the new West. That's true, and will always be the case, to a degree. People were clearly limited in moving into the old West by the costs of doing so and even by their handicaps. Social and family circumstances have always limited people's ability to take advantage of emerging opportunities. At the same time, it is folly to let the claim of some people's limitations obscure the essential point: A growing number of Americans have new unexploited opportunities that are likely to become more numerous, not more restricted, because of the unfolding nature of the new West, which, at its foundation, is a discovery process.

I say that with conviction because of commonly acknowledged facts. The price of computing power has fallen precipitously for decades now by at least 25 percent a year, and the fall is not likely to be abated in the near future. Indeed, the fall might accelerate in the years ahead at the same time that the computer features and add-ons continue to mount. Many programs have become progressively more powerful. At times, they have become more complicated to use, but that is generally because users have demanded more complicated features, not so much that basic uses have become more complicated.

Admittedly, people often fret over the difficulty of using their computers. Nevertheless, many programs at the heart of the complaints can be used, and are being used, by children, even pre-kindergarten children. There is every reason to believe that the programs and computers will become more user friendly, more intuitive. Computers *can* become more friendly, given their greater power. They *are* likely to become more friendly, given the demand for ease of use and the considerable profits that that demand represents.

If there is a problem with people entering the new West, then it is a rapidly diminishing problem as the "trips" become more affordable—*even to the poor and other disadvantaged people*. In the early 1980s, the price of a personal computer with limited capabilities was virtually out of reach to people at the annual poverty-income threshold. However, by the mid-1990s, a family of four living at the poverty threshold could buy a far more powerful computer than could be purchased a decade earlier with less than 5 percent of its annual income. Given that the computer can last for several years, even that figure overstates the burden of entering the new West. The Windows operating system can help a lot of computer users, but it is an obvious obstacle for many, especially the blind. Nevertheless even their particular problem is overcome with JAWS, a Windows-based program designed to "see" the screen and speak the names of the icons. With such a program, the blind can literally navigate in cyberspace more freely than they can navigate within the confines of their homes and workplaces.[31]

I am sure that there are those who object to such calculations based on the claim that the poor cannot "afford" to free up the several hundred dollars required for a baseline computer. I am not so sure how serious that argument should be taken. No doubt, it should be weighed, but kept in perspective. Many far poorer people of a hundred years ago were able to find the resources to move into the only available West they knew. Moreover, the objection misses the central point: The burden of moving into the new West is shrinking.

Besides, Americans must realize that "affordability" is too often couched in the wrong perspective: how much something costs juxtaposed with how much a person or family has earned. That makes for a rigged debate. The proper perspective is the one most likely used by the pioneers: *how much a given investment can return to the investor.* The actual cost, the dollars that must be put down, is relevant but largely immaterial when considered in isolation from the flow of *future* benefits it can yield. The overwhelming majority of Americans, no matter what their circumstances, can afford those things that yield a flow of future benefits that exceed the costs of the item that is bought.[32] Indeed, it is far more accurate to suggest that they cannot afford *not* to buy those things where the future flow of benefits exceeds the costs. They may be "poor," but they can be *less poor* when they assess their purchases in terms of what they can yield.

Although not all Americans need enter the electronic age, it's a fair bet that many Americans, even the poor, must. They *must* because they *must* meet the competition from all those other people who are taking advantage of the available opportunities in the new West. I suspect that Americans in all income brackets will continue to face the challenges of the vital forces at work. The genie is out of the lamp. That is fact, not fiction from the movie. Stuffing the genie back in the lamp is simply not an option, no matter how much people might wish the contrary.

31. Michelle Vranizan, "New Windows Programs Being Made for the Blind," *Orange County* [Calif.] *Register,* February 20, 1995, p. 24 (business section).

32. Of course, the flow of future benefits (or income) must be appropriately discounted.

Concluding Comments

Frederick Jackson Turner got into trouble with his scholarly colleagues because of his myopic focus on one explanation for national institutional development—the pioneering of the West. He overlooked a number of other "vital forces." He assumed the western lands were "free," which they could never be, given the difficulties of getting to the land and then making it useful. Perhaps his focus was necessary, and the criticisms unavoidable, given the limitations of space and time to develop any thesis and his intent, which was to draw historians of his time away from their own concentrated focus on European influences at work on the American character and political institutions.

The thesis developed here may suffer much the same criticisms. The attention has been narrowly focused on one "vital force," albeit the vast and expanding new world of cyberspace. Clearly, more than the old West was at work in the nineteenth century. Far more than the virtual economy of the new West will be at work in the twenty-first century. The internationalization of social networks and the economy means nothing short than that the "west" is virtually everywhere in all kinds of ways. The point in need of repeating is that the future is full of unexplored and unexploited opportunities, not just in computers (although computer technology may be at the bottom of developments in many fields), but also in an array of developments in science, medicine, construction, space, and environment. And we can anticipate future scientific and practical developments that will open fascinating worlds of opportunities that cannot be imagined now. The opportunities for business are now immense, given the possibilities of linking far more business locations and then monitoring and controlling the remote workplaces by information technologies in what has been described as "cottage multinationals," far-flung enterprises that are, at the same time, "big" and "small."[33] Real estate companies are setting up to sell properties across the country via computer hookups. North Carolina has set up its own information superhighway over which state business can now be done. Mecklenburg County, North Carolina, has video links between its jails and the courthouses, obviating the need for prisoners to actually go to court. Grocery stores are linking their pricing decisions, made in their headquarters, to the shelf labels in their stores.[34] Commerce of all kinds,

33. "'Being Digital' Appears as Next Curve on Information Highway," *Orange County* [Calif.] *Register*, March 14, 1995, p. D9.

34. Barrett Seaman, "The Future Is Already Here," *Time*, Spring 1995 (special edition), pp. 31–32.

from interactive magazines to books, are being sold on the worldwide web. Once someone is able to create secure "electronic checks," "electronic cash," and "digital credit cards," one that cannot be easily reproduced, forged, or stolen by net robbers, business in net order (as distinct from what is now ordinary mail order) should take off. A number of firms have solutions in the works as this page is being written and another firm announced the opening of the Security First Network Bank (http://www.sfnb.com) as this chapter was being sent through its final revision in late 1995.[35]

"What will they think of next?" is a question that must pass the mind of everyone who reads reports of product and service developments in cyberspace. The speed of the developments is truly amazing, so much so that there is no point to my even trying to list the "latest" developments here. Those developments will be old hat by the time these pages are in print. Bill Gates, the CEO and founder of Microsoft, was on target when he confessed in his book *The Road Ahead* to being "thrilled by the feeling that I am squinting into the future and catching the first revealing hint of revolutionary possibilities [in communications]. I feel incredibly lucky that I am getting the chance to play a part in the beginning of an epochal change for the second time."[36]

If fifty years from now, people are not talking about developments and worlds of opportunity that could not have been imagined fifty years earlier, they will be the first generation of people in a long, long time who will not have done so. The problem future generations will face is not one of lack of opportunities, but one of seizing, with some sense of gusto, the opportunities that will be close at hand.

Granted, like the old West, getting to (or in) the new West will not be without cost. Computers are now relatively inexpensive and getting cheaper, but information, which fuels work and play in the new virtual economy, is not without cost. As in the past, people will simply have to find ways of coping with their costs. The pioneers of yesteryears did it. Future generations should be able to do the same, given the relatively

35. One means of sending payments through networks would be to have the cash stored on what is being called a "PC card," credit-card–type card that would be loaded with cash at a bank, for example, and then inserted into a slot in a personal computer for use on the network. Payments would be deducted from the card's balance. Similarly, electronic checks could be sent with "digital signatures," which would be verified by a credit-card–type card that would be inserted in a computer [Em A. Strassel, "Dutch Software Concern Experiments with Electronic 'Cash' in Cyberspace," *Wall Street Journal*, April 17, 1995, p. A7E; Saul Hansell, "A Checkbook for Computers Is Planned," *New York Times*, August 23, 1995, p. C2].

36. Bill Gates, *The Road Ahead* (New York: Viking, 1995), p. 11.

lighter burden they will have to bear and the relatively greater luxury in which they will make their treks.

At the same time, it will present perils and problems. The virtual frontier is ill-defined, and the virtual economy is, and will remain, a messy one, with a lot of people doing stupid and criminal things (just as in the real world). And things will likely get messier as more people enter their computer gateways. Frankly, no one can know exactly where the virtual frontier and how the virtual economy will develop. If wc knew where and how Americans will explore and exploit this whole new world, how they will deal with both the opportunities and perils, it would probably not be nearly as valuable, on balance, as it will likely be. What we can surmise is that the frontier *will* move and the economy *will* continue to develop, to expand outward, and to profoundly affect people's psyche (in many ways that, as of now, are not even recognizable).

We have focused here in cyberspace, primarily because it represents an immense array of opportunities to which people can relate. In the end, however, our examples, are just that, examples—metaphors—for a whole constellation of new arenas, new Wests, that are and will be open to generations of Americans through technology. My purpose in using the metaphors has not been to bedazzle (many of the facts are old hat now) but, more fundamentally, to use the metaphors to reconstitute the way we think about the world—and, if possible, to break the stranglehold that visions of a closed real West had on the American psyche, to motivate people to think in terms of what is possible, not what isn't.

All in all, this whole new world has, for many Americans, been or will likely soon be a liberating force, much like the whole West was to generations of Americans who thought about going and who actually went. It will be no less of a force than the old West was, meaning it is one with which people will have to contend because of the many places they can be at once. As you will see in chapter 6, this new force is relentlessly constraining and directing not only business policies but also government policies.

6

ECONOMIC TECTONICS

> Money moves over, around and through them [national borders] with the speed of light. The flows of capital are now in the range of 30 to 50 times greater than world trade. The world's capital market that moves along this electronic highway goes where it is wanted and it stays where it is well-treated. . . . As long as our free-market system permits and delivers an acceptable rate of return on investment in an environment of political stability that is competitive with other areas of investment, the capital will keep coming.
>
> Walter B. Wriston,
> "On track with the Deficit"

SOME OF the most important and powerful forces at work in the physical and social worlds are often some of the more obscure, difficult to detect by the usual senses. Why is the planet inhabited with the species that now exist, for example? Why do volcanoes erupt? Why do the continents look the way they do? Answers have abounded over recorded history.

At one time, few doubted that the planet Earth and all that lives on it were created in a frenzy by one or more gods in a week or so. They believed that, although naked, fully formed people were set more or less as they are today to find their way in a world full of temptations and to propagate. Volcanic eruptions were even attributed to the hot and volatile tempers of the gods. These were relatively easy answers to com-

I am indebted to Dwight Lee who co-authored the article that forms the foundation of this chapter ("Countervailing Impotence: How Technology Has Undercut Galbraith's Theory of Countervailing Power," *Society*, November/December 1992, pp. 34–40.

plex phenomena, with mysterious forces afoot in the world "explained" by equally mysterious (for some) religious forces.

Having shucked religious explanations for physical events, scientists also presumed for centuries that continents either emerged more or less into their present form as Earth cooled and/or were reshaped gradually by the upwelling of land masses through volcanoes and earthquakes. Few scientists stopped to think that the whole of the earth's crust may have literally been on the move. Understandable. No one had actually seen a whole continent move. For that matter, no one had observed a specie, much less human beings, evolve. Maybe it was simply natural for people to think that things were always the way they are.

It was left to Charles Darwin to give order to the history of unobserved experience, to explain how the present collection of species evolved over the millenniums through the process of natural selection. The process of evolution was and is fundamental to the way the world has developed, but it took a monumental leap of imagination and insight for anyone to see the underlying, transcendent forces at work, which explains Darwin's preeminent position in biological science. The evolutionary process is tediously slow, its power beyond the direct experience of mere mortals in any given generation.

Since the 1950s, scientists have discerned that not only were species evolving, but the environment—indeed, the whole of the earth's surface—has also been evolving in response to fundamental geophysical forces at work on the shapes and contents of whole continents. Scientists now have better explanations than "the gods did it" for why things are the way they are. They have explained broad-based geophysical changes in the world by forces that were out of sight and mind to earlier generations of scientists, and even remain so today.

Plate tectonics, the tiresomely slow but persistent and powerful shifts of continents across the globe, has been given credit for many events observed by contemporary scientists on the earth's crust. Plate tectonics helps to explain, for example, the location of earthquakes and volcanoes (which tend to be concentrated along ridges that run down the middle of the Pacific and Atlantic Oceans and along fault lines that run along China's coast up by Japan across the Bering Strait and down the West Coast of the United States). The science of plate tectonics also explains why seashells can be found buried beneath mountains far from the U.S. coast (those portions of the crust were once on the sea floor), and it explains why the coastal shapes of continents appear, even to the untrained eye, as though they were intended to fit together into one global jigsaw puzzle (which they did a very long time ago).

More fundamentally, plate tectonics reminds us that easy answers are not always the best answers, that we can't always trust what we can observe on the surface of everyday experience. It mandates that we look below the surface for deeper, more fundamental forces that extend backward into history and that shape the world we live in and that must be accommodated, not reshaped or muted.

Through the millenniums, all life has adjusted to one extent or another to the power of plate tectonics and evolution. The exact nature of human societies and economies today are to one extent or another attributable to the slow but persistent forces of plate tectonics, and evolution is as indisputable as it may be difficult to observe. At the same time, we understand that social and economic institutions are the products of far more forces than those of evolution and plate tectonics, but that they may be no less important or apparent by way of casual observation.

In this chapter, we begin our exploration of "economic tectonics," a line of reasoning that looks underneath the social fabrics of everyday experience for slow but persistent and powerful fundamental forces at work on the nature of economic and societal institutions. Economic tectonics focuses on two fundamental forces. The first force, which is the exclusive subject of this chapter, is technology, mainly as it relates to capital mobility—the ongoing quasi-independent power that can feed upon itself; that, as recognized in the last chapter, can offer untold opportunities and higher incomes; but that, over long stretches of time, forces a fundamental restructuring of public and private institutions. In discussing this first force, I draw heavily from themes that my friend and co-author Dwight Lee and I developed at length in an earlier book that carried an elusive but, upon reflection, a descriptive title, *Quicksilver Capital.*[1]

The second force of economic tectonics, the exclusive subject of chapters 7 and 8, is "cultural evolution," a theory of economic development that posits that many societies prosper today because they long ago adopted—albeit gradually, often by accident and trial and error—fundamental rules for behavior of group members that proved productive, enabling all members of those societies to be better off than their counterparts who did not (and still do not) follow the same rules.

Neither the force of technology nor cultural evolution can be denied, although they may perhaps be muted marginally by human design. We will argue here that governments as well as businesses must accept the

1. See Richard B. McKenzie and Dwight R. Lee, *Quicksilver Capital: How the Rapid Movement of Wealth Has Changed the World* (New York: Free Press, 1991).

constraints that technology has imposed on their economic freedoms. From the perspective of traditional political studies, fiscal problems are either the consequence of politics or the way votes are counted. From the perspective of this chapter, the fiscal binds that governments face can be attributed, in part, to the more fundamental, slow, but persistent shift in the technological plate, which has freed capital, but not governments, from the constraints of specific geographical locations.

Plus, I will argue in chapter 7 that the continuing prosperity of successful societies depends upon the members' continued allegiance (even blind allegiance) to commonly accepted rules of behavior. The central problem for these societies in maintaining their economic success is that the adopted rules are difficult for anyone who comes under their purview to justify or explain, given that they evolved, were refined and reconstituted so gradually over such a long stretch of time, far beyond the experience of members of any given generation.

Those who know F. A. Hayek's work will see in chapter 7 that I have borrowed heavily from the "master." I do so unabashedly, mainly because his thoughts are so profound and in need of a wider audience, with perhaps some revisions and extensions. My theme in that chapter, however, is largely his: *The social order, including most notably our economic institutions, "arose from unitentionally conforming to certain traditional and largely* moral *practices, many of whicn men tend to dislike, whose significance they usually fail to understand, whose validity they cannot prove, and which have nonetheless fairly rapidly spread by means of an evolutionary selection."*[2] The institutions' value lies in that they have worked, but their fragility is grounded in the fact that they often cannot withstand serious analytical scrutiny and challenge by those who must obey them.

An underlying theme of this book is that there persists a paradox of progress: Economic opportunities will likely abound in the future. Then why do so many Americans feel an angst when they survey their future economic prospects? Again, an easy answer has been repeated by others almost to the point of boredom: that Americans no longer have secure jobs and incomes, and governments are too fiscally tight to help. Those are the surface answers. But why are Americans' jobs no longer secure, and why are governments in such tight fiscal binds? A significant part of the answer is revealed below: Ongoing technological developments have shaken up markets, requiring them—and the firms that must operate within them—to reconstitute, to reinvent themselves, even to rethink the nature of the firm, what the firm can do in the new world order. In

2. Ibid.

the process, those technological developments, which are pressing economic evolution forward, have caused many people to fear the future, mainly because their *specific* economic roles in the future are less certain.

As argued in chapters 7 and 8, another part of the answer, another of the moving plates, is that commonly accepted rules of behavior are no longer given blind allegiance and have, as a consequence, begun to break down within *some* (but hardly *all* or *most*) groups. Of course, the breakdown of rules may be partially attributed to ongoing technological developments and the way markets are being reshaped. These "plates" may go a long way toward explaining the sense of lost aspirations, but not always in the anticipated ways.

Countervailing Economic Powers

In the early 1950s, John Kenneth Galbraith wrote a book on American capitalism in which he argued that big government is a predictable response to the power of big business. As business became more concentrated with fewer but larger firms dominating the marketplace, Galbraith saw a larger government as the natural and most effective source of "countervailing power," or a force that would neutralize that growing power of concentrated capital.[3]

It is doubtful that big business ever possessed the power Galbraith believes it did, and it is debatable whether big government can be effective at countering or augmenting the power that big business does have. However, for reasons which Galbraith did not anticipate, his thesis is more powerful for explaining modern conditions—including many people's lost aspirations—than even he realized, but in reverse. There are good reasons for believing that the structure of business prompted government to grow in size and power during most of this century. But those same reasons also help explain why many Americans have lost their jobs and why governments now face severe budgetary problems, revealed, for example, in mounting deficits, cutbacks in services, and efforts to privatize a broadening array of services, from education to trash pickup to incarceration of prisoners to provision of public housing.

Growth in government power was indeed a predictable consequence of the accumulation of large concentrations of industrial wealth. Amassed industrial capital provided a target of opportunity that proved irresistible to many unions and those who derived benefit from govern-

3. John Kenneth Galbraith, *American Capitalism: The Concept of Countervailing Power* (Boston: Houghton Mifflin, 1952).

ment growth. Why? An answer lies in the evolving nature of capital over the last couple of centuries, especially over the last fifty years or so. At one time capital was more like a caterpillar, slow and sluggish, not like a butterfuly that can take to the wing.

Capital as a Caterpillar

The hallmark of the Industrial Revolution was the growing use of capital (plant, equipment, and machinery) that permitted people to produce more than was possible with muscle (human and animal) power. As capital innovations allowed the power contained in flowing water, expanding steam, wood, and coal to be focused on such tasks as lifting, spinning, grinding, and digging, the ability to convert human effort and natural resources into valuable products increased dramatically. Economic productivity has continued to increase with improvements in our ability to employ capital to tap and harness old energy sources and convert previously useless resources into new sources.

Beginning in the early stages of the Industrial Revolution and continuing into the second half of this century, increased productivity meant investments in larger machines, bigger furnaces, and longer assembly lines, all of which required bringing more people together into ever larger productive units. In other words, the productive process was characterized by escalating economies of scale. By the late nineteenth century, firms had reached truly gigantic proportions, and the trend toward larger firms continued well into the twentieth century as conglomerates and multinational corporations produced an increasing share of domestic output and employed an increasing share of the domestic workforce. Not surprisingly, Professor Galbraith's approval of the rapid growth in unions through the early 1950s in face of what he saw as the growing economic power of the "New Industrial State," and the need for additional "countervailing power" of government struck a popular chord, as evidenced by the robust sales of his books.[4]

It is easy to prompt debate on the question of whether public concern over the size of firms and industries has ever been justified. On the one hand, there is no doubt that people, both as consumers and as workers, benefited enormously in the last half of the nineteenth century as those industries in which the greatest economies of scale could be realized became dominated by a few large and extremely productive firms.

4. John Kenneth Galbraith, *The New Industrial State* (Boston: Houghton Mifflin, 1967).

Although the most concentrated, and therefore visible, result of the productivity of these firms was the enormous wealth of a few entrepreneurs (pejoratively referred to as "robber barons"[5]), by far the greater portion of the wealth created was distributed widely in the form of better products, lower prices, higher salaries, and improved working conditions.[6]

Of course, for the very reason that the general public realized so much benefit from large enterprises, the firms may have possessed some measure of power over customers and workers. The firm that produces a better product at a lower cost than the competition has the power to attract eager customers, while charging a higher-than-minimum-cost price. Likewise, firms that use labor more productively than the competition have the power to attract eager workers, while paying a wage lower than that which reflects the full productivity of those workers in those firms.[7]

Moreover, firms that were achieving the economies of scale and were growing relentlessly could offer their employees a great deal of security. Employees could look forward to long-term, even career-ending employment with the firm they joined as a young worker. They could also enjoy the security of knowing that wage increases could be absorbed by the economies that come with larger scale and/or could be passed along to consumers in the form of higher prices (given the dominant market position of the firms who could offset price increases by increasing the demand for their products).

Employees and employers could also strike something approximating lifetime pay contracts under which the employees might be "underpaid" (or paid less than their true market value) early in their career with the prospect that their wages would jump rapidly with productivity improvement and longevity, resulting in the workers being "overpaid" later in their careers (with some portion of their earnings being withheld for retirement). Of course, such deals meant that over the course of their lifetimes, workers could possibly earn more than they would have

5. Matthew Josephson, *The Robber Barons* (New York: Harcourt, Brace & World, 1934).

6. See, for example, Robert Puth, *American Economic History*, 2nd ed. (Dryden Press, 1988), chap. 12.

7. Over the long run, competition erodes the market power of even the most productive firms as markets expand and technology is disseminated. But competition in the real world is never as effective at eliminating excess profits as is the sterile competition of the textbooks, which would also eliminate much of the incentive to innovate better products and superior technologies.

earned had they been paid simply in line with their market worth. This is because the pay scheme would provide more incentives than otherwise to increase productivity, which is the source of all wage gains.[8] Moreover, as did their employers, workers of many American firms in the New Industrial State could relax—even become "fat and happy" to a degree—confident that their competition would be held at bay by the problems of duplicating the economies of scale and by the cost of transporting competitively priced products from across the oceans.

Whether or not the increased size of business enterprises made a larger government desireable is debatable, but it surely made it possible. Large firms may have possessed some market power by virtue of their large concentrations of capital, but they also found themselves more vulnerable to the power of government as a result, a point that Galbraith pressed.

The large concentrations of business capital motivated by large economies of scale, and the wealth they created, were both highly visible and securely anchored in place. The greatest part of a firm's assets were in the form of large machines and production facilities that were practically immobile because of both their size and their dependence on proximity to markets, critical natural resources, and navigable harbors or rail routes. In this earlier era, capital was epitomized by steel and concrete and by huge factories. Belching smokestacks were symbols of capitalism at its finest (that is, before the damage done to the environment was recognized). This "old capital" was then much like a caterpillar on a large spring leaf, fat and happy, maybe a little sassy. By committing themselves to investments in large concentrations of capital, businesses increased their ability to produce what Marxists delight in calling surplus value. But by making those capital commitments, businesses reduced their ability to avoid sharing that surplus with their workers (especially those who were unionized) and with government.

Large concentrations of capital not only created economies of scale in the production of wealth, they also created economies of scale in the extraction of wealth. Workers understood that under the threat of strike or other labor action, they could boost their wages, at least marginally, by tapping the concentrated, deep-pocket, difficult-to-move capital. Governments came to the same conclusion, only they could tax this "old capital" with efficiency. It is far more costly per dollar collected to tax the

8. This thesis is developed at length by Edward P. Lazear, "Why Is There Mandatory Retirement?" *Journal of Political Economy* 87 (1979): 1261–84. For a discussion of how workers' productivity can be raised by "twisting" their career pay schedule, see Richard B. McKenzie and Dwight R. Lee, *Managing Incentives* (under development).

profits and wages generated by many small and scattered firms than it is to tax the profits and wages generated by a few large and concentrated firms (especially since the withholding system requires businesses to undertake much of the work of tax collection). And because large firms with major commitments to plant and equipment are less mobile, and therefore more captive, than smaller, less capital-intensive firms, government can take advantage of economies of scale in taxation with a significant degree of impunity.

Also, by offering increasingly attractive and plentiful employment opportunities, larger, more efficient firms attract large numbers of people out of self-employment, further easing the task of the tax collector. The earnings of those who are employed by a firm are easier to tax than are the earnings of those who are self-employed, if for no other reason than the firm has a strong motivation to report accurately, as costs, the salaries and wages they pay. This vulnerability of the employees of large firms to higher effective taxes is equivalent to yet additional vulnerability of large firms to governments intent on expanding (following the advice of social reformers like Galbraith).

As large corporations began emerging during the end of the nineteenth and beginning of the twentieth centuries, the federal government took what today would be considered an insignificant percentage of Gross Domestic Product (GDP). Consider the fact that in 1902 the federal government spent 3 percent of the GDP (compared to about 22 percent in the mid-1990s), with most of the revenue at the turn of the century coming from import duties and excise taxes. The federal government was not oblivious, however, to the revenue-enhancing opportunities that big business offered. The political pressure to impose a tax on corporate profits gathered strength, and the first corporate income tax went into effect in 1909.

A federal tax on personal income was enacted in the late nineteenth century to take advantage of the increasing percentage of the workforce receiving visible salaries and wages, but it was declared unconstitutional. Wages and salaries soon represented such a mother lode of wealth, however, that Congress initiated a constitutional amendment permitting a personal income tax, which was ratified in 1913. Corporate and personal income taxes quickly became the dominant sources of federal tax revenue and powerful engines for propelling rapid growth in the federal government.

The corporate income tax accounted for 11 percent of federal government tax revenue in 1916, and this percentage escalated quickly, in part due to the demand of World War I, but with the escalation continuing after the war. In 1925, 36 percent of federal revenues came from the corporate income tax, with this percentage reaching 47 in 1928. The revenue from the personal income tax followed a similar pattern. In 1916 this tax accounted for 13 percent of federal revenues, increasing to 33 percent in 1925 and 34 percent in 1930. Not surprisingly, as the highly lucrative corporate and personal income taxes became the dominant sources of federal revenue, the federal government increased rapidly in size as measured by the share of the national income it captured through taxation.[9] No wonder Galbraith could have faith that his advice for more government growth in the 1950s and 1960s could be heeded.

Additional tax revenue was not the only source of increased government power that was made possible by the growth of big business. Government power is measured in terms of control over resources, and securing tax revenue is not the only way government exercises control. By regulating private-sector decisions in general and business decisions in particular, government can direct resources just as surely as it can through the expenditure of tax revenue. And large firms with large concentrations of fixed capital make it possible for governments to realize economies of scale in regulation just as they made possible economies of scale in taxation. As it is more difficult for government to tax business profits when firms are small, widely scattered, and unanchored with large capital commitments, so it is more difficult for government to regulate business decisions under these conditions. Certainly, it was after the emergence of large business firms that the regulation of business by government (in the form of market-entry controls for transportation, production restrictions for agriculture, and safety management in mining and construction, for example) began in earnest, with this regulation escalating during this century as the size of businesses continued to increase.

The conventional wisdom is that with the emergence of big business, government regulation increased because of public demands. There is an element of truth in this prevailing view. But how much could the de-

9. By the middle of the 1930s the federal government had more than tripled the share of GDP it was spending when compared to the beginning of the century. It is common to argue that federal expenditures grew rapidly from 1915 through the 1940s because of the demands placed on the federal government by war, the Great Depression, and as Galbraith and others would argue, by the need to counter the power of big business. Although there is an element of truth to these "demand-side" explanations of government growth, any complete explanation of government growth has to recognize the importance of "supply-side" influences. See James B. Kau and Paul H. Rubin, "The Size of Government," *Public Choice* 37 (1981): 261–74.

mand for government to protect the public against business have increased as large businesses began springing up in the late nineteenth century, given that those who purchased from and worked for these businesses benefited enormously from the economies of scale being realized?[10] There was, is, and always will be demand for government to provide benefits in any number of ways and under any number of guises, but the supply of these benefits is always limited by constraints on government's ability to control resources. The demand for government may vary over time, but changes in demand cannot be expected to carry the entire burden of explaining changes in the size of government. Even if the emergence of big business did increase the demand for government, it did far more to increase the supply of government by making it easier—meaning, less costly—for government to capture and control resources, an outcome that spurred its growth.

In this earlier era in which Galbraith formulated his theory of the New Industrial State, he, along with many worker groups, could press for greater government involvement in the economy, a principal purpose of which could be to make Americans feel more secure. If workers faced domestic competition, then government could regulate away some of the competition (as was done, for example, in trucking and airlines). If firms and their workers faced international competition, then government could protect them with import barriers (tariffs and quotas). If workers suffered unemployment, then government could add a new social welfare program or extend the number of weeks unemployment benefits would be provided. After all, government could finance the added expenditures by draining off some of the surplus generated by immobile capital. Workers and employers with political clout could look to a secure future, assured that if they encountered a problem, they could rely on the extended hand of the government to relieve them of their burden to adjust, or solve their own problems.

But times have changed—substantially. American workers understandably feel the press of competition, and many are no doubt distressed by the inability of their governments to help them. Indeed, more than ever, government in the United States, as well as in many other countries around the world, seems intent on deregulating capital,

10. Certainly consumers and workers did not capture all of the efficiency from big business, at least in the short run, and the desire to capture more of these gains could account for an increase in the demand for regulation. Business itself, of course, exerted some demand on government for protection against competition. This is a demand, however, that obviously had nothing to do with enlisting government as a contervailing power to that of big business.

eliminating import protections, and generally catering to captial—and curbing the social safety net at a time when many workers feel far less secure in their jobs. Why? A deeper understanding of the changing predicament of business, their workers, and governments can be gleaned from a study of economic tectonics, more specifically, the changing nature and mobility of capital. However, a key to an understanding of the process is to recognize in the wisdom of Walter Wriston, former CEO of Citicorp, who in the epigraph to this chapter posits, "Borders that were once the cause of wars are now becoming porous."

Capital as a Butterfly

If big business ever had much power over consumers, that power is currently fading—fast. Witness the financial difficulties of such Galbraithian giants as Eastern Airlines, LTV, W. T. Grant, Sears, General Motors, U.S. Steel (or USX), and even IBM. With the emergence of a global economy, product markets have expanded geographically. The result is that consumers are not as dependent on local suppliers as was once the case. The very technology lauded in previous chapters for expanding opportunities has a downside for firms, their workers, and governments: It is increasing the worldwide mobility of products and productive resources, and increasing opportunities for consumers in the process.

Consider that the mobility of much capital is inversely related to its size, and then consider the continuing effect technology is having on the size of capital. The most dramatic example to the downsizing of capital is found in the computer field. Mainframe computers purchased by universities in the early 1960s filled suites of offices and had a meager 8 K of internal memory. Today, a good subnotebook computer has far more memory and computing power than those big mainframes had less than thirty years ago—no, less than a single decade ago. With the miniaturization of computers has come the downsizing of other types of capital. In textile production, air-jet looms have replaced fly-shuttle looms with the result that the same amount of fabric can be produced in one-third the space. Metal fabrication plants used to require large numbers of workers and long production runs in order to achieve maximum efficiency, which is now realized with six machines and six people. In addition, the floorspace for some "flexible manufacturing systems" has been reduced by 60 percent.[11] Even the need for inventory and storage space has diminished

11. See Ramchandran Jaikumar, "Postindustrial Manufacturing," *Harvard Business Review*, November/December 1986, pp. 69–76.

as "just-in-time" delivery, made possible by better communications and more flexible production techniques, is becoming the norm.

Technological advances not only allow production to take place in less space, they allow production to take place on a smaller scale. For example, the textbook publisher McGraw-Hill can justify printing individualized texts for classes with as few as ten students by making use of advances in computerized printing. A Texas computer manufacturer, whose slogan is "Mass Production in Runs of One" allows customers to phone in orders for computers with detailed specifications that are transmitted immediately to the assembly line. Even men's and women's jeans can be cut-to-fit at the factory to the particular shapes of individual customers.

With less space required for production, and the economies of scale diminishing, the efficiency of small firms increases relative to that of larger firms. The increased relative efficiency of smaller firms also reflects improvements in transportation and communication that reduce the advantage in bringing large numbers of workers together under one roof in order to coordinate their efforts. A company can now consist of many small plants scattered around the globe, operating with the same degree of productive coordination and efficiency that in the past required the close proximity of people and equipment. Obtaining products and services that were once supplied "in house" from outside suppliers—or "outsourcing"—is seen as an efficient practice by an increasing number of firms. Technology is increasing the feasibility of self-employment as individuals can productively operate out of their homes, or small offices, independently providing services to firms that in the past would have had to employ them directly to fully utilize their talents.[12] The result is that many businesses are becoming smaller, less dependent on location and proximity to population and industrial centers, while it is easier to shift operations entirely or in part to other locations worldwide.[13] When businesses are gaining in size (for example, McDonalds), their growth tends to be through the expansion of the number of small units (franchises) that have categorically different relationships to the corporate headquarters than the plants of yesteryear did. Many large firms have transformed themselves into organizations that have been appropriately dubbed "cottage multinationals," with many small production units linked together, and with the ability of the parent company to move or close any one unit with little loss of firm output.

12. From 1970 to 1988 nonagricultural self-employment increased 63 percent while nonagricultural employment in total increased only 47 percent.

13. For evidence on the tendency toward smaller businesses, see David L. Birch, *Job Creation in America* (New York: Free Press, 1987).

Factories made of steel and concrete still dot the landscape, but their economic dominance seems to be more a feature of the underdeveloped, or rather misdeveloped, economies of eastern Europe than of the western world. The caterpillar has turned into a butterfly. The critical assets of companies are no longer steel and buildings. They are more often than not the information and the brainpower at the companies' disposal for creating the quintessential company asset—good ideas for doing things better, faster, cheaper, and more profitably at the most favorable location on earth (and it won't be too long before we can add "in space").[14]

Knowledge is not only the major productive input in many firms, it is often the primary output as well. As George Gilder has stated succinctly, "The displacement of materials with ideas is the essence of all real economic progress."[15] Management guru Tom Peters drove home the transformation of the production by noting in his seminar, "Welcome to a world where, in the words of one executive I know, 'If you can touch it, it's not real.' I don't know about you, but that's a tough concept for an old (me) civil engineer (me, again) to get."[16] Few things are as elusive and less subject to control by worker groups or by taxing and regulating authorities as ideas and knowledge. Information, knowledge, and ideas can be moved around the globe at the literal speed of electrical impulses, which means that compared to physical capital like plant and equipment that are fixed in place, many new forms of capital can escape appropriation by worker groups and government with relative ease by going to more hospitable climates.

The rapidity with which capital has become more mobile and forced a restructuring of business around the world has, no doubt, undermined the employment security of workers. It has forced many American workers to give up prized jobs with what were perceived to be invulnerable Galbraithian firms that, because of their market position, could "over pay" in cash and benefits. It has also forced American workers to compete with other, often lower-paid, workers from around the world for the jobs and wages they covet. Many have been thrown out of their old

14. One measure of the increasing importance of this capital (which when embodied in individuals is commonly referred to as human capital) is the increasing premium being paid to more educated workers. See Kevin Murphy and Finis Welch, "Wage Premiums for College Graduates: Recent Growth and Possible Explanations" *Educational Researcher* 18, no. 4 (May 1989): 17–26.

15. George Gilder, *Microcosm: The Quantum Revolution in Economics and Technology* (New York: Simon and Schuster, 1989), p. 63.

16. Tom Peters, *Tom Peters Seminar: Crazy Times Call for Crazy Organizations* (New York: Vintage Books, 1994), p. 13.

jobs—sometimes in their peak earning years, after they had built up years of seniority—and into new jobs that don't pay as well, don't have as many benefits, and are far less secure—*simply because virtually all employment is less secure.* Others who forewent wages early in their career, with the expectation that they would be compensated with higher-than-market income late in their careers, have found that their expectations cannot be realized, that they will not get the overpayment they expected, mainly because their firms are strapped to meet new forms of competition from other firms around the world that are paying straight market wages.

Many American workers have accordingly had to give up on their fondest dreams, simply because the markets that extend to the ends of the globe will no longer afford them the incomes to which they thought they were entitled. Economic tectonics is, in effect, causing the evolutionary process to speed up, which in turn is forcing workers and managers alike to pick up the pace of adaptation, to adapt to new conditions spawned by the technology itself, and then to adapt to the vast array of adaptations people are making around the world, with adaptations giving way to adaptations, ad infinitum. The economic system is, from the process, becoming ever more complex and sophisticated.

Countervailing Impotence

What should workers do to counter the economic tectonics afoot in the world? We can all lament the affected workers' hardship, but there is little that affected workers or anyone else can do about the matter—other than not waste a lot of energy fighting the forces afoot. The butterfly has taken wing; the tectonic plate is on the move; the world has changed and will not likely return to its old ways. The message is that life must adjust—will adjust, as it always has, in spite of the grumbling that always tends to accompany adjustments to externally imposed demands. Once more there isn't really much that either governments can do to hold the forces at bay (other than get out of the way) and to bring back workers' lost security, mainly because governments also have, in the process, become competitors and face many of the same types of constraints that workers do.

The writing is on the (international) walls for all workers of the world to follow: *Become more productive. Work harder and smarter. Get more education and skills. Get competitive. Do more than others have been doing or will likely do. Stop complaining.*

In many people's minds, Ronald Reagan and Margaret Thatcher were directing world events during their political eras by redirecting their countries' economic policies. The critics charge that during the 1980s, the "blind" were leading the "dumb." That is a highly dubious proposition, but not for reasons others give. It is probably far more accurate to say that Reagan and Thatcher were *responding* to the very economic forces footloose in the world and identified above than to say they were *directing* world political and economic forces. Reagan and Thatcher somehow heard the clarion call of escalating capital mobility on an international scale and intuitively, if not explicitly, understood that the phenomenon ultimately meant that they must enable businesses in their countries to become more competitive by making their countries' policies more competitive.

If the move toward market-based solutions for social problems in the 1980s had been limited to the United States and the United Kingdom, the critics' charge that it was "all Reagan's and Thatcher's fault" might be given credence. However, the movement was worldwide, stretching from all of Europe to Australia to New Zealand and back to Chile and from the United States to Poland and the former Soviet Union, covering the full ideological spectrum from highly capitalistic economies to fully socialistic ones.[17]

Many governments have not yet fully faced up to the fact that the world has changed, that governments do business within a *given* parcel of land. On the other hand, businesses can do business, must do business, on practically *any* parcel of land. All the while, businesses must treat governmentally imposed taxes and regulations as any other cost of doing business and must respond accordingly—that is, move elsewhere if governmentally imposed cost conditions warrant it.

What does that critical observation mean for national governments? For state governments? For city governments? In general, states must realize that their role is now, more than ever, one of "greasing the skids" for businesses who operate or might operate in their area; it is one of making sure that state and local policies do not hamper the competitiveness of the businesses that operate inside their borders.

In bygone eras, politicians and policymakers could sit around glibly chatting about what they *wanted* to do, or what their constituents would allow them to do, totally disregarding what other governments in other parts of the country were doing. They were free to follow their fondest wishes because capital could not move, except at a snail's pace. If an

17. For details on what countries were adopting what market-based policies, see McKenzie and Lee, *Quicksilver Capital*.

interest group wanted an added tax or a subsidy, the only relevant issue was typically whether the politicians had the votes. Now, they have to think twice, if not three and four times, about such matters.

More to the point, they must think competitively, which is something they are not yet fully used to doing. Politicians and policymakers must, like all good businesses, begin to ask, What are our competitors doing? Who are the relevant competitors? What will the market bear? What is the responsiveness of our customer/citizen base? Does the proposal make economic sense, that is, make a profit in a well-defined bottom-line or in some broad social sense?

In the end, political leaders and policymakers must realize that the governments they lead can no longer be satisfied with meeting the best of policy and delivery standards in this state or even this country. They must begin to look around the world to determine who has the very highest standards for government performance and begin to seek to meet those standards. This is because, as in business, governments are in competition with "the very best" in the world for the capital they need. They must seek to lead, not follow, in the policy formulation process. They must realize, at the very least, that the growing mobility of capital necessarily makes cuts in tax rates potentially more attractive. Why? Because the greater responsiveness of capital means that they will have more capital in their jurisdictions with the greater prospects that the expanded base, potentially at least, will more than offset the impact of the rate cuts.

The new world economic order certainly means that government officials must look long and hard at proposals to raise tax rates, because the higher rates can spell a lower tax base and less revenue, exactly opposite of that intended.[18] Clearly, if the path of higher tax rates is followed, state and local officials and policymakers must double their efforts to ensure that the expenditures more than compensate for the higher taxes. Regardless, they must temper the extent of their tax-rate increases. Similarly, workers must recognize the competitive bind their governments are in and then be willing to temper their demands on their governments to solve their problems. Workers must realize that in the new world economic order, they will be called on to solve more of their own problems, to get out of their own fixes.

As the 1990s began, the country was embroiled in a fierce political

18. The tie between higher state tax rates and slower economic and job growth has been studied by David L. Littman, "States Tax Constituents Away," *Wall Street Journal*, March 8, 1991, p. A10; and Gerald W. Scully, *Constitutional Environments and Economic Growth* (Princeton, N.J.: Princeton University Press, 1992).

debate over trade liberalization through NAFTA (North American Free Trade Agreement), under which the trade barriers among Canada, the United States, and Mexico would be gradually eliminated. The American partisans in the debate scored points on how many jobs would be created (the pro-NAFTA forces) or destroyed (the anti-NAFTA forces)—*as if the country had a meaningful political choice over the matter.*

The United States never really had a choice over whether NAFTA would pass; its only choice was when it would pass. The bill was actually passed by a surprisingly generous margin, but if it had not passed then, it very likely would have eventually. If the United States had turned it down, Canada and Mexico would surely have finalized their own pact. Capital from around the world, especially Japan, would have flowed into Canada and Mexico, taking advantage of profitable opportunities left unexploited by the United States. The United States would not have been as competitive in world product markets, an outcome that would have increased the economic and political pressure for adoption of a revised NAFTA. Indeed, NAFTA was proposed as a competitive response by Canada, the United States, and Mexico to the greater efficiency being achieved (and threatened) from trade liberalization in Europe and South America. It should be no surprise that the growing mobility of capital over the last forty or fifty years has been accompanied by growing trade liberalization; the former has been causing the latter.

Washington is constantly buzzing with glib talk about "soaking the rich," which means making them pay their fair share of taxes (whatever that is), and/or "making businesses pay" for whatever fringe benefit is deemed valued by workers. Those making the reform proposals don't get it. They don't realize that the "rich" are generally rich because they have control of an unusual amount of physical and human capital that can be sent hurtling to other points on the globe if they wish. Moreover, escalating capital mobility means that businesses do not have to pay for the mandates imposed upon them; they can simply pass along the costs of the mandates to their workers in the form of lower pay and fewer fringe benefits.

In his 1983 book *The Next American Frontier,* Secretary of Labor Robert Reich wrote eloquently about how the country desperately needed an "industrial policy," through which governments would tax some firms in order to help others.[19] By 1991, he had recognized the force of capital mobility on a global scale. In his book *The Work of Nations,* he retreated from his full-blown industrial-policy agenda, arguing that the country

19. Robert B. Reich, *The Next American Frontier* (New York: Times Books, 1983).

could not afford to tax some firms for the benefit of others.[20] Why? Capital was too mobile. The taxes would drive some firms away, and the subsidies from other firms could easily be transferred abroad. That part of his message was right on target, something everyone should read.

Nevertheless, Reich continued to argue that what we need to do now is raise the taxes on the wealthy, reasoning that people are not mobile. He overlooked the fact that the brainpower and knowledge of what he calls the "fortunate fifth" of the population is some of the most mobile of capital; it can be sent overseas in literally a flash. Clearly, we can still tax those who bring their incomes back home. However, we will have lost in the process the brainpower that is so crucial to a modern economy.

The point that needs to be remembered is that intentionally redistributive policies—designed to bolster the incomes of this or that group, whether workers or capitalists—must be developed with the utmost care. Officials and policymakers must take care to ensure that their efforts are not out of line with the policies in place elsewhere and are designed to serve effectively some broad social objective, not strictly the narrow interests of those who are on the receiving end of the redistribution. Otherwise, officials and policymakers can expect to find their fiscal troubles mounting as capital moves or is created elsewhere.

Those who are concerned about the plight of the poor must realize that there are economic limits to how much society can do for the poor, given the mobility of capital. Similarly, the poor must realize that there are limits to how much they can expect from the benevolence of governments and those who are not poor.

For that matter, everyone associated with government—all those who draw from government in various forms (myself included)—must accept the tightening grip of the *economic,* as distinct from *political,* limits to what governments can do. Hence, every proposed program must be evaluated in terms of the other programs that will have to be given up. To work within those limits, people of all political persuasions must begin to ask how government services can be provided more effectively and at lower cost, not so much because that is a way of reducing government involvement in the economy (which might be helpful), but as a way of government doing more for the benefit of capital, for the purpose of attracting more capital and of inducing the creation of more homegrown capital that will have less reason to leave.

Proponents of privatization of various government services, from gar-

20. Robert B. Reich, *The Work of Nations* (New York: Random House, 1991).

bage collection to the distribution of public housing units to the provision of education, make an important point: Just because a service must be funded by the public treasury, it need not be delivered by public agencies. The proponents' goal is to make government more efficient by choosing from an array of alternative delivery systems (government included), the purpose of which must be to make governmental jurisdictions more competitive vis-à-vis other governmental jurisdictions and for increasing the likelihood of the existing capital base remaining and additional capital flowing in.

Although some people might like to believe the contrary, many governments don't have much choice about privatization; they must do it (unless they come up with more productive strategies for increasing their competitiveness). The proponents and opponents in debates over school vouchers have both missed an obvious point: Public schools are rapidly losing their privileged monopoly position; they are becoming competitive, as people and capital become progressively more mobile across school districts. The growing competitiveness is vividly revealed in the attention so many people give to the comparative scores on national exams in various states and countries. We know we have to improve the public education system, or else the country will suffer from a failure to produce the capital of the future and from a failure to attract capital from other parts of the world. American public schools are now having to compete with each other simply because Americans can move to alternative school districts and many are doing so, with harsh effects being felt by those school districts that have not gotten their education act together. Moreover, public schools in the future will have to compete to a growing degree with unheralded forms of private education, those that can be obtained through computers, on CD-ROMs, or by way of the Internet and the World Wide Web.

The only relevant unsettled question in the educational voucher debate is no longer *whether* the voucher system will be broadly accepted as a part of the country's education system, but *when* it will be accepted (or supplanted by a superior solution). It will be accepted. Why? Those states and local governments that seek to prosper by making their jurisdictions more attractive (or less unattractive) to capital will seek the benefits of an even more competitive educational system by overriding the objections of the public educational establishment and installing some kind of voucher system. Of course, it may be that the public educational establishment may switch to support of the vouchers, mainly because they too can benefit from working and living in a more prosperous economy. At any rate, when some states begin to adopt the voucher system, other states will surely follow suit. They will have to do so in order that their jurisdictions will remain competitive.

Accordingly, Minnesota presented a competitive challenge to the rest of the country by being a leader in instituting statewide school choice, an experiment that has forced other states to follow suit. Similarly, Minneapolis has issued another challenge to many other communities around the country and world by discarding the traditional bureaucratic management system for public schools and turning over day-to-day operations to a private company whose officials will be paid based on performance. That move was reported in the *Los Angeles Times*, and probably many other newspapers around the country, for good reason.[21] The state's experimentation with educational innovation was a direct consequence of reports in the early 1980s of the economic difficulties the state was then facing and may still be confronting (although the reviews on Minnesota appear to be mixed)—of the firms and jobs that are leaving the state.[22] At the same time, the very fact that the city and state continue to experiment with new approaches to education should be causing other communities to take notice and ask, "What do the officials in Minneapolis know that we don't know? How will the state's actions affect our ability to compete in the world market for capital, that is, plant, equipment, headquarters, and jobs?" Those are the types of questions that people in Minneapolis probably had to ask of other communities and that led them to the reforms that have been put in place.

By the same token, in spite of criticism, Wisconsin has competitively challenged surrounding states (if not all states) by daring to impose a two-year limit on payments going to welfare recipients.[23] Other states in the Midwest must recognize the Wisconsin experiment as a two-barrelled threat: Wisconsin's welfare limit can make government (and doing business) in that state more efficient. In addition, because the payment limits may send welfare recipients to other states, the Wisconsin experiment can make government (and doing business) in other states more inefficient. No wonder Congress passed in 1996 a two-year limit on welfare benefits.

21. Rhonda Hillbery, "Private Firm to Run Schools in Minneapolis," *Los Angeles Times*, November 5, 1993, p. A4.

22. See John Herbers, "Costs Cited in Loss of New Companies," *New York Times*, April 12, 1983, p. D1; Harvey Meyer, "Goodby Minnesota," *Minnesota Ventures*, May/June 1992, pp. 21–31; Peter Applebome, "South Raises Stakes in Flight of Jobs," *New York Times*, October 4, 1993, p. A12.

23. See "Welfare Reform, Done Harshly," *New York Times*, November 8, 1993, p. A14.

Regardless of how inattentive they may be, communities all over the world are being led, to paraphrase the venerable Adam Smith, *as if* by an "invisible hand"—an economic tectonic plate of sorts—toward reforms that are market based, because they are market driven. The power of those market forces may be tempered somewhat from time to time by political decisions, but it is certain that they will not be denied.

States and communities (and countries) ought to begin to actively work *with* those market-based forces, recognizing that the ultimate economic security comes from having a more productive and lower-cost venue than can be had elsewhere. This means, paradoxically, officials need to rethink their efforts. In the past, they have devoted most of their energies to asking "How can we create and save the most jobs?" Instead, they should begin to ask "How can we begin to help business promote cost-effective job destruction?"—not to kill off jobs for job's sake. Rather, the purpose should be to ensure that the cost of production is lower than elsewhere in the country and world. Economic development strategies designed to make firms more productive means enabling them to operate "leaner and meaner," which implies fewer workers for any given output level, which in turn will inevitably mean, at times, that jobs will be destroyed. Ironically, job destruction is oftentimes the most effective way to have a healthy growth rate in jobs.

In spite of its economic troubles in the 1990s, Japan remains, in the minds of many observers, an economic powerhouse. Yet, it reached its exalted status by destroying practically every job in existence in the 1950s, if not 1960s. Those American firms and industries that have found ways of producing more with less (including fewer workers) should be praised, not damned as they so often are. Historically, job destruction and economic prosperity have always gone hand in hand.[24]

Likewise, government officials often spend all of their efforts trying to attract firms and, where possible, erect barriers (for example, onerous plant-closing laws) to their exiting. They should contemplate the prospects that easing the exit barriers can be a way of increasing the emergence and inflow of new business. Firms that must be footloose to meet their competitors in their product markets will not ignore the costs of exiting from markets in their relocation decisions. Also, new firms will consider the costs of closing down in their decisions to expand. In other words, loose talk about increasing the costs of plant closures in order to "save" jobs should not be accepted simply because of good intentions. The former Soviet Union did a magnificent job of "saving" jobs for more than seventy years, and look where its jobs program landed the several

24. See David Birch, *Job Creation in America: How Our Smallest Companies Put the Most People to Work* (New York: Free Press, 1987).

republics involved in that not-so-grand social experiment, in the exalted ranks of third-world economies.

The Bidding War for Firms

For at least the past twenty years, more and more municipal and state governments have been actively pursuing companies all over the globe that have, in effect, plants and jobs for sale. Governments have been forced to do so. Capital has become crucial to local economic prosperity, and, as has been argued here, capital has become progressively more mobile over the years. Understandably, firms have begun to realize that they have more than their goods and services to sell; they have their location decisions that can be put up for state and municipal auction. Moreover, many firms realize that their competitors have put their location decisions up for sale, which means all must follow suit or suffer a competitive disadvantage, given that those firms that do sell their location decisions for the price of tax abatements, worker-retraining programs, and subsidized loans will have lower costs than those firms that resist, for whatever reasons.

Accordingly, a new economic phenomenon has emerged with force since the early 1980s. Economic development "posses" from many communities and states, often headed by governors, are scouring the globe for discontented firms who are ready and willing to move and to listen to a "better deal." At the same time, firms have radically changed the way they make location decisions. They no longer do them quietly for fear that the news will drive up land prices in the targeted sites. Rather, they broadcast their intentions in the media with the expectation that government officials will come "a courting," pockets lined with government-backed economic incentives.

BMW put its proposed U.S. assembly plant up for sale in 1992. After a fierce competitive battle, South Carolina "won" (if that is the right word), but only after agreeing to provide BMW with keys to its public treasury, from which the automaker will be able to draw tens of millions of dollars in benefits.[25] Not to be outdone, in 1993 Mercedes Benz put its proposed U.S. assembly plant up for bids. Alabama won the bidding war after agreeing to provide an estimated total package of benefits worth $300 million to Mercedes.[26]

25. See Lyn Riddle, "Former Textile Town Draws International Fare to the New South," *Los Angeles Times*, August 25, 1992, p. A5; and Doron P. Levin, "What BMW Sees in South Carolina," *New York Times*, April 11, 1993, p. F5.

26. Helene Cooper and Glenn Ruffenach, "Alabama's Winning of Mercedes Plant Will Be Costly, with Major Tax Breaks," *Wall Street Journal*, September 30, 1993, p. A2.

What should workers and communities and states do? The answer is no less simple than it was earlier: They must join the competitive fray in one way or another. They cannot hold back the force of capital mobility. Again, the genie is out of the lamp but unlike the genie in *Aladdin,* this genie can't grant people their fondest wishes—control over the forces afoot.

Was the deal that the state of Alabama made with Mercedes Benz a good one? Frankly, it is difficult for an outside observer to say. The making and taking of offers oftentimes crucially depends upon intangible factors, for example, differences in attitudes among competitors and the symbolism of the deals. What is clear is that if the deal was not a good one for Alabama, the market will not be very forgiving.

This means that in their search for businesses, communities and states must act very cautiously and judiciously for a number of reasons. The mobility of capital requires that they strike deals that are profitable in the strict sense of that term: The benefits to the states and taxpayers must exceed the concessions that are made. If the costs are greater than the benefits, then communities and states can be assured that the deals they make with firms like Mercedes Benz will make it tougher for governments to provide the agreed-upon benefits. Mercedes Benz might move in, but other capital will move out and still more capital that might have moved there will go elsewhere.

Communities and states must be cautious for another, not so obvious, reason. Because of political forces, many of the bidding wars will likely involve large plants with large job bases. After all, "jobs" have become the raison d'être for many public policies emanating from the halls of Congress and state capitols. But firms with a lot of jobs are not always the firms that will be around in the future; many will fold simply because they have lots of jobs to sell (and too little productivity). Popular wisdom notwithstanding, the world economy suggests that the most viable firms in the future will be those with very few jobs. The fewer the jobs, the better, but regrettably, economic development boards often have a sharply contrasting rule that guides their searches (which has a way of being translated to the more inefficient, the better). In other words, I suspect that the politics of the moment will likely cause many states to make some poor investments.

Communities and states should also remember that most of the job growth in the country is occurring not in large firms (they are, generally speaking, downsizing), but in small firms, those most unlikely to be candidates for special deals from economic development boards. Unless undertaken with great care, bids for large plants can stifle the growth of small plants, primarily because small firms will be forced to cover the costs of subsidies provided to large firms and because the small firms will be hamstrung in their efforts to compete with the large firms who have secured the subsidies. The net growth in jobs in Alabama will not be equal to the supposed 1,500 jobs that will be available in the Mercedes plant, plus the jobs in satellite industries; it will likely equal that total minus some number of jobs lost in small firms that do not benefit from the existence of the Mercedes plant but who will be forced to help Mercedes pay its bills.

As stark as these problems might be, there is a more onimous reason that communities and states should proceed cautiously in their competitive battles for plants, headquarters, and jobs: *Communities and states that by their agreements indicate they are willing to pay firms to move in, are also communities and states that should be willing to pay firms to stay.* If Alabama is willing to pay to have 1,500 jobs move in, it should be willing to pay to keep 1,500 from moving out—and profit-hungry firms, with footloose capital being wooed by other states and communities, should be expected to bargain with their governments over staying put. Consequently, communities and states cannot continue to evaluate their agreements with only the particular costs and benefits at issue (as appears to have been the case in Alabama and South Carolina). They must consider the prospects that they will have to up their payments to keep other firms that threaten to move out.

Michigan has for a long time indicated a willingness to pay firms to move in. That fact obviously didn't escape the attention of General Motors, which in 1980 announced plans to close two of its Fisher Body plants in Detroit and replace them with a new $630 million Cadillac plant. Its plant-closing announcement was accompanied by none-too-subtle threats to move the plant out of the city unless a suitable site could be found. Six thousand jobs were at stake, a fact that caused state and city officials to launch a campaign that ended with the condemnation of a section of the city known as Poletown, encompassing 327 acres, 127 businesses, 16 churches, and 1,753 residences—and the expenditure of literally tens of millions of federal, state, and city tax dollars, partially for the benefit of GM stockholders.[27]

Everyone knows California has had economic difficulties, caused in

27. Detroit bought the property for about $200 million ($150 million of this amount coming from the federal government) and sold the property to GM for slightly more than $8 million. See Sheldon Richman, "The Rape of Poletown," *Inquiry*, August 3 and 24, 1981.

part by the downsizing in the defense establishment and in part by what businesses see as an antibusiness climate. The state has been scrambling to slow the out-migration of businesses. Recognizing that fact, Taco Bell, which is headquartered in my hometown, Irvine, California, took note in 1993 of the willingness of city and state governments to buy firms and to keep them from moving out of town. The lease on Taco Bell's gleaming office tower in Irvine was up in 1996, a fact that prompted the company to announce in 1993 that it was considering a move. No one could be sure how serious Taco Bell was; everyone, however, understood why they were taking bids. The firm wanted to make money, and it just might have been able to make more money by selling its location decision than by selling tacos. Taco Bell also needed to stay competitive in a fiercely cost-conscious fast-food market, and it had to make sure that its market share was not harmed by firms who received special treatment that Taco Bell didn't. Covington, Kentucky, thought it could buy the (re)location decision for $50 million, but couldn't. However, Fort Worth, Texas, made a bid of more than $10 million in benefits, which Taco Bell *and* the state of California took very seriously, mainly because Taco Bell almost took the Texas bait. California returned with a bid that Taco Bell ultimately accepted.

The restaurant chain's headquarters remains in Irvine, but the story has not yet ended. You can imagine that other California firms are thinking they should try the same ploy. The costs will surely mount.

It would probably be far better for governments to recognize that the tail is no longer wagging the dog to the degree that it once did. Businesses, and for that matter, individuals, no longer have to sit and take the wagging; they can move. In the power to move lies the foundation of a much more prosperous and competitive, if less secure, economic future.

The Bush–Clinton Reversal

George Bush was elected to office in 1988 on the political coattails of Ronald Reagan. Voters assumed that Bush would continue the pro-market policies of his predecessor and mentor, but he did not. He charted a substantially different policy course, one filled with tax increases (in 1990, the largest in history), hikes in the minimum wage, and regulatory expansions (including stiffer environmental laws and a broadening of the employment rights of handicapped Americans, the definition of which covers alcoholics and drug addicts and obese people). In 1992, he was defeated, partially because of the violation of his own "no new taxes" pledge, by Bill Clinton who successfully convinced voters that the Reagan–Bush policies had landed the country in a persistent recession in the 1990s and that it was time for a change. However, Clinton extended Bush's anti-market policy course. Clinton pressed for and got a major tax-rate increase on the richest taxpayers. He extended environmental, drug, communication, and antidiscrimination regulations. In 1994, he also indicated his clear intentions to install a national health-care system, to seek another round of increases in the minimum wage, to fortify environmental laws, and to strengthen the bargaining position of unions.

From all surface political signs, the global international economic forces of capital mobility clearly at work in the 1980s had dissipated by the early 1990s. But there are seven good reasons to believe that they were still at work as strong as ever, just out of sight and mind to political leaders who remained convinced that they could tilt against them.

First, it should be noted that in the early 1990s, the United States and world economy went into a resession and then began a far slower recovery than historical experience would have suggested. The sluggishness of the recovery is, without much question, partially attributable to the anti-market policies adopted that helped to redirect—slowly and quietly, but persistently—the world's capital base toward the newly liberated economies of eastern Europe, the former Soviet Union, and China, as well as those western economies that had continued on the path of economic liberation, most notably Mexico and much of South America.

Second, job growth in the recovery was lackluster, a reflection of the fact that mandated worker costs were escalating and that entrepreneurs were seeking to economize on the use of labor. A price was being paid by workers for the anti-market policies, and that consequence would surely show up later in political drives to reverse the policies, to delay passage of other anti-market policies, and to adopt other offsetting pro-market policies.

Third, the downsizing of large firms (and capital) continued unabated in the 1990s, meaning large firms were continuing their goal of becoming "meaner and leaner," better able to respond to market forces *and* hostile government policies and to negate many of the efforts of governments to extend their control.

Fourth, the economic pressure to liberate international trade was fully evident in the political debate over the passage of NAFTA in the United States. The pro-Nafta partisans conceded to world economic forces, arguing successfully that trade liberalization was absolutely necessary in order to revive the North American economies; to spur economic growth in the West; to respond to the liberation of trade in Europe, South

America, and Pacific Rim countries; and to offset the consequences of the previously adopted antigrowth policies of higher taxes and expanded regulations of recent years.

Fifth, the power of capital mobility in the world was nowhere more clearly revealed than in the escalating competitive bidding of states for plants and the capital base they represent. None of the states involved wanted to make the concessions (which, as indicated above, ran into the hundreds of millions of dollars for a single plant), but they all admitted they had to be a part of the competitive fray. Political leaders at all levels of governments must also be a part of the competitive fray for capital when they consider other policies that might not affect so directly and intensely the location and relocation decisions of firms who control the world's capital base. The force of competition does not stop with a few isolated, well-publicized instances of government concessions. The force is constant, unrelenting.

Sixth, both Mexico and Orange County, California, governments allowed their financial houses to run amuck for years. Mexico couldn't control its expenditures. Orange County couldn't resist the temptation to seek unusual returns by what amounted to speculation in derivatives. The economies of both areas were battered by the reaction of the capitalists who began to seek financial cover elsewhere. Both economies had to temper their enthusiasm for taxes as quick fixes, revealing the relentless pressure of the quicksilver capital at work on national and local economies.

Seventh, even the Clinton administration has yielded to the rhetoric and policy dictates for the need for countries to become competitive. In spite of proposed plans to greatly expand federal expenditures, federal spending receded as a percentage of GDP, falling to levels below those achieved in the 1980s under conservative Ronald Reagan.[28] In addition, the Clinton administration has not gotten its way politically. It has had to set aside its expansive political agenda. A major surface reason for the shift in Clinton's aspirations was the dramatic political realignment of Congress in 1994, from Democratic to Republican domination, but no doubt the political realignment was being augmented by more fundamental forces, one of which was the one emphasized here, "quicksilver capital," that has made expansive government policies impractical and unattractive to the electorate.

Governments and their leaders must recognize and yield to the global economic forces afoot in the world. They won't go away. It is probably no understatement to suggest that many worker and firm insecurities

28. See Richard B. McKenzie, "Clinton Confidential," *Reason*, November 1996, pp. 40–43.

have arisen in the country over the last decade or so precisely because the global forces outlined here have taken hold with a rapidity that has not been equaled in history, even during the era of the first industrial revolution two or three centuries ago. Workers, firms, and governments have had a tough time trying to reorient their thinking; they have naturally sought to deny the forces or to work against them, which has, for some, only worsened future prospects and economic insecurities. To repeat, the time has come to "go with the flow," simply because there are not many viable options. However, economic security in the future will only arise from entering the competitive fray with gusto.

Concluding Comments

The new world economic order is for real. Capital mobility is for real. The more intense competition for the private *and* public sectors is for real. Economic tectonics are at work on the evolutionary process we call business and government. Most private firms have responded to the new world economic order by restructuring and even reinventing themselves. Governments have begun, albeit at times grudgingly and with occasional reversals, to be responsive to the forces at work in the world.

What workers, businesses, and governments need to do is more of what they have been doing—recognizing that their aspirations cannot be fulfilled by simply ignoring world competition. What governments need to do is to think anew about the policies that will work effectively to promote the development of the income and wealth base practically everyone wants.

The successful workers, businesses, and governments will be those that get ahead of the (international) learning curve, that no longer just respond to what everyone else is doing, but that seek to actively promote a local environment that allows capital—human and physical—to be competitive with the best in the world. As odd as this may seem, the new world order requires job destruction through efficiency improvements—lots of it. It requires busted dreams for some. It requires that people work harder, that they be more alert to changing market conditions and opportunities, and that they be prepared to adjust repeatedly at their own expense.

This is a position that doesn't sit well with many Americans. Most Americans understandably would prefer to be told that the new world economic order is not for real, that all their problems will fade away, that their problems can be made better by government nursemaids. Nevertheless, the position, albeit seemingly heartless and strident, is one that squares with real-world experience on a daily basis.

7

THE RULES OF PROSPERITY

> To understand our civilization, one must appreciate that the extended order resulted not from human design or intention but spontaneously: it arose from unintentionally conforming to certain traditional and largely *moral* practices, many of which men tend to dislike, whose significance they usually fail to understand, whose validity they cannot prove, and which have nonetheless fairly rapidly spread by means of an evolutionary selection—the comparative increase in population and wealth—of those groups that happened to follow them.
>
> F. A. Hayek,
> *The Fatal Conceit: The Errors of Socialism*

HE WAS TALL, white-haired, and elderly, having lived and worked long past the end of a normal distinguished career. I was half his age, just entering some of my more productive years. He had come to the States in the early 1980s to do some rare interviews with major magazines. I was there to shuttle him from one interview site to the next.

He could not have known my name. I was in awe of his, having read and admired much of what he had written. I had thought that he would be hard to talk to and that, given recent illnesses that had left him frail, he would be slow to respond to probing questions. He could not have been nicer, more cordial, more perceptive. He was a true, old-fashioned scholar and a gentleman. When pressed by editors, he never failed to explain the world he envisioned in terms that others had missed. In those brief hours I saw his work come alive as he reflected deeply on the simplest of questions. I also saw my own intellectual perspective on the world change anew.

Before my brief stay in New York City with the late F. A. Hayek, Nobel laureate in economics, I had always thought, as most economists do, that the world's overarching economic problems arise from too few resources available to satisfy too many wants. He insisted to the editors and me that the problem was more internal, a matter of being able to create and sustain civilized society in spite of the limits of the human mind to comprehend the complexity of the world within which we had to live. From childhood, I had been told time and again that wisdom emerged from the acquisition of knowledge. He insisted that its fountainhead was elsewhere, from a most unlikely position, that is, in the recognition of how much we mere mortals do not know—and cannot know—about complex society. He reminded me of a passage from one of his works that says something to the effect that freedom's ultimate social value lies in the fact that we don't know what people will do with it. What a thought! It took a long time for me to understand what he meant.

With knee-jerk speed, economists frequently point to prices and markets as the source of solutions to social problems, to the total exclusion of ethical concerns. Hayek stressed much the opposite. Of course, he was troubled then, as he had been all of his career, with the proclivity of governments to concede to their "fatal conceit" (his phrase) and believe that they could productively supplant markets with centralized direction of one sector of the economy or another, but he was obviously even more troubled by the slow fraying of the ethical foundations of markets, the growing lack of appreciation for and adherence to the fundamental rules of social order. To Hayek, economics and prosperity had to start with ethics, that is, with generalizable rules of reasonable behavior.

The social dilemma, which, as I will explain, is the cause of so much contemporary angst, is apparent in the above epigraph: *We must appreciate rules of reasonable behavior—call them ethics or morals—that we don't like, can't understand, and can't validate.* Moreover, the rules must be reasonably stable over the short run, but they must also be flexible over the very long run. That's quite a thought, too. It is at the heart of this and the following chapters as we try a substantially different take on the paradox of progress, the reasons for growing pessimism in an era of abundance.

Bill Clinton was elected president in 1992 using the pat campaign phrase: "It's the economy, Stupid!" That perspective is parroted in one form or another by a variety of Washington-based policy wonks. My overriding point in this and the following chapter is that some Americans' problems are more fundamental than "the economy." Their problems stem from the fact that a form of "moral tectonics" has arisen, and the stress has begun to show. Economic tectonics, described in the last chapter, are forcing a reconstitution of the rules on which markets and other social institutions are founded. As a result, uncertainty abounds. For some groups of Americans, the moral order, the constellation of undergirding rules of reasonable behavior, has begun to dissipate at far too rapid a pace or has fallen practically apart, leaving too many of the affected people with the prospects of a dreadful economic fate—unless group members reform their ways, which may not be possible. These Americans have reason to fear the future, but not so much because they have been victimized by others. In a real sense, they have been victimized by no one; then again, they have been victimized by their own collective tendencies to follow their most base instincts, jettisoning in the process the necessary rules of reasonable behavior.

To understand these points, however, we need first to acknowledge the extent to which social and economic interactions are grounded in ethical, as well as legal, precepts. I focus here on markets for two reasons. One, matters of markets are my specialty. Two, and more important, people seem to think, as does Clinton, that the country's basic problems are "economic"—that is, jobs, incomes, and so on. We need to understand that many economic problems are symptoms of more deep-seated changes, ethical in nature, that may appear on the surface to have nothing to do with markets and the economy. Furthermore, we need to recognize the inherent difficulties of reconstructing, or just fortifying, rules of behavior once they have begun to crumble. To appreciate the analysis, standard arguments in criticism and praise of markets must be revisited.

Markets and Their Critics

Critics of market economies protest that markets are worse than moral vacuums because of their dependence on the profit motive. Marx made an intellectual fetish of the extent to which profit-hungry firms would exploit their workers, always willfully holding them close to the subsistence-income level. Many modern economists don't protest Marx's vision of money-grubbing capitalists. Indeed, many fortify, albeit inadvertently, his and other critics' assessment of markets by default—that is, by constantly exalting the importance of profit making in achieving economic efficiency to the neglect of the underlying social *setting* (legal and moral) within which pursuit of self-interest, or profit seeking, *must* take place.

Modern critics continue to condemn markets for their excessive reliance on greed as the primordial driving force. They seek a more humane world, one that would be more rationally organized and that would require that a greater number of economic decisions be driven, explicitly, by good intentions. After all, good results require good intentions, or so the critics seem to think.[1]

The critics do make an important point that needs to be accepted by the most ardent market proponents: Good intentions often do make for good results. The world needs good intentions and actions. We can see the truth of those claims in the work of a host of family, charitable, religious, and communitarian efforts. Successful families thrive on love, but not necessarily greed. The Salvation Army has the best of intentions, to help the downtrodden, and should be commended for the souls it saves from self-destructive behavior. People drop money in the Army's red pots precisely because they believe that the people ringing the bells and ladling the soup have concern for the people they help.

The critics err, however, when they suggest that few good results can be achieved by profit seeking, a claim that seems to be taken as a case for political action to rectify problems. A lot of good works are done—good products offered, services rendered, and real income raised—by people who, when they are doing their good works, have little more than money on their minds. In the process of becoming the country's largest retailer, Wal-Mart's main goal was probably to make as much money as it could for its shareholders. Along the way, however, it provided ever-expanding hordes of Americans with deals they could not match elsewhere.

Futhermore, political processes are not activated by any more superior motives than are markets. People in governments have good *and* bad intentions, just as do people operating within markets. There is clearly precious little, if any, evidence that people who work for governments are morally superior (or inferior) to the people who work for private firms. People are simply people, regardless of where they happen to work, and they all must be constrained at times in what they do and how they do it. Competition needs to be heralded as a force for social constraint not because it is the only form of constraint—hardly—but that it reduces the need for other necessary forms of constraint, legal and moral, that have their own practical limits.

1. See, for example, Robert B. Reich, *The Work of Nations: Preparing Ourselves for the 21st Century* (New York: Random House, 1991); Kevin Phillips, *The Politics of Rich and Poor: Wealth and the American Electorate in the Reagan Aftermath* (New York: Random House, 1990); and Robert Kuttner, *The Economic Illusion: False Choice Between Economic Prosperity and Social Justice* (Boston: Houghton Mifflin, 1984).

The paradox of markets is that in order to make a system that permits the pursuit of self-interest work tolerably well, the participants must first check, by various means, the pursuit of self-interest. Markets can be efficient but not without nonmarket, even nonrational, bounds being imposed upon them, not the least of which go by the names of honesty and integrity, a willingness to play by generally recognized rules of restraint. That is one principle that is rarely mentioned in Economics 101, mainly because economists don't seem to understand it, but Hayek did. So did Adam Smith, a point stressed below.

The purists who insist that markets are moral vacuums or that markets are relentlessly guided to perfection through profit seeking have trouble understanding the angst of our time. Once we concede, however, that more than profits matter—that, in fact, "rules matter" and matter a great deal—then we are in a position to see that the turbulence and uncertainty of our times can be related to the slow but persistent changes in the underlying structure of rules that are having both good and bad effects.

Adam Smith Reconsidered

In making their assessments of markets, critics and proponents alike defer to the venerable Adam Smith, who in 1776 insisted in his *Wealth of Nations* that those who supply our personal needs do not do what they do out of love for their customers. On the contrary, they do it out of self-interest or, worse yet, "self-love." A passage from Smith is frequently cited: "It is not from the benevolence of the butcher, the brewer, or the baker, that we expect our dinner, but from their regard to their own interest. We address ourselves, not to their humanity but to their self-love, and never talk to them of our own necessities but of their advantages."[2]

The critics are right about the emphasis on private gain in markets, but only in part. The role of private interest has been grossly exaggerated. Even Adam Smith can be faulted on that score, to a degree, but he also has been misinterpreted and misunderstood on that same score. Smith

2. Adam Smith, *An Inquiry into the Nature and Causes of the Wealth of Nations* (New York: Modern Library, 1937), p. 14. The critics then might reflect, musing over the words of Alexis de Tocqueville, on the ongoing contradiction between Americans' willingness to profess being motivated almost exclusively by their personal agendas and, at the same time, their willingness to remind every citizen that "it is the duty as well as the interest of men to make themselves useful to their fellow creatures" (Alexis de Tocqueville, *Democracy in America,* as cited in Reich, *Work of Nations,* p. 24).

never felt that "self-interest" was the only motivator in human endeavors. He wrote fondly of the important role of love, benevolence (or "beneficence"), and respect for family, friends, and community in getting things done. Within the context of a family, for example, personal greed may be of little consequence in directing the actions of family members to help others. In fact, narrowly focused greed by family members can be destructive, giving rise to fights and the dissolution of the family, which often happens, of course.

Love, benevolence, altruism, and concern for others (call the motivating force what you like) can be all that is needed to gain the cooperation of others within the family, mainly because the members may value the welfare of others within the family as much as they value their own welfare. As a consequence, family members can give freely of themselves for the benefit of members, and they can, for the most part, work cooperatively to achieve their commonly shared goals.

The same might be said of friends and, to a lesser extent, members of the broader community in which people live: A person can still be concerned about relevant others. He or she can detect the impact of his or her own actions on the welfare of friends and people in the immediate community and can reasonably expect that favors can be returned in kind, although no formal agreement may ever be made. People simply live by unstated pacts that have the implied provision: "I will help you when you are in need," assuming all relevant others will follow suit when necessary. No doubt, cooperation within the family or broader community draws on a combination of forces, selflessness as well as self-interest, but selflessness is probably of greater importance than many economists might like to think. Indeed, it may be the overwhelming dominating force.

At the same time, Smith was rightfully concerned that the powers of love, benevolence, and altruism have well-circumscribed practical limits. People simply can't be concerned with *all* others in the broader world to the same degree as they are with their loved ones. There are operational limits, so to speak, to the power of love, benevolence, and altruism, beyond which their driving force can be expected to fade. It is then that some other motivator must come into play in order for the "extended order" to actually be extended. When Smith spoke of the importance of self-interest to the "butcher, the brewer, or the baker," he did not intend to say that self-interest is the only motivator in the context of securing our personal needs. He was simply seeking to point out that we often need the cooperation of far more people than those in our family, friends, and immediate community to obtain the things we want.

We often seek the cooperation of far-flung people across the country or globe who have talents that we don't have, who can do things for us that we can't do, or who can do the things more cheaply than we can do them, but who, at the same time, know and care little about us. In that broader context—call them markets—we cannot expect our "dinner" by appealing exclusively to the benevolence of the "butcher, the brewer, or the baker" because the appeals would likely carry too little force, given how far removed those people are from us and how many similar appeals they (the butcher, brewer, baker, or whomever) would have to accommodate.[3]

At the same time, Smith probably chose his words with less care than he should have. He was probably wrong to be so absolute and negative in his position: "We address ourselves, *not* to their humanity but to their self-love, and *never* talk to them of our own necessities but of their advantages."[4] In dealing with others, most of us often do speak to those with whom we have dealing (aside from dealings that have been routinized and reduced to paper or electronic orders) in terms of their humanity and of our necessities, or, at least, such concerns, to one degree or another, are rarely totally absent from our efforts to gain cooperation.

Our shared human experience, our "humanity," invariably means that we feel some of the pain that others feel when they hurt. We rejoice in the successes of others in business and sports whom we do not know. Pictures of gaunt children who are too weak to brush the flies from their bodies enlist emotional and financial responses precisely because "self-love" is not all that matters. News stories of people who have been duped out of their life savings do cause concern. Even well-heeled entrepreneurs who go bankrupt can give rise to concern by others.

At virtually all times, we work from a constellation of motivations, some more or less selfless and others more or less selfish. Our greatest difficulty (and one experienced by Smith) is in putting into words just how our motivations mix and mingle in varying combinations within different circumstances. Nevertheless, our dealings with many others is made possible by our ability to vary our motivations to meet the particular needs of the situation. That is to say, we expect business people to do what they do for more than greed, and we observe that they, like others, frequently do. People who run businesses, like their customers, want

3. Just prior to the famous passage about the butcher and the baker, Smith acknowledged that an individual "has not the time, however, to do this upon every occasion [that is, seek others' good will]. In civilized society he stands at all times in need of the cooperation and assistance of great multitudes, while his whole life is scarcely sufficient to gain the friendship of a few persons" (*Wealth of Nations*, p. 14).

4. Ibid., p. 14.

more from life than to consummate the transactions and make as much money as they can. We expect, seek out, and find that people generally behave fairly reasonably within the constellation of motivations they have and the constraints they face, all of which make up what I mean by the *context* of market and other types of transactions.

The Moral Context

Even market proponents do not always fully appreciate the context, which is necessarily legal *and* moral, within which market participants must operate. Adam Smith certainly did. Few of markets' critics and proponents realize that prior to *The Wealth of Nations*, Smith wrote another treatise, *A Theory of Moral Sentiments*, that may be more important than his later work primarily because of the extent to which the former elevated, even justified, moral concerns and strictures as transcendent, constraining forces within the world. Had he not written the former book, it is virtually certain that Smith (who was a professor of moral philosophy, not economics) would have been more cautious in the words he chose in *The Wealth of Nations*.

In the earlier work he seems to preach (and I use that word advisedly) that no social system—including the market system—could ever work very well without some *framework*, legal and moral, that contains, tempers, and directs the power of self-interest. He wrote eloquently about the "impartial spectator," what we might call our alter ego, to whom we might defer for judgment on the appropriateness, the rightness or wrongness, of what we might do. I suspect that without the prevalence of impartial spectators, Smith would not have been so sanguine about markets as viable forces for the accumulation of personal and national wealth. In fact, Smith staunchly maintained that

> without the restraint which this principle [that is, the impartial spectator] imposes, every passion would upon occasion, rush headlong, if I may say so, to its own gratification. Anger would follow the suggestion of its own fury; fear those of its own violent agitation. Regard to no time or place would induce vanity to refrain from the loudest and most impertinent ostentation; or voluptuousness from the most open indecent, and scandalous indulgence. Respect for what are, for what ought to be, or for what, upon certain conditions, would be, the sentiments of other people is the sole principle which, upon occasion, overawes all those mutations and turbulent passions into that tone and temper which the impartial spectators can enter into and sympathize with.[5]

5. Adam Smith, *The Theory of Moral Sentiments*, in *Adam Smith's Moral and Political Philosophy*, ed. Herbert W. Schneider (New York: Harper & Row, 1970), p. 275.

Smith railed against governments not because he thought the people who run governments are any worse human beings than anyone else, but because he feared (as his experience had shown) that self-interest would not be sufficiently checked in that institutional setting; that, if given the chance, governments might, as they had, abuse the powers at hand, just as business people might do. He recognized the important roles for government, but given the tendency of people in all areas of life to follow their "passions," governments had to be constrained, limited in the scope of their allowable activities.

In order to assess the importance of the *context*, all we have to do today is look around the world to see the consequences of replacing markets with open-ended, centralized bureaucratic and political direction, ostensibly intended to produce a more humane and productive world. The several economies of eastern Europe and the whole of the former Soviet Union were economic basket cases in the late 1980s when they collaspsed, not because the pursuit of private interest had been destroyed (it still was at work in all sorts of ways that were inefficient and counterproductive, resulting in waste and destruction). Rather, those economies collapsed because they no longer had an appropriate legal and moral environment, or context, within which private interests would be adequately constrained, tempered, and directed toward unknown ends.

Those Eastern Bloc economies did not simply arise naturally from the interaction of well-intended people; they were created, somewhat artificially, and imposed on the people of the former communist-bloc countries. In the process, the system of course destroyed private property, which in itself was sufficient to cause great economic harm. More important, the newly created context gave rise to a new form of moral tectonics that began to move within and among the peoples of the former communist-bloc countries and that had the effect of undermining the necessary moral fiber of those societies.

The fundamental problem of communism is that it abruptly disrupted the constellation of motivations and arrangements that people had, though their personal and market dealings, worked out for themselves for their benefit. Instead of seeking to develop and fortify forms of *natural* cooperation among members of families, circles of friends, and the broader community, Soviet citizens were forced to pay their allegiance to the far-flung *state*, which, because people's contributions to the goals were inconsequential and insignificant, given the enormity of the state, was in itself not much of a motivator. Instead of being a moral beacon, it had proved to be a source of official oppression, if not terror.

In the end, the Soviet system collapsed because it arose from the needs of the leaders with little attention to the needs of those the system was supposedly intended to serve. Throughout the communist world there was a great deal of truth in the worker's adage, "We pretend to work, and they pretend to pay us," a saying that must have reflected upon the spiritual vacuum within the citizenry. The citizens of the communist countries had lost the necessary drive and will to work for efficient ends.

Americans, however, need not look beyond the borders of their country, and possibly the borders of their own communities, to see the power of the *context* within which people pursue their interests. Communities abound where markets and cooperative arrangements work exceptionally well without coercion, where people diligently work away, ostensibly pursuing their own goals but serving the ends of others. There are also communities—consider depressed areas of any major metropolitan area—where markets and other social arrangements work very poorly, where social and economic problems abound and fester, because the moral and legal *context* has dissipated. People in those degenerate communities may, at some fundamental level, behave no differently than people elsewhere; they still seek to do the best they can with what they have within the context at hand. The problem is not that people do not know how to trade; all too often it is that the context for trades is corrosive. The lack of moral fiber (for lack of a better turn of words) of too many people (not necessarily close to all) within those communities works against progress; the community members, unwittingly, work for economic retrogression.

The Constructive Context

What makes for a constructive context? That's not a really hard question, although the extent to which the critics avoid it might make one think it is. The context needs markets, lots of them, for reasons Smith gave. But it needs to be acknowledged at the start that markets are founded on exchanges, lots of them. Exchanges cannot be made if there is nothing to trade. In order for trades to occur, people contemplating the trades must have recognized *rights* to things that can be handed over to others.

Markets are everywhere and at all times constrained by rules of property, which, on the one hand, amount to nothing more than definitions of who owns what and, on the other hand, set limits on what people can do with what they possess. I "own" the pen in my vest pocket, which means that you do not have the authority to take it from me. At the same time, my rights to the pen do not extend to my using it as a weapon. These rules of property can be formal—that is, written down—as in the case of automobile ownership, or they can be informally accepted, as in the case of an umbrella that someone lays down on a table in a busy restaurant for a few moments and no one bothers. People in the restaurant understand that the umbrella is "owned" by the person who puts it there.

There must be some reason or some stated or implicit common consensus that leads people to respect the rights that others have for the property. Otherwise, many trades would never occur; few markets would emerge and, if they did emerge, would not work as effectively as they could. Many people would be reluctant to produce anything for fear that the product of their sweat would be taken away. Others would be fearful of giving up what they have in their possession in trade for something else for fear that what they received would not remain theirs for very long.

Property rights can be formalized, codified, and enforced by governments, in which case penalties (in cash, time, and reputation) can be imposed for violations. To the extent that governments are unable to regulate property, of course, fewer trades will exist. Fewer people will engage in production and fewer people will save and invest, fearing that their efforts would be for naught. More people, however, would follow their private interests (or, should we say, instincts) into taking what others have produced.[6]

Where crime is a problem, markets tend to break down, or work less effectively and efficiently than they would otherwise. To make them work properly, crime must be expunged to the extent possible, which means that markets must be carefully constrained with formal limits—that is, rules—on what people can do. Such observations make clear that "free enterprise" is one of the greatest of all oxymorons; there is much that is not "free" about the system.[7] Indeed, it is a highly regulated system—if not more regulated than any other conceivable system—which, no doubt, explains why many people don't like it: They want to

6. Indeed, it is altogether reasonable to speculate that without something other than government enforcing property rights—for example, simple respect for recognized rights—markets might never emerge even with the prospects of government enforcement. At the very instant that the rights were initially defined, people would predate against the property of others, overwhelming the power of the government to enforce limits on people's behavior. In fact, the enforcers, seeing their job as futile, would join in the predation.

7. As Adam Ferguson has reasoned, "liberty or freedom is not, as the origin of the name may seem to imply, an exemption from all restraint, but rather the most effectual application of every just restraint to all members of a free society whether they be magistrates or subjects" [quoted in F. A. Hayek, *The Fatal Conceit: The Errors of Socialism* (Chicago: University of Chicago Press, 1988), p. 3].

be freer to break the rules of property, through crime or government appropriation, and take what others have produced.[8]

Having acknowledged the role of formal property rights in market systems, I do not mean to imply that I have described the full scope, or even a minor portion, of the *context* within which markets must operate in order to be effective and efficient. We need restraints on governments, as Smith reasons, to check the "passions" of those who might govern. Moreover, government enforcement of people's rights cannot be all-pervasive, because it would then likely be too intrusive (and would, then, be unchecked). Much of what people own cannot be protected by formal rules that are enforced by governments. Why? A lot of things in many (but hardly all) places—from toothpicks to napkins to straight pins—simply have too little value (or can be replaced too easily) for states to justify the cost of formal, legal protection. More resources would clearly be absorbed, in other words, in legal protection, than in their replacement when or if they are taken.

A lot of property has ill-defined boundaries, meaning it is not always clear where one person's property begins and another person's ends. Consider the case of a high-powered stereo system that someone "owns." In households and neighborhoods, it is not always clear just what the stereo's owner can do with the stereo, how loud and at what times, for example, the stereo can be played. People can own "clothes," but wearing identified items (punk-rocker chains at a wedding) is not always appropriate. It is simply impossible for governments to draw the numerous lines on what people can do with their property. Moreover, it is often far more cost effective for people to come to understandings on how they should behave and on where to draw the line on their own behavior. *Competition* is a hallmark of efficient markets, but, as in all competitive arenas, there are always necessary boundaries to the ways people can and should compete.

The actual rules of behavior that undergird the simplest of efficiently operating competitive markets extend far beyond the furthest possible reach of any government. This ill-defined but massive constellation of *informal* rules includes virtually all general behavioral dictums that pervade the world's religions, not the least of which are that one should not

8. Even criminals, inclined to break any and every rule made, can be expected to favor the market system—to the extent that others play by the rules of property—because there is more that is saved and invested, more produced, *and* more to be stolen. However, there is an obvious limit to how much crime even criminals would want tolerated. Too much crime can lead to too little production, and too little property for criminals to steal at acceptable costs.

try to gain competitive advantage by killing or maiming competitors or, for that matter, by lying, cheating, bearing false pretenses, and so forth. Markets don't work very well when people lie and cheat whenever they can, and they probably wouldn't work very well if the government had to close off lying and cheating by imposing penalties, given that much lying and cheating would be beyond the purview of governments. The fact that people themselves impose a variety of sanctions and penalties (from looks of disapproval to group exclusion to termination of further dealings) on rule violators adds to the value of the rules by improving the efficiency with which people can interact and make exchanges by increasing the predictability of people's behavior.

Markets probably work best when in fact the participants follow something akin to the Golden Rule, which, in so many words, implies that one should deal with others much as he or she would want to be dealt with. Integrity and respect for the person and property of others are key, unheralded cornerstones of rules that work for efficient markets, as well as virtually all other areas of human behavior. Diligence and bona fide sincerity are other key attributes of efficient markets.

A commitment to personal responsibility—meaning that the consequences of actions are knowingly and willingly accepted—is absolutely vital if markets are to work smoothly and efficiently. A society cannot allow people to be free to do as they wish, presuming that they have the required detailed information of circumstances to make all necessary decisions, and at the same time, allow decision makers to avoid the costs and unpleasant consequences of their decisions. At the same time, personal responsibility must be more than a legal concept with attendant enforcement. Personal responsibility must be accepted as a guiding principle (and duty)—in spite of daunting incentives individuals may have to shift the effects of actions to the "state," a multitude of others, or more generally, "society" at large. Shifting of responsibility can simply reduce the incentives people have to deal honestly, considering the costs of their deals to themselves and those with whom they deal.

Assumption of responsibility can also have a positive impact on how hard and how diligently people work because of the rewards that can come from thinking, "I did it." Even when "a man's conviction that all he achieves is due solely to his exertions, skill, and intelligence may be largely false," notes Hayek, "it is apt to have the most beneficial effects on his energy and circumspection."[9] Indeed, there is value in exaggerat-

9. F. A. Hayek, *The Constitution of Liberty* (Chicago: University of Chicago Press, 1960), p. 83.

ing the importance of personal responsibility given that people have an all-too-strong incentive to be derelict in their duty to be responsible for their actions. They can, in effect, reason all too readily: "In spite of the fact that everyone behaving responsibly can improve the social welfare, it is still true that my *individual* irresponsible actions have no detectable impact on the workings of broader society."

Although economists rarely ever mention their value, markets are greatly dependent upon common, everyday rules of reasonable conduct, such as being pleasant; helping out; persevering; going the second mile; working in earnest; showing courage, loyalty, interest, and concern; offering encouragement; sharing gains; and a host of other major and minor rules of behavior. The rules of reasonable conduct also include the order of respect given individuals and groups (for example, the elderly), the code of who can speak with authority (the respect given to intellectuals), and the multitude of "good manners" (from who goes in the door first to how and when people are expected to eat at the dinner table) that we follow in dealing with others without much thought.

There are many rules that we understand; we explicitly agree to them, in order to achieve well-defined ends, such as restraining democratic processes that we set up for our own time and purposes. The reasons for these rules can be, as they have been, subject to logical discourse.[10] But then there are a multitude of other rules—constraints—on our "passions" that are not so easily explained. Hayek could not have been more perceptive than he was in the epigraph that leads this chapter. In that passage, Hayek insists, as he did with me when I was with him in New York, that in order to understand much of the world we live in, its stresses and strains, we must first acknowledge that civilized society was not designed, per se, not in so many of its most important, pervasive, endearing, and enduring features. Civilized society arose somewhat spontaneously as people began to adhere to a pattern of "traditional and largely *moral* practices" that, ironically, are disliked and unappreciated, whose value cannot be proven. Hayek adds,

> It is no accident that many abstract rules, such as those treating individual responsibility and several property, are associated with economics. . . . Adam Smith was the first to perceive that we have stumbled upon methods of ordering human economic cooperation that exceed the limits of our knowledge and perception. His "invisible

10. For an analysis of constitutional precepts from the perspective of economic theory, see Geoffrey Brennan and James M. Buchanan, *The Reason of Rules: Constitutional Political Economy* (New York: Cambridge University Press, 1985).

> hand" had perhaps better have been described as an invisible or unsurveyable pattern. . . . Almost all of us serve people who we do not know, even of whose existence we are ignorant; and we in turn constantly live on the services of other people of whom we know nothing. All this is possible because we stand in a great framework of institutions and traditions—economic, legal, and moral—into which we fit ourselves by obeying certain rules of conduct that we never made, and which we have never understood in the sense in which we understand how the things that we manufacture function.[11]

Similarly, it is no accident that proponents of markets remain some of the strongest proponents of morality, not so much religious tenets, per se (although religion has often been helpful in fortifying markets), but generally acknowledged rules of reasonable behavior.

Modern critics of the way society works have been adept at exploring how markets "fail"—that is, don't work as efficiently as advertised.[12] They have not been so adept at exploring the changes to the critical underlying institutional, especially moral, setting on which markets are founded. The reason is that the rules are the consequences of an evolutionary process, or trial and error, that take generations to develop, which means their value is hard to explain. It is in the ongoing tectonic changes to that underlying, moral institutional setting that we can find reason for pessimism for the future.

Cultural Evolution

People are good at designing and redesigning relatively simple "things"—cars, boats, buildings, toothpicks, and so on. People are also reasonably adept at designing games and organizing relatively small numbers of people into associations and firms. As the Founding Fathers demonstrated, they also can, on occasion, be pretty good at developing constitutions, or the broad rules for making a sequence of future political decisions. However, there is much about civilization that people could not possibly design, not the least of which are the complex overlapping

11. Critics, such as John Kenneth Galbraith and his students, have pointed to the market power of large firms that, when exercised, means that production is restricted while prices are raised. The critics also stress that markets are beset with "externalities," or spillover effects that lead, at times, to too much of certain goods and services being produced and, at other times, too little.

12. The so-called external cost of pollution means that someone other than producers will bear the cost of production and that the products will be underpriced and oversold. The so-called external benefit of community beautification efforts means that beautification will be underpriced and undersold.

webs of forever changing interrelationships we have with others close to us and those far removed from us, and the myriad rules that constrain and direct our everyday behavior. However, as the philosopher David Hume stated more bluntly and prophetically, "The rules of morality are not the conclusions of our reason."[13]

Hayek spent his career explaining why that is so, which is remarkable only because the essence of his explanation is so straightforward: *People simply don't have the intelligence to design complex and extended human arrangements, nor has anyone actually designed the arrangements, at least not in their essential details.* No one person knows enough about what others want or about how others want to operate and work, what trade-offs they are willing to make, or what adjustments will be made in order to be very good at complex institutional design. No one person could possibly understand what works, especially when it comes to a complex web of rules of behavior for a multitude of people.

Indeed, much of the information required for complex human institutional design is unknowable, simply because so much of what needs to be known is subjective and subject to change, if not rapid fluctuation. People often don't know exactly what they want until they seek to satisfy some ill-conceived unease. While people might be able to imagine exactly how they may be able to relate productively to a relatively small number of other people (within their family, friends, and community), they cannot know the details of the diverse ways the people with whom they relate will relate to many other people and how those people in turn will relate to an unknown multitude of others.

Critics might retort: "Well, we admit that the intelligence of individuals is severely circumscribed, but their individual limitations can be overcome by utilizing the brainpower of a number of institutional designers who can work together, with the aid of very large computers, to construct complex institutional settings." Yes, Marx and Lenin thought they could plan an entire economy larger than most continents, and then much of the rest of the world, with all the guiding principles laid out in a few hundred pages of text.

The fundamental problem of broad-based institutional design is, again, that so much of what needs to be known is unknowable; there is no such thing as "societal knowledge" independent of what people, as individuals, know. Even if the requisite information for design of what Hayek calls "extended order" could be assembled in one place (which is impossible), it would easily overwhelm the capacity of the largest con-

13. Quoted in Hayek, *Fatal Conceit*, p. 3.

ceivable group of institutional designers to handle intelligently. In Hayek's words, "Knowledge exists only as the knowledge of individuals. It is not much more than a metaphor to speak of the knowledge of society as a whole. The sum of the knowledge of all the individuals exists nowhere as an integrated whole. The great problem is how we can profit from this knowledge, which exists only dispersed as the separate, partial, and sometimes conflicting beliefs of all men."[14] Institutional designers would inevitably face the plain fact that "not all the knowledge of the ever changing particular facts that man continually uses lends itself to organization and systematic expositon."[15] In order to reduce the design problem to manageable proportions, the designers would likely seek *sameness,* not the *diversity* of ways people work productively together, and they certainly would be inclined to reduce the flexibility and, hence, efficiency of the system.

How, then, did civilization, as we know it, emerge? Hayek's quick answer is that complex societies *evolved,* gradually and persistently, albeit through a lot of fits and starts, trials and errors, as people used the liberty at their disposal to do as they wished. (To say that rules "evolved" is not to say that the evolutionary process is mindless with no one ever trying well-thought-out rules, only that a lot of what was tried was scrapped, set aside, as it was supplanted by superior rules.) As people interacted with others, using the information at hand, they progressively formed more complex webs of interrelationships based on tried rules (some of which worked and some of which did not) that eventually became commonly accepted (and, only then, partially codified). But they have never been able to codify or even just articulate the fine details of the diverse ways people interact; they could not, given their complexity and the span of time over which the details of the complex web were constituted. In this sense, no one person or group intentionally *designed* the "extended order" we now observe around us (in much the same way that no one *designed* the array of species in the natural world).[16] At any one time, people can productively tinker with only a few of the ways people interact and the rules they follow. For the most part, they must allow the extended order to emerge "sponta-

14. Hayek, *Constitution of Liberty,* pp. 24–25.

15. Ibid., p. 25.

16. Hayek maintains it is misleading to assert "that man has created his civilization and that he therefore can also change its institutions as he pleases. The assertion would be justified only if man had deliberately created civilzaton in full understanding of what he was doing or if he at least clearly knew how it was being maintained" (ibid., p. 23).

neously," meaning not so much "abruptly" as "naturally" from internal forces that feed and react to one another. This is not to say that during any period a subset of people (the Founding Fathers, for example) cannot impose a rules system, only that they can productively scope out the broad framework, with the details of the order to be worked out by subsequent interactions of people in their private or political affairs.

The absence of intentional design of the extended order implies that people, at some distant point in the past, had literally to stumble upon many, if not practically all, of the most important rules they now follow: "What are chiefly responsible for having generated this extraordinary order, and the existence of mankind in its present size and structure," Hayek writes, "are the rules of human conduct that generally evolved (especially those dealing with several property, honesty, contract, exchange, trade, competition, gain, and privacy.)"[17]

Similar to natural evolution, many variations of the rules were tried over vast stretches of time in different places. Some rules worked; most rules that were tried probably did not. Those groups who stumbled upon, accepted, and found ways to sustain efficient rules survived and prospered, while those who inadvertently tried inefficient rules did not. Some groups languished or regressed simply because they did not follow the right rules (or maybe followed too few rules, meaning constraints, or were not able to sustain the efficient rules that were tried). Unlike natural evolution, however, the rules [that "largely consist of prohibitions ('shalt not's') that designate adjustable domains for individual decisions"] were not, for the most part, passed down by instinct, meaning genetic direction. Rather, they were passed along "by tradition, teaching and imitation." In fact, Hayek observed that "mankind achieved civilization by developing and learning to follow rules (first in territorial tribes and then over broader reaches) that often forbade him to do what his instincts demanded, and no longer depended upon common perception of events."[18] Fortunately, children are born helpless, requiring long years of parental nurturing and rearing in the ways of the family and communities they have joined. During their formative years, they can be taught or can learn from experience what is expected of them and how to behave with respect to others.

However, the learning process may be fortified by genetics. James Q. Wilson argues that the evolutionary process causes people to acquire an inherent "moral sense," that reflects a combination of self- and other-

17. Hayek, *Fatal Conceit*, p. 12.
18. Ibid.

motivated behavior.[19] People who are always motivated by self-interests will not likely prosper and out-compete other groups, given that so much can be produced and gained through the cooperation of many people; they will tend to fall by the wayside. Wilson points out that if two people are in the woods and are approached by a tiger, the winning strategy for the survival of either or both is not likely to be self-interest over the long run. Each runner might reason that all that he or she had to do was to outrun the other person, not outrun the tiger. The tiger would stop after capturing the first runner. However, the problem with that strategy is that the tiger could then just pick off one runner at a time. The successful groups are likely to be those who cooperate, who, in the case of the tiger, stand their ground together. Getting the runners to cooperate requires more than self-interested behavior, given the incentive inherent in the noncooperative strategy. The noncooperative, self-interested incentive must be neutralized, either through the members of the group understanding the difference between "right" and "wrong," or achieving a sense of "how they ought to act when one is free to act voluntarily. . . . By 'ought' I mean an obligation binding on all people similarly situated."[20]

Hayek's vision of cultural evolution leads to several observations about rules of extended order.

1. The benefits of the rules that are extant are realized as successive generations adopt and gradually improve upon the rules and as they survive and prosper. The people within any given generation cannot always fully appreciate the value of the rules; their full value is realized over multiple generations, only when they are followed by those generations. The full value of the "several rules" of private property, for example, emerge only when those rights are commonly accepted and when people act upon those rights to trade, save, and invest and then pass down wealth to succeeding generations. (In "econospeak," the benefits of the rules are largely "external" to the people who must follow them and bear the costs of restraint.)
2. There is no necessary logic to, or rational reason for, many of the rules of successful extended orders. They just work. What constitutes good manners is not always evident. Some forms of behavior—for example, a polite smile on meeting someone—simply synergize working relationships.

19. James Q. Wilson, *The Moral Sense* (New York: Free Press, 1993), p. xii.
20. Ibid.

3. Individuals may naturally dislike many of the rules, primarily because the rules constrain their individual behavior and deny them the immediate pleasure that might come from following their more basic instincts and impulses. Rules against stealing, lying, and premarital and extramarital sex, as with rules against overeating, are especially constraining as well as difficult to rationalize and, apparently, to follow. Each individual may rightfully reason that his or her violations of the rules would have an inconsequential impact on the long-term development of society. One person stealing from the local grocer would, *by itself*, obviously have no perceptible impact on the course of civilization. Hence, there is an ever-present temptation for everyone to violate the rules, which necessarily means that most of the rules of reasonable behavior are fragile and tenuous at best and in need of continuous fortification. Violations can be self-enforcing, leading to more violations with the gradual erosion of the rules' social value. Cheating on tests can lead to cheating by a growing number of students, given that each student has a greater need to protect his or her relative position in points. Stealing is rampant in riots simply because each person is less likely to be caught.
4. Given the absence of a rational basis for many of the rules of the extended order, the rules are subject to destruction by overly critical rational evaluation (for example, by social scientific and cost/benefit analysis). A poor person who appraises the costs and benefits of the theft of food can easily justify his or her actions, when those actions are considered separate from everyone else (or just every other poor person) making similar calculations.
5. Given the inherent and abiding incentives for people to violate the rules of extended order, the rules must be inculcated—that is, instilled as basic virtues, religious precepts, or absolute societal dictums, not subject to radical questioning. Parents often teach their children the Ten Commandments, or some other similar set of religious dictums, *as if* they were sent from God or *as if* they are beyond dispute under virtually all circumstances. Allowing people to question the rules can lead to reenforcing violations.
6. Rules must have some rigidity. Otherwise, they can lose much of their value in making the behavior of others predictable. At the same time, they must retain some flexibility. Rules must have some give or ability to change with circumstances. As his students attest, the late Frank Knight, University of Chicago economist/social philosopher, held high the social importance of "relatively ab-

> solute absolutes," which is what some rules must be.[21] They cannot be absolute, never subject to violation or change. As a practical matter, there are no absolutes (other than that statement), or so Knight argued; there are always exceptions or conditions under which rules should be violated or adjusted in one way or another. But, then, there are good reasons for treating some rules almost *as if* they are inviolate or not subject to change. Some rules can be adjusted, but only after careful thought or much experience that a change is required. The Ten Commandments or rules of markets can be viewed as "relatively absolute absolutes," subject to change but only after compelling evidence that they should be violated. The problem with admitting to relatively absolute absolutes is that the prospects that some rules can be adjusted in one way or another can lead to the corruption of the rules, given the delicate balance between flexibility and inflexibility that must be maintained and the inherent incentives people have to violate the rules for reasons that are not so compelling. (The incentives to violate the rules of reasonable behavior are no less powerful than the incentives that made the rules necessary and productive.) Moreover, we cannot always understand the long-run consequences of violating any rule, given the multitude of adjustments people will make with one another and in other rules in the interlocking network of rules.

In small groups, rules can be self-enforcing. Violations can be easily detected and blame can be assessed. But allegiance to rules can break down in larger groups, simply because the actions of individuals are difficult to detect and, often, inconsequential. In larger groups, people have daunting incentives to disobey the rules or, in some way, to get around them—that is, to cater to the temptation of not suffering the costs that individuals must incur when abiding by the rules. (Again, in "econospeak," everyone has an inclination, from a purely rational perspective, based on the costs and benefits perceived individually, to "free ride" on the rules while at the same time hoping that all others abide by the rules.[22]) Fortunately, experimental research in economics reveals that people are not as rational as economists speculate. People

21. As noted by James M. Buchanan, who was one of Frank Knight's students, in his classes.

22. The incentives individuals have to "free ride" in the context of small and large groups is analyzed by Mancur Olson, *The Logic of Collective Action* (Cambridge, Mass.: Harvard University Press, 1965).

are, at times and to a degree, willing to forgo gains that can be had by violating group rules and other efforts to pursue common, shared objectives.[23] People's tendencies to cooperate may be "natural," a consequence of genes, but their tendencies seem to be the consequence of considerable efforts to instill the value of rules.

How are the rules instilled? Probably the best answer is "in a variety of ways." Fortunately, given that children develop slowly for a relatively long period, there is time for repeating the necessity of following rules so frequently that they can be imprinted, to one degree or another, as a basic value or virtue, constraining, to a potentially tolerable degree, people's future choices. Children often look to their parents for the rules they follow and imitate, simply because they wish to avoid the arduous task of finding their own constraining rules that are acceptable to others.

Children also learn the ways of their culture through stories, poems, and songs. "The Little Engine That Could" is clearly intended to teach perseverance. The Berenstain Bears is a whole series of children's books intended to teach within families and communities the rules of reasonable behavior, from the necessity of picking up one's things to the need to share and cooperate with others. Aesop's fables are full of moral lessons. "The Goose That Laid the Golden Egg" teaches that people need to control their desires. When the man and wife cut the goose open in hope of increasing their riches, they discover their goose, in Aesop's words, "was just like any other goose. Thus, they neither got rich all at once, as the had hoped, nor enjoyed any longer the daily addition to their wealth."

Adults pass along rules, showing where and how the rules can be good for those who follow them. Following many rules makes good, logical sense, given other people may be following the same rules. However, parents also exaggerate—at times, inadvertently, and at other times, purposely—their value to their children. Almost all parents tell their children that undesired behavior, from lying to stealing, does not pay, when in fact they, the parents, know that such behavior often does pay. Contrary to all societal admonitions, lies often give advantage to those who purvey them. Even crime frequently pays, often handsomely. Few shoplifters ever get caught and punished; drug dealers can get rich. Nevertheless, to the extent that children buy into the mythology that lying and stealing do not pay and hold to it, society can gain the benefits of more production and trade at lower cost.

23. See Richard Thaler, *Winner's Curse* (New York: Free Press, 1992), especially chap. 2.

The mythology that obeying rules is intrinsically valuable to *individuals* can pay for society taken as a whole, but, ironically, not necessarily for all the individuals taken separately. The irony of rules is that rational results for all concerned can be achieved from irrational or nonrational acceptance of the rules by individuals. Efforts by individuals to find a rational basis for their *individual* allegiance to the rules cannot only be in vain, but can be destructive, given that the absence of rational foundations for many rules can cause individuals to forgo allegiance to them. Once the rules start to prevail, they can be self-enforcing and self-extending. People can follow rules because other people do, and they can do so for the same reason that they speak the same language, get up at approximately the same time, or use the same currency: It is cost effective. They also don't like the sanctions (from frowns to ostracism) that are often imposed (inspite of the fact that it may not be rational or cost effective for them to do so) on those who violate the rules.

Religious training can be especially useful in promoting adherence to rules, mainly because most religions presume the existence of an omnipresent, omniscient, and omnipotent God who defines rules for acceptable behavior which he (or she) expects people to follow. Without God's presence (in fact or as a perception), people may figure that they can violate the rules with impunity. With God around, however, believers must figure that he can record (with some reasonable probability) all violations and impose appropriate penalties, thus giving people meaningful personal incentives to obey the rules. If everyone obeys the rules, then their social benefits are realized. Everyone is better off, a fact that may be attributed to God's presence (regardless of whether he exists).

I do not need to get into a dispute over whether or not God exists; that issue is irrelevant for my purposes. I need only point out that if he does exist, he can serve a very useful social function of getting people to observe reasonable rules of behavior. If he does not exist, but people behave *as if* he does exist (out of respect or fear), then the pretense of his existence can have much the same effect—improvement in social welfare that comes from efficiently operating markets and other social processes as people abide by reasonable rules of behavior. If he does not exist, people would want to create Him and carefully nurture the view that he does exist (as they may have done) to garner the benefits of an extended order.[24]

24. This line of reasoning is developed at length by me in "The Economic Dimensions of Ethical Behavior," *Ethics*, April 1977, pp. 208-21.

Concluding Comments

Regardless of how people induce allegiance to rules of reasonable behavior, they must do it in order to survive—and certainly to prosper. If people were as self-interested as a superficial reading of Adam Smith might suggest or as rational and calculating on every possible margin, markets or any other social processes would not work very well at all. Clearly, many trades would not be made, because each trader would fear that the other would take what is offered without handing over what he or she agreed to give up in the exchange. Once all agreed to respect the property rights of others, for example, everyone would immediately violate those rights, knowing that the enforcers of the rights would be overwhelmed with violations.

The fact is that people have prospered because they have overcome their own rational inclinations and have accepted rules that circumscribe the realm of rational actions. They have stumbled upon efficient rules of property and ethics, and they have found ways of sustaining those rules, in spite of their tenuous nature.

I hasten to add, however, that such comments are no longer fully relevant for segments of our civilization. As we will se in chapter 8, some rules of reasonable behavior that have worked for the extended order have begun to lose their force within segments of society. For those groups, the extended order has begun to contract. The economic futures of some, as a consequence, look bleak. That is a dismal assessment to which we can now turn.

8

MORAL TECTONICS

> For 60 years, since the New Deal, Americans who wanted to solve national problems have thought and talked about government programs and policies. And now this mode of thinking and talking suddenly seems inadequate, maybe even archaic. Today, government is increasingly beside the point: not because government has changed but because our problems have.
>
> Jonathan Rauch,
> "America's Crack-Up"

When Los Angeles shook in January 1994, freeway bridges crumbled, gas lines busted, fires broke out everywhere in the vicinity of the epicenter, tall buildings swayed and cracked at their foundations. The earthquake of 1994 forced many L.A. commuters, famed for their allegiance to their automobiles, to telecommute to their downtown offices or to reconfigure their trips to lower the increase in their commute times.

Television newsrooms were left in shambles. Nevertheless, reporters and camera crews lost little time getting to the hardest hit areas, ready and eager to convey their and others' impressions on the deaths, damage to people's emotional security, and the destruction to the area's physical infrastructure—meaning roads, bridges, communication facilities, and water and gas lines. Getting pictures and sound bites that would pull on viewers' emotions were easy assignments, given the magnitude of the destruction, and vivid (perhaps somewhat exaggerated) reports on the area's economic losses were sent across the country and around the globe within minutes of the jolt.

Because of such natural disasters, we can fully appreciate the value of the nation's *infrastructure* to the economic health of the country. We can see secondhand, as L.A. residents endured firsthand, the havoc that comes with its demise, especially when it is sudden and is caused by jarring shifts in the earth's tectonic plates, totally out of the control of those who must suffer the consequences.

It is all too easy for us to think that the *physical* infrastructure is the only infrastructure that is important to a thriving economy. We can *see* the physical infrastructure, even *touch* it, and we know what to do when it is in disarray: *repair* it, which we generally know how to do. Within sixty days of the earthquake, a major overpass on L.A.'s busiest freeway that was left broken in pieces in the quake's aftermath had been reincarnated stronger and more shock-resistant than ever, thanks in part to a multimillion-dollar bonus the construction company received for beating the tight reconstruction deadline. The economic losses from the January earthquake were painful but, thankfully, they were relatively short-lived for the overall California economy.

But is the *physical* infrastructure the only infrastructure of consequence, or even the most important infrastructure that an economy must sustain? The last chapter suggests not. Common sense suggests not, or else the L.A. area, or any other area that is socked with a natural disaster, could not possibly bounce back as quickly as it did. Jonathan Rauch, a perceptive freelance journalist whose words head this chapter, suggests that the physical infrastructure is hardly the one that Americans must worry about.[1] He and others have begun to catch on that the economy has a *moral*, as well as *physical*, foundation that for segments of society may be crumbling in a slow but relentless rumble.

The Great Physical/Moral Divide

The country does have some bridges that are falling apart and maybe thousands of miles of the interstate system are in need of substantial repair. However, most of the bridges and miles of roads have never been in better shape. John Tatom, an economist with the Federal Reserve Bank of St. Louis, argues that contrary to the claims of critics, the country does not really have a widespread physical "infrastructure crisis," as our bridge-and-road problems have been characterized, probably with political intent.[2] We may have misallocated some of our infrastructure expen-

1. Jonathan Rauch, "America's Crack-Up," *Los Angeles Times Magazine*, July 26, 1992, pp. 22–23, 31–32.

2. John A. Tatom, "Is an Infrastructure Crisis Lowering the Nation's Productivity?" *Review* (Federal Reserve Bank of St. Louis, November/December 1993): 3–21. Tatom reports a slowdown in the *growth* of the net public capital stock since the late 1970s but not an absolute decline in it. He also found no connection between the slowdown in

ditures (for example, spent too much on dome stadiums and too little on back-road bridges), but the "net stock of public capital" has continued to grow, albeit at times at a slower pace, in total and per capita real dollar value since at least World War II. The slowdown in America's overall productivity growth rate cannot be attributed to changes in the growth rate of the infrastructure, contrary to what critics have charged and much of the public has accepted. Furthermore, our infrastructure expenditures will surely surge in the 1990s and beyond as even more budget dollars are devoted to the creation of the heralded "electronic superhighway," that might just rival the freeway system in terms of importance in the country's future overall infrastructure. That infrastructure is expanding apace as more and more people and businesses buy computers with modems and create their own web pages and make use of others. Moreover, hordes of special-interest lobbyists who ply the halls of the nation's seats of political power are fully prepared to lay down substantial campaign contributions to ensure that politicians do not forget the interests of the infrastructure industries. Politicians love to "bring home the bacon," which now is more often than not reinforced concrete and redesigned domestic and global telecommunication systems.

What we don't have as a country in the way of physical (infrastructure) assets doesn't seem to be a major problem, especially when compared with what so many other people in the world do without. We have plenty of "stuff" and continue to produce more "stuff" year by year. If the country's central problem were merely physical, we would surely be blessed, because we would clearly know how to fix it. Nevertheless, the country is fraught with problems that seem to be growing and that seem to be at the heart of so much angst Americans have over their futures.

Rauch argues that it may be time for us to openly recognize that we have another form of infrastructure, a *moral* one, that in the long run may be far more important to the country's future prosperity than the physical infrastructure. Yet it may be more difficult to define, discuss, sustain, and fix.

The problem with the sustainability of the *moral infrastructure,* or the underlying complex webs of rules that restrain individual behavior for collective ends, is severalfold. People may appreciate the moral infrastructure for its own sake (because, for example, of religious values), but

---

the growth of the infrastructure and the slowdown in the growth in worker productivity.

not for the economy's sake; the connections may be too tenuous. Few economists, among others, have ever stopped to think that morality may be at the core of an efficient market economy; they like to think that they do *science*, not normative philosophy, that an economy can function well without a moral base so long as property rights are legally enforced and unfettered exchanges at freely floating prices are permitted and encouraged.

The moral infrastructure is not concrete, literally and figuratively. We can't touch it, clearly see its boundaries, or know exactly how to repair it, given that, as stressed in the previous chapter, it may have evolved gradually over the ages and may never have been the product of human design—and may not be subject to deliberate human reconstruction with the best of design intentions. Its fraying (which may be hard to distinguish from the expected evolutionary accommodations to changes in conditions), slow but persistent, may go undetected until considerable damage has been done. Then once its fraying has become recognized, there may be few individuals or interest groups (given the free-rider problem) with the necessary motivation to repair it or to see that others help with the repairs. And, unfortunately, we can't turn to government to make things right with the moral infrastructure, because government may also draw its viability, or lack thereof, from the underlying moral structure. Moreover, an infrastructure can't simply be superimposed on people; it must evolve upward from people as they interact over long stretches of time. An imposed moral infrastructure from on top would also likely be too rigid and too uniform across wide variations in conditions, unable to continue its own evolutionary process. When it comes to morality, there are, regrettably, no "quick fixes," the type that Washington loves to feed on.

Nevertheless, the strains and stresses from this changing moral infrastructure may be no less real and no less destructive than those physical strains and stresses that built up and caused the 1994 L.A. quake. A form of *moral tectonics*, the quiet unseen shifting of the fundamental ground rules of society, may be a root cause of many Americans' angst, for much the same reasons that L.A. quake victims lost their swaddling sense of security in the sudden rumble they felt. The main difference between earth-based plate tectonics and the more elusive moral tectonics is that in moral tectonics the destructive energy is only rarely released in sudden jolts—for example, rioting and looting in city streets. Most often the destruction comes gradually bit by bit, instance by instance, through the often minor transgressions of isolated individuals, the net effects of which result first in imparied productivity and income growth and then in outright retrogression, growing fears and worries, and pervasive pessimism about the future.

For the most part, this book has been upbeat. I see unbounded potential for *most* Americans, but only for those who are able and willing to seize the expanding array of opportunities. To seize them, however, many Americans will have to stay with or return to their moral roots to fortify the rules of reasonable behavior within their own groups. Otherwise, prosperity will pass them by.

Rules of behavior are not all that matter, of course. But they matter a great deal more to the economy and future prosperity than most people might suppose. As stressed in chapter 7, rules of self-restraint ultimately make a prosperous market economy possible simply because they reduce the cost of interactions and increase people's predictability. However, society is at all times involved in a delicate balancing act between unleashing the productive power of pursuit of self-interest and its confinement.[3]

In my view, the distinction between the "haves" and "have nots" may not be a totally defunct social division. Clearly, many people's economic problems are a consequence of what they don't have in the way of incomes, education, and opportunities. Poverty is not something that is always easy to overcome. Some people are falling behind economically not because of things they may or may not have done but because market forces have turned against them. The incomes of many hardworking union members are falling because the world has become more competitive for all workers. By the same token, the distinction between the "haves" and "have nots" based on incomes and material well-being has probably become overused, if not antiquated, as well as a facile description of a human division whose value has dissipated. Again, that isn't to say that people aren't partitioned in many large and small ways by incomes and wealth. All one has to do is to drive through Los Angeles, or any other major urban center, and see the sudden changes in the look, feel, and prosperity of adjoining neighborhoods.

However, the importance of the gaping material divides in society have been greatly exaggerated. Sure, there were poor people who rioted and looted stores in South-Central Los Angeles in 1992, in the wake of another quake, the first verdict in the Rodney King/police beating trial.

3. This social dilemma is developed at length by Geoffrey Brennan and James M. Buchanan, *The Reason of Rules: Constitutional Political Economy* (New York: Cambridge University Press, 1985).

However, not all of the people who rioted were poor by the income standards of this or other countries. There were many desperately poor people in L.A. and around the country who were horrified at the actions of their much more well-off compatriots. Furthermore, almost all of the "have not" Americans today have far more materials and incomes to work and advance with than the "have" Americans did in our not-too-distant past, facts that must make us wonder if it is what people have, or do not have, that determines their behavior, including what rules they follow. Contrary to conventional wisdom, hordes of low-income Americans still do move up the income distribution while others languish.

All of this is to say that the great divide of have and have nots is, more than we may like to admit, largely irrelevant to the new world order, and that material divide, while still relevant, is surely becoming progressively less relevant for explaining the changing economic order, including the angst. That does not mean that the divides are missing. On the contrary, I see a division emerging all right, but it is an old division that has been at work on the income and wealth gap. The division that seems to be crystallizing is the age-old one between those who are willing to live by tried-and-true fundamental rules of reasonable conduct and those who are not. This division is starkly self-evident in the difference in behavior of inner-city gang members who have virtually no respect of life, limb, and property of others outside of their immediate order and the members of inner-city church circles who never miss an opportunity to pass along a kind word or return forgotten property to its rightful owner.

The latter group exists in the kind of extended order that I discussed with reference to the work of F. A. Hayek in the last chapter. Whether rich or poor, members of this latter group can expect to prosper because they can draw on the cooperation of people in far-off places through community associations and markets. These latter group members have, at least, the *potential* of escaping from their circumstances, even if they are in dire circumstances. Members of the former groups, however, exist in a highly reduced order and may find the future dimmed by the fact that they will not be able to participate in the extended order until they change their ways and adopt more reasonable rules of behavior. Their potential for escape is no doubt limited, not so much by their limited incomes and resources, but by the fact that their rules of behavior are relevant only to the boundaries of their immediate group. Members of gangs, and similar groups, are out of step with the dictates of the moral infrastructure that binds outside groups together.

The Moral Infrastructure

The very mention of a *moral infrastructure* may conjure images of unthinking religious, if not dogmatic, strictures, maybe those precepts central to the constant wailing of the so-called religious right or the moral majority. Such an infrastructure necessarily has a religious quality to it, but religious dicates are not all that Rauch has in mind, mainly because he—and I—do not wish to be detracted by knee-jerk religious conflicts over semantics and religious affiliation. What he means by *moral infrastructure* is that set of fundamental, pervasive, guiding principles, precepts, or morals (call them what you will) that we intuitively understand make for the good, honorable, just, as well as efficient society precisely because they enable us to link up, form nets and communities, and work together not perfectly, but with some reasonable degree of predictable fluidity.

Everyone probably has a lengthy list of favored precepts, but it is likely that many lists have a number of precepts in common. Rauch chose to isolate five such common precepts mainly to frame the discussion:

1. Lawfulness and honesty.
2. Education.
3. Thrift: saving and investment.
4. Diligence: the willingness to work hard and do one's best.
5. Strong family: meaning a family that is dependable for its members, especially children.[4]

Rauch was no doubt on target when he concluded, "In the longer term, a society, or an individual, that gets all five right cannot be stopped, absent bad luck. A society, or an individual, that gets them wrong cannot be saved, absent good fortune."[5]

Personally, I like his list for starters, short and sweet, well-suited for the audience he was addressing. Not to quibble, but only to be more complete and avoid misunderstanding, I would add honor, integrity, acceptance of consequences (for good and bad) that come with actions, basic respect, sense of duty, and acceptance of differences. The implied rules of reasonable conduct make economic progress possible.

The Evidence of Moral Tectonics

America's most fundamental problem may not be so much with the economy per se as with the country's underlying moral infrastructure

4. Rauch, "America's Crack-Up," p. 22.
5. Ibid.

that now has serious fissures, mainly due to what seem to be shifts in some of the underlying social and intellectual tectonic plates. Evidence on the decay is necessarily fragmentary and incomplete, but all around us, a point Rauch stresses. The demise of the virtue of lawfulness and honesty is apparent on nightly television newscasts, if not in real-life scenes that pepper neighborhoods and business districts.

Nearly 15 million violent and property crimes were reported in 1991 (that's a major crime for every 17 Americans), with the total of the two categories up 15 percent from 1982 (and that data does not include the likely immense number of crimes that went unreported).[6] During the 1982–1991 period, total violent crimes rose 45 percent, while property crimes rose 12 percent. No wonder the country employed in 1992 more than 2 million people in "protective services," with more private security guards than public police officers in the total.[7]

The National Coalition Against Domestic Violence reports that a woman is battered every 15 seconds in the country and that a quarter of the murders of women are committed by their spouses. The murders of O. J. Simpson's wife and her friend, allegedly at the hand of Simpson, captured the imagination of the media and the public in mid-1994, especially given Simpson's chase scene on an L.A. freeway in prime-time television. However, the crime was nothing particularly novel by 1994, given that the L.A. County prosecutor files a murder case against an abusive husband every nine days.[8] However, spouse battering is hardly for "men only." Half of spousal murders are committed by women. According to one 1985 survey, men and women assault each other in about equal numbers (with 2 million assaults by women on their husbands and 1.8 million assaults by men on their wives). Moreover, women were responsible for 54 percent of spousal injuries that were

6. All statistics not attributed to specific sources were obtained from Department of Commerce, Bureau of the Census, *Statistical Abstract of the United States: 1993* (Washington: Government Printing Office, 1993).

7. The overall crime *rate* (crimes per 100,000 Americans) did not, of course, rise as rapidly, given population increase, but it still rose more than 5 percent over nine years. Murders were up 8 percent; forcible rape, 24 percent; robbery, 14 percent; and aggravated assault, 50 percent. The total property crime *rate* rose only 2 percent between 1982 and 1991, but that was only because burglaries fell by 16 percent. Larceny/theft rose by 5 percent. Given that automobile theft rose by 50 percent, it is apparent the criminals were reallocating their scarce resources, perhaps with the profits from all crimes rising.

8. As reported in "Spouse Battering: The Crime Wave Too Often Forgotten," *Los Angeles Times*, June 21, 1994, p. B8.

judged to be "severe."[9] And these statistics do not include reports on a host of other crimes and dastardly deeds, including, for instance, more than 2 million (reported) cases of child abuse.[10]

Between the end of World War II and the mid-1970s, the percentage of the population in the nation's prisons drifted up irregularly but slightly, only to take a sharp upward turn in the early 1970s, mainly due to drug-related crimes.[11] Prison overcrowding is now a major political issue in spite of the fact that we keep building more prisons. Thc typical American prison has 15 percent more prisoners than it was built to handle. However, that percentage hides differences among states. Texas prisons have four times as many prisoners as the state's prisons were designed to handle. Florida has two and a half as many. In 1978, there were 71 Americans in jail for every 100,000 people in the population; eleven years later, the number of inmates per 100,000 Americans was up to 171, an increase of 140 percent.[12] Although the count of serious crimes began to fall off modestly in the early 1990s (by 3 percent between 1992 and 1993, to be exact), the long-run trend in crime is a particularly pressing problem among young people, especially young males within African-American communities. In 1991, over three-fourths of all crimes against others were committed by people age eighteen to forty-four, which suggests that the aging process is the best known antidote for crime.[13]

Americans lead the industrial world in crime. Our rape rate is 27 times that of the Japanese. Our robbery rate is 157 times theirs. Our robbery and rape rates are four times the rates in Germany. And the cost of all the crime? At least $600 billion a year, according to one estimate,[14] a tidy total that exceeds the gross domestic product of many industrial coun-

9. The reason for the widely held view that spousal abuse is for women only is that women are nine times as likely to report their abuse [as reported by Judith Sherven and James Sniechowski, "Women Are Responsible, Too," *Los Angeles Times*, June 21, 1994, p. B9].

10. Ibid.

11. See David Copal, "Prison Blues: How America's Foolish Sentencing Policies Endanger Public Safety," *Policy Analysis* (Washington: Cato Institute, May 17, 1994).

12. Ibid., pp. 3–4.

13. In 1990, white females had a homicide rate of just under 3 per 100,000 females; their black counterparts had a homicide rate five times higher. White males had a homicide rate of 9, but black males' homicide rate was nine times higher—and 25 times the homicide rate of white females. Crime among the nation's youth, especially the African-Americans, has become epidemic, casual, and vicious, with teenagers killing for as little as a pair of sneakers or a wrong look. More than a fourth of all black men under age twenty-five either have been in prison or are in prison.

14. Copal, "Prison Blues," p. 23.

tries. However, the computed costs may be only a minor percentage of the total cost of crime and, more generally, dishonesty, given that automobile, health, and workman's compensation insurance fraud is rampant.

The stories are common: One person backs his or her car into another car at three miles per hour in a parking lot with barely a scratch on the bumper. However, the occupants in the car that was hit all claim that the "violent crash" caused untold "pain and suffering." A city bus is disabled by a minor collision; nevertheless, the personal-injury claims are some multiple of the number of paid riders, primarily because people (as video tapes revealed) scrambled to get on the bus *after* it was disabled in order to participate in any settlement claims.[15]

In spite of the starkness of the easily tabulated reported crimes, the country's moral foundation is felt in much smaller, more subtle, but often more profound ways. In the early 1960s, most colleges and universities had honor codes that really worked. Supervision of most tests was casual if not nonexistent. Cheating was spurned and tolerably rare. Even in the late 1960s (when I began teaching), students could be left alone to take tests in their classes, provided they were separated by vacant seats. Now, few university or college professors anywhere in the country, even in many seminaries, would dare give unmonitored tests. Even with safeguards, professors quietly acknowledge that cheating is likely an epidemic on their tests, especially in large lecture hall settings. Few professors now try to correct the problems. Not too many years ago, cheating was "wrong." Now, it's a game that students regularly play and win. Once the bastion of honor, the military academies are regularly beset with cheating scandals.

According to a Harris poll of 5,000 young people in the early 1990s, less than 2 percent of the respondents said that people in science or the media were the "most believable authority in matters of truth." Three to 4 percent named people in religion or their parents. Most of the young people said, "Me." However, 67 percent of the high school seniors indicated they would willfully inflate expense accounts, half said they would inflate an insurance claim, and two-thirds indicated they would lie to accomplish a business objective.[16] According to another survey reported by the *Wall Street Journal*, more than half of the students who work while

15. See Philip K. Howard, *The Death of Common Sense: How Law Is Suffocating America* (New York: Random House, 1994).

16. As reported by Lawrence W. Reed, "Government Steps In to Fill a Values Vacuum," *Orange County Register*, June 5, 1994, p. 1.

in school admitted to stealing from their compaines. More than 35 percent of the responding students confessed to regularly stealing more than $10 a month, with nearly 7 percent taking more than $50 a month.[17]

But there are problems that are simply more subtle than what young people do in classes or at work. Simple "respect" for the potential sensitivities of others can be a terrifically productive virtue. The scene at a local shopping center could have been almost anywhere in large-town USA. It happened to be near my hometown. A group of teenagers in punk clothing were standing around razzing one another as teenagers are inclined to do. The problem is that they seemed to be competing with one another on just how crude they were willing to be in public (with the "f—" word being frequently used). They had no regard for the interests of the many people, young and old alike, who passed by them. Indeed, they seemed to be daring passersby to say anything—and no one did say anything (possibly because there was a serious chance that a confrontation, even if stated politely, could have escalated beyond words).

I understand this is a small matter—in itself—but I also understand that the scene reflects a nontrivial change in the way people conduct themselves. *Respect* has lost it guiding force. The lost respect can also be assessed in terms of how often an umbrella can be left on a restaurant booth and is not held until the person returns. The loss is also seen in the frequency with which smokers snuff out their butts on the floors of public buildings. In Washington, respect for the rights of others has all too frequently fallen prey to raw political power. What counts there is not people's rights, but their power, or lack thereof.

Many Americans have always tried to shift the blame for what they do wrong and to make others responsible for what goes bad in their lives. At the same time, it used to be a matter of some pride for the overwhelming majority of Americans to bear the burden of their own actions, to accept blame and responsibility and to start anew. Responsibility is now denied simply by defining irresponsible behavior as a disease or mental disorder. When the American Psychiatric Association first published its reference manual for mental disorders in the late 1970s, *Diagnostic and Statistic Manual of Mental Disorders*, 106 mental disorders were then described. When the APA published the fourth edition fifteen years later in 1994, the manual's coverage had exploded to more than 300 disorders, in spite of the fact that several disorders (for example, homosexuality) had

17. As reported by Rochelle Sharpe, "Labor Letter," *Wall Street Journal*, June 14, 1994, p. A1.

been deleted.[18] The manual, of course, covers many serious mental problems, not the least of which are schizophrenia and depression. However, the don't-blame-me mentality has resulted in the inclusion of highly dubious, if not laughable, disorders. The manual includes, for example, the "Disorder of Written Expression," which covers people's problems with poor grammar, punctuation, disorganized paragraph construction, and handwriting. Or consider the "Oppositional Defiant Disorder," which covers children who exhibit any four of the following behavioral traits: display temper, disregard adults' rules, annoy others, blame others, or act touchy, angry, or hateful. There are probably extreme cases of all of these problems that are worthy of medical attention, but is also a sure bet that the looseness of the disorders' definitions, and the lack of strict scientific measurement of them, can lead to gross abuse by people who want to evade legal responsibility for what they have done or simply want to pass the buck.

Then there are the legal defenses that we dare allow the courts to entertain. Lorena Bobbitt cut off her husband's penis while he slept, but to listen to her, she was the victim. She used the "abuse excuse." Her husband caused her to do it, because of years of abuse. In effect, his problem was self-inflicted. Lyle and Eric Menendez shot their wealthy parents at point-blank range, and then went on a spending spree with what they thought would be their inheritance. After being trapped in the flaws of their own alibi, they pleaded guilty, but not without a novel defense: They *had* to kill their parents, for fear of being killed by them, given years of alleged sexual abuse that the parents were (supposedly) worried would come to light. The person caught on tape smashing a brick against the head of a beleaguered truck driver in the middle of the 1992 Los Angeles riot claimed that he was not to blame because the mob made him do it.

But, it should be stressed that the problems highlighted here are not a problem *only* for the poor or inner-city youth; they permeate many segments of society and link up various groups across ethnic and cultural boundaries. As this chapter was being finalized, some hate mongers from the heartland of the country took it upon themselves to redress governmental ills by blowing up a federal building in Oklahoma City, taking nearly two hundred lives. Apparently, the codes of conduct that bind terrorists together to do their dirty work meant that many others could be sacrificed.

18. As reported by Stuart A. Kirk and Herb Kutchins, "Is Bad Writing a Mental Disorder?" *New York Times*, June 20, 1994, p. A11.

When people fall off ladders, they blame the ladder maker, regardless of how they used the ladder. When bike buyers crash when taking a test ride, they sue the dealer for mistakes that were theirs. When fast-food customers spill hot coffee in their laps while driving, they sue the restaurants. When women have the smallest problem with their pregnancy, they sue the attending physicians and anyone else who might take over the financial responsibility for their problems. People's willingness to lie for money and position have become legion. While we might argue for hours over the fine points of all of these examples, we still know that they represent flaws that are growing at the core of some (but not all) segments of society.

Little need be said here about the lost virtues of frugality and investment because so much has been written elsewhere about it. The savings rate of many Americans continues to drop. Many use their credit as if there is no tomorrow or as if they don't care or don't intend to care for themselves later in life. In spite of continuing growth in the real-dollar budgets for education, many American schools are downright dreadful, partly because of social conditions in and outside the schools, but also partly because many students simply do not study. Furthermore, teachers can't make them study, and many parents don't try. Students can claim, as many do, that they don't study because of peer pressure.

What many American students don't know is legion; how they stack up against students in other countries in terms of both the time they devote to studying and how well they perform is a national disgrace. Geography educators report that students can't locate major countries on a globe. Economy educators have found that students think that "national" in bank titles means that the banks are owned by the federal government. Math educators report that Americans students can't solve simple addition problems, much less basic algebraic problems. English teachers have found that most American students can't read or write very well. For example, in a 1992 U.S. Department of Education survey, fewer than 20 percent of the American students could write a detailed, well-developed assignment. That finding, as well as many others, is understandable, given the amount of television they watch. Eighty-three percent of the responding fourth-graders reported watching more than an hour of television a day.[19] However, only 16 percent reported spending more than an hour a day on homework. What is frightening is that so many of the students themselves don't seem to care. They blame their schools, while the schools blame larger society. However, American

19. As reported by Jeff Leeds, "Study Finds Johnny Can't Write Too Well," *Los Angles Times*, June 8, 1994, p. A22.

businesses must care, given that nearly a third of them report that they are unable to restructure their companies to become more competitive because their employees would be unable to cope with the greater educational demands.[20] No wonder many American workers feel great angst.

The fact is that personal responsibility has become for far too many Americans a lost virtue. Who or what is responsible? People's environment is. Racism, sexism, elitism, and lack of income are the causes. People no longer *choose* to do what they do. The are *forced* to do whatever by something or someone else. Many Americans have assumed the mantle of the *victim*. For example, one commentator, who was seeking to explain the "code of the streets," excused violent behavior in a way that has become familiar: "The inclination to violence [on the streets, mainly in inner-city communities] springs from the circumstances of life among the ghetto poor—the lack of jobs that pay a living wage, the stigma of race, the fallout from rampant drug use and drug trafficking, and the resulting alienation and lack of hope for the future."[21] Although there may be a measure of truth in the proposition that sordid conditions cause unethical and intolerable behavior, the converse is probably far more accurate, that unethical and intolerable behavior is the seedbed of the sordid conditions.

The crack-up of the American family in many segments of the population is evident in the long-term upward trend in the divorce rate, in the growing number of deadbeat dads and moms who refuse to help with supporting their children, and in the increase in the number of single-parent households. In thirty years, the percentage of children living only with their mother in the house has tripled, from under 8 percent in 1960 to 22 percent in 1990 (with the percentage of children living with both parents slipping from 81 percent in 1960 to 58 percent in 1990).[22] Fortunately, there is some evidence that family problems may be stabilizing, given the modest reversal in the divorce rate since the early 1980s (the rate of divorces per thousand married women was 20.5 in 1994, compared with 23 in 1980).[23] However, other evidence is not so comforting. The lack of responsible family values, as well as personal restraint, is

20. As reported in Louis V. Gerstner Jr., "Our Schools Are Failing. Do We Care?" *New York Times*, May 27, 1994, p. A15.

21. Elijah Anderson, "The Code of the Streets," *Atlantic Monthly*, May 1994, p. 81.

22. As reported by David Blankenhorn, *Fatherless America* (New York: Basic Books, 1995), p. 18.

23. As computed by the Population Reference Bureau, Inc. and reported by Steven H. Holmes, "Traditional Family Stabilized in 90's, New Study Suggests," *New York Times*, March 7, 1996, p. A1.

equally evident in the number of teenage girls who get pregnant only to abort the fetuses. The sad truth today is that in spite of condoms being given away like balloons at school and on street corners and in spite of the availability of cheap abortions (that resulted in close to 2 million abortions a year in the mid-1990s), 30 percent of all births and 68 percent of African-American births are illegitimate. If present trends continue, by the turn of the century, according to William Bennett, a former head of the country's drug war, illegitimate births will constitute 40 percent of all births and 80 percent of all African-American births.[24]

Reasons for the Crack-Up

Where did America go wrong? More accurately, what has gone wrong for many Americans? There is no simple, single answer—there are, in fact, many possible answers—and there is no simple, single solution, if there is a solution at all (in the sense that there can be an orchestrated set of changes in policies and institutions that can be imposed externally, that is, from the seats of political power). All that we can do here is highlight possible explanations for what went wrong and then consider how circumstances will likely be rectified. However, we must keep in mind that a country's moral infrastructure—its code of reasonable rules of behavior—is always on the move, adjusting to a multitude of changes, not the least of which is technology. What seems to be the central problem today is the speed with which the moral tectonic plates are moving.

The Market Economy

The market economy is surely partly to blame for the problems Americans face. It has given rise to fabulous increases in people's incomes and stores of wealth, the positive attributes of economic growth long trumpeted by economists. Practically everyone has had an opportunity to live better than they could have imagined.

At the same time, the negative attributes of growth should not go unnoticed. Increased incomes and wealth have made crime an attractive, if not irresistible, enterprise, because is has made it more profitable. Prosperous market economies simply create more to steal, more tools of the criminal trade (from crowbars to pagers to planes), and more opportunities to dispose of the "loot" that is taken.

24. William J. Bennett, "Getting Used to Decadence: The Spirit of Democracy in Modern America," *Heritage Lectures* (Washington, D.C.: Heritage Foundation, 1993), p. 3.

Crime can be self-perpetuating, given that an increase in crime induced by greater wealth can reduce the probability that any one person will get caught, thus reducing the assessed *expected* cost of crime and increasing the assessed *expected* net gains from crime. We have noted that rules of reasonable conduct are tenuous at best. When everyone begins to exploit the opportunities to lie, steal, and cheat, it is all the more tempting for any one person to forgo resistance to the temptations to lie, steal, and cheat. In this regard, "some" crime can be like the proverbial hole in the dike that can eventually cause a break in the entire dam. In parts of America, the "dam" has literally broken.

Regrettably, the components of the moral infrastructure that have given way are unlike a real dam. They are not so much concrete and steel that can be resurrected by the decisions of political leaders. A multimillion-dollar bonus spurred the reconstruction of a major bridge after the L.A. earthquake of 1994; such a bonus will not have much impact in the case of the moral infrastructure. There is no one to whom a bonus can be offered, and the bonus can't be offered to everyone. Rather, the components that have been washed away will likely come back gradually, if at all, as people rediscover exactly what they have lost—hard to define rules of conduct—and how to sustain them. There is no quick fix here; the fix can only be generated gradually, from the bottom up, as people work their way into and through the reconstructed webs of rules over time.

Some people have obviously not been able to cope with their economic gains. They have used a portion of their gains to "buy" more leisure (and less diligence) for themselves and their children, if not downright laziness; irresponsibility; disrespect for others; and disregard for normal rules of honor. Professional athletes and rock stars who have become models of dishonor for their drug habits are simply the rawest examples of how income and wealth can eat away moral fiber.

However, middle-class suburbanites have also succumbed to the corrupting influence of income and wealth. Many have reared their children with few demands being placed on them for hard work, honesty, integrity, and frugality. They have in fact insisted that schools, social clubs, and even churches be devoid of means of discipline that might fortify tried-and-true virtues.

Markets have reduced our direct dependence on people within our immediate families, groups of friends, and communities. They have enabled people to get what they need from many others in the extended order of exchanges, reducing the incentives they have to abide by the local rules of conduct in the greater societal web of rules. Breaking the rules of commitment simply have fewer direct detectable penalties for those who break them. When couples divorce, they can simply obtain, at little added cost, in markets what they depended on their former partner for (from meals to cleaning to yard work). Markets have, in other words, reduced the cost of breaks in interpersonal commitments, which are so necessary for the survival of the moral infrastructure.

The developing market economy has given rise to the so-called welfare state, perhaps more accurately described as the "redistributive state," by drastically reducing the number of poor people, thus increasing the opportunity that the remaining poor have to garner income from the nonpoor. When most people are poor, as they were a century or more ago, there was little income to redistribute to anyone. The cost of redistribution would then be high, because redistributive programs would exact an enormous tax on those few people with enough income to transfer to others. When few people are poor, there is a great deal of income to redistribute and the tax burden on the nonpoor is not so great, making redistribution all the more palatable, resulting in more benefits for each of the remaining poor.[25] The problem is that the redistributive state can be all too readily converted to the "dependency state" with many of those on the receiving end of the transfers becoming accustomed to their handouts, especially given that the public handouts may be made with weak, if not zero, demands that they, the recipients, uphold reasonable rules of behavior and contribute to the public good.[26]

At the same time, the dependency state can be expected to administer its programs by corralling the dependents in, for example, large high-rise housing facilities. Given that the dependents are likely to lack many of the required rules of reasonable conduct, which partially explains their destitution, we should not be surprised that such facilities breed degradation.

The Disruption of Everything

Without much question, historians of the future will look back on our era with amazement, given the breadth and depth of the technological and

25. This line of argument, with empirical support, has been developed by Amihai Glazer, Richard B. McKenzie, and Thomas Roemer, "The Relation Between Poverty Rates and Welfare Benefits" (Irvine, Calif.: Graduate School of Management, University of California, Irvine, 1994). The authors found in a cross-state study of poverty benefits that as the number of poor people falls, the per capita real proverty benefits rise (after adjusting for a number of variables that might influence poverty benefits).

26. Charles Murray has eloquently described how the country's efforts to help the disadvantaged have undermined responsible behavior (*Losing Ground: American Social Policy, 1950–1980* [New York: Basic Books, 1984]).

structural changes afoot in society. They will probably talk about the telecommunication/computer/information revolution that we have been experiencing and will continue to experience for sometime into the future as being on par with the agricultural revolution of several centuries ago and the industrial revolution that ended barely a hundred years ago. The revolutionary forces at work in the world have had tremendous positive effects, as we have stressed, but they have also unsettled the rules structure of whole groups as different societies have come into closer contact with one another, with greater potential and actual conflict and competition. Ethnic, religious, geographical, and nationalistic groups are intermingling by way of travel but also by way of mass communications. Kenichi Ohmae and Walter Wriston, both of whom were cited earlier in this book, stress that national boundaries have become porous, with human and physical capital moving among countries almost as if the geographically based national borders were no longer as important as they once were. Their theories apply also to groups, with their boundaries, defined as much by their commonly accepted rules, becoming as porous as, if not more porous than, national boundaries—for much the same reasons. No doubt the ethics, or lack thereof, on nightly television can pose a threat to many codes of personal conduct, partly because they might cause defections from the rules.

The observed variations in rules across societies has, naturally, caused many people to rethink the rules they will accept, and has given rise to uncertainties and angst among the affected peoples. It is difficult to say how the contacts will play out in the reconstituting of whole societies. All we can say is that there will be, as there already has been, some degree of reconstitution of the rules. The technology has, no doubt, forced new directions in the evolution of rules, the moral foundations of societies.

The Rationalization of Everything

The modern era has been characterized by drives to rationally understand and evaluate everything. Economists, in particular, have done a great job of explaining how markets work—aside for validating the moral foundation of market economies. As noted in chapter 7, if the "rules" are mentioned, they are mentioned in the context of laws that must be enforced by governments. On the other hand, economists have perhaps inadvertently instilled the values of *marginal analysis,* under which people are supposed to take actions only after carefully weighing the marginal costs and benefits of each circumstance. They probably have overlooked the fact (as developed in the last chapter) that most rules of reasonable behavior are not grounded in such calculations, but rather in the evolutionary success of the societies that happen to adopt them. A society whose individual members carefully weigh the costs and benefits of stealing, cheating, and lying are likely to be societies full of stealing, cheating, and lying. A society whose central, guiding ethic is the net balance of costs and benefits is likely to be a society with little restraint.

Milton Friedman, who is probably the most widely recognized and revered economist of this century, wrote an article in 1970 for the *New York Times Magazine* that contained an eminently valuable but equally misinterpreted point. Friedman's central theme is captured by the article's title, "The Social Responsibility of Business Is to Increase Its Profits."[27] While Friedman adequately qualifies his argument to mean that firms should profit maximize within the confines of laws and ethical customs, he has clearly been misinterpreted by both his critics and admirers who still insist that his point is much simpler than he intended: *There is no higher goal for business than profit*—which could not be the case. If firms did nothing but profit maximize, even at the expense of violating rules of reasonable conduct, they would surely destroy the ethical foundation of the system that is designed to promote profit maximization.[28]

Economists generally have not fully appreciated the paradox of maintaining the market economy that they espouse. In order for pursuit of self-interest to be profitable and efficiency enhancing, people must first be willing to restrain the scope of their self-directed behavior (a point developed in the previous chapter). Instead of seeking to make the distinction between legitimate and illegitimate self-seeking behavior, economists have presumed that their analytical methods were generally applicable to every nook and cranny of human existence, which they simply cannot be.

Even more generally, intellectuals have sought to scrutinize all rules of behavior to see if they make sense. They have failed to understand Hayek's essential point developed in the last chapter: Most rules of behavior cannot be fully rationalized, explained, or understood in purely logical terms. Most rules exist because they enable the societies that live by them to survive and prosper over mulitple generations. The most important argument for the existing rules is that they have worked. If they are subjected to close short-term scrutiny, they most surely will all too often be found wanting in particular cases by those who

27. Milton Friedman, "The Social Responsibility of Business Is to Increase Its Profits." *New York Times Magazine,* September 13, 1970, pp. 32ff.

28. For a critique of Friedman's thesis, see Dwight R. Lee and Richard B. McKenzie, "Monitoring Costs and the Efficient Provision of Community Goods," *Journal of Business Ethics* 13 (1994): 969–78.

try to find intellectual soundness in them for their individual circumstances.

Bigness in Social Entities

The growth in big economic entities, public and private, has had a predictable impact on the moral infrastructure. It has caused fraying for reasons that both liberals and communitarians should appreciate. Rules of behavior work best in small groups where love, mutual respect, concern for others, and interpersonal sanctions work to reinforce the rules. In small groups, the consequences of individual actions can be detected and assessed by the acting person and the relevant others in the group. In large groups, however, the consequences of actions cannot be detected with the same strength by anyone, and the larger the group, the more difficult it is for the acting person and others to detect and assess consequences that *individuals* have per se.

This fundamental observation is central to the "logic of collective action" best articulated by University of Maryland economist Mancur Olson in his classic work,[29] but other economists have relied on some variation of the same point, not the least of which, as discussed in chapter 7, is Adam Smith. Smith would definitely agree with philosopher David Hume that the "notion of morals implies some sentiment common to all mankind, which recommends the same object to general approbation, and makes every man, or most men, agree in the same opinion or decision concerning it."[30] However, constitutional political economist James Buchanan reasons that while each individual may be expected to abide by ethical precepts in small groups, "there is some increase in group size that will cause him to modify his ethical rule and become a private maximizer."[31] He cites examples of the efficacy of moral codes at work:

> Volunteer fire departments arise in villages, not in metropolitan centers. Crime rates consistently rise with city size. Africans behave differ-

29. Mancur Olson, *The Logic of Collective Action* (Cambridge, Mass.: Harvard University Press, 1965).

30. David Hume, *An Inquiry Concerning the Principles of Morals,* included in *Hume: Selections,* ed. Charles W. Hendel Jr. (New York: Scribner, 1927), p. 28. Hume added, "It [the notion or morals] also implies some sentiment, so universal and comprehensive as to extend to all mankind, and render the actions and conduct, even of the person most remote, an object of applause and censure, according as they agree or disagree with that rule of right which is established" (ibid.).

31. James M. Buchanan, "Ethical Rules, Expected Values, and Large Numbers," *Ethics,* October 1965, p. 8.

> ently in tribal culture than in urban-industrialized settings. There is honor among thieves. The Mafia has its own standards. Time-tested honor systems in universities and colleges collapse when enrollments exceed critical size limits. Litter is more likely to be found on main traveled routes than on residential streets. Even the old adage, "Never trust a stranger," reflects recognition of this elemental truth, along with, of course, additional ethical predictions. Successful politicians organize "grassroots" support at the precinct level.[32]

The very fact that communities, cities, businesses, schools and universities, bureaucracies, and governments in general have grown in size, in expenditures, and in the number of people served has no doubt inadvertently undercut the force of binding moral precepts. Misbehavior can simply go undetected, which means that the expected value of misdeeds has increased. Students in large lecture halls cheat for two (of possibly many) reasons: First, the probability of being caught in such settings is practically nonexistent and the probability of being kicked out of school if caught is just about as low. Second, students understand that others in the class are cheating, meaning they may have to cheat just to prevent their relative grade from falling.

People who faithfully meet their church pledges think nothing of lying on their state and federal income taxes because their failure to pay taxes will have no detectable impact on the services received, *regardless of how much other taxpayers fail to pay*, mainly because the relevant group of taxpayers is so large and the impact of the individual's contributions, or lack thereof, is so small. Other Americans don't worry about the social (moral infrastructure) consequences of their lawsuits against large companies, regardless of how ill-founded they may be, because their court awards *by themselves* will have no perceptible impact on product quality and price. Large companies' pockets are too "deep."

The fact is that one of the tectonic forces at work on the moral infrastructure has been the growth in sizes of social and economic units. Few have thought to sound the alarm: "Look, the much-heralded 'economies of scale' can drive the economy to greater and greater efficiency, but there can also be a long-term downside, a slow but persistent undermining of the moral base of the economy." We simply have paid too little attention to the long-term impact of size on community values. Fortunately, this problem may be abated with the advent of smaller firms, if not smaller governments and groups.

32. Ibid.

Special Role of Government

Growth in government efforts to solve social problems, which has been nothing short of dramatic in the last half of the twenty-first century, has been particularly troublesome. It has probably forced people to overextend themselves in concern for others who are distant from them in space and culture, reducing their perceived responsibility for people who are in need and are close at hand. It has centralized economic power, increasing the temptations politicians face to violate rules of reasonable behavior as they use the powers of government for their own personal ends. Growth in government has helped to make unethical behavior common, a model to be followed by others.

My good friend and co-author on other books, Dwight Lee, argues in a penetrating monograph, appropriately titled *Malice in Plunderland*, that modern big and expansive governments go further and literally encourage unreasonable behavior. All interest groups in Washington want favors.[33] They can get the favors, of course, by offering money, which in itself subverts the credibility of democratic governance, but interest groups can also secure benefits by loudly proclaiming their needs in the streets of the nation's capital or in the halls of Congress and securing all the media attention possible. The meek, mild, and strictly honest interest-group representatives are not likely to gain much attention, especially when they must compete for attention from the agressive, boisterous, and disingenuous. Washington politics simply drives people to take extreme positions, based on contorted truths, further eroding the credibility of the system, if not a very scarce resource, people's inclination to be moral.

Intellectual Tectonics

To a degree, the methods of science are to blame for the breakdown of the moral infrastructure. Tremendous technical progress has been made by the search of external, objective causes of, for example, chemical reactions and physical changes. For instance, if chemical A is combined with chemical B under given pressure and temperature, a reaction of a certain magnitude and in a certain form can be expected. Alternately, earthquakes occur because of the buildup or pressures from the movements of tectonic plates.

Social scientists have sought to advance our understanding of human

33. Dwight R. Lee, *The Political Economy of Social Conflict, or Malice in Plunderland* (Los Angeles: International Institute for Economic Research, 1982).

behavior by duplicating the methods of science proper, seeking to identify the external, objective determinants of human action. Why do people do what they do? It's because of objective, meaning measurable, factors: their incomes, genetics, and history, for example. *Behaviorism* is the most extreme variant of prevailing intellectual paradigms that have dominated social policy discussions for the past half century. Under behaviorism, people do nothing out of their own choices or volition (free will simply does not exist). People's behavior is fully determined by a multitude of external, objective stimuli that extends from the important (i.e., a person's sex) to the seemingly unimportant (e.g., the intensity of the lighting in a room).[34]

Regrettably, such a social philosophy detracts from the role of the underlying code of conduct as an explanation for why people do what they do and as a source of general prosperity. Why is it not considered by social scientists? Because the code is difficult to measure and it is not codified (printed and available for careful examination by scientists). That is, it is not "objective." The scientific approach to the study of behavior also obviates individuals from accepting responsibility (because actions are attributed to anything and everything other than personal choices, which are necessarily subjective). When we say that race, sex, income, or whatever is the "cause" of some person's place in life, we literally give people a ready-made, external excuse for anything bad that happens to them. We also give them grounds for passing the buck to others and for seeking solutions to observed problems outside themselves. We destroy the concept of personal blame. Blame is spread so thinly over so many potential environmental, genetic, and historical factors that it is basically obliterated. This is especially true when we glibly attribute blame to "society," which literally amounts to blaming everyone and, at the same time, no one. We obviously reduce the incentive people have to adhere to the underlying rules of reasonable behavior. They can claim the modern scientific equivalent of "the devil made me do it."

Granted, it may be, as Hayek points out, that many behaviors are the consequence of identifiable external factors and/or even luck. However, the assignment of personal responsibility is not intended to mitigate past behaviors but is intended to press people to override past conditions and to seek different, better outcomes in the future. The denial of personal responsibility averts the potential for progress, for improvement, not only for those whose actions might be changed but for everyone else.

34. See B. F. Skinner, *Beyond Freedom and Dignity* (New York: Bantam Books, 1971).

The assignment of *personal* responsibility is ultimately designed to achieve *social* benefits, a serendipitous result indeed for the people who must adjust their ways.

Granted, people may not be individually responsible, in any meaningful way, for many things that happen to them. Environmental factors may often weigh heavily. But that isn't to say that exaggerating, even grossly, the importance of assigning responsibility to individuals doesn't have merit. Such exaggeration can cause people to be more responsible than they otherwise would be, and hence contribute more to the social welfare. Correcting the exaggeration can inadvertently cause people to be less responsible and society to be less prosperous.

The Required Social Mythology

To some difficult-to-define extent, it is quite clear that the vitality of the rules of reasonable conduct is founded on a commonly shared mythology that individual adherence to the rules truly counts in some measurable, concrete way—when in fact the individuals' actions, taken separately, may be of absolutely no consequence. Nevertheless, if everyone acts *as if* their actions count, there can be realized benefits for all, which can make belief in the rules self-fulfilling. The deterministic theories (even economists hammering on the nonconsequences of individual actions in large-group contexts) have probably served to undermine the durability of the necessary social mythology that rules count for society *and* for individuals taken separately.[35]

For much the same reasons, the fading of Americans' adherence to strict religious dictates and the growing secularization of religion, coupled with the individualization of God (or the view that God is "what you want him to be"), have very likely further eroded the moral infrastructure. As theologian Richard John Neuhaus has stressed, "Making sense assumes that there is some truth about the matter in dispute. But when it comes to morality, it is widely assumed today that there is no such thing as truth," to which he later adds, "Clear thinking about moral truth flounders on the rock of relativism and subjectivism. In a radically individualistic culture, we do not discern and obey what is objectively true. Rather, each of us decides what is true. We *create* the truth."[36] We,

35. One study found economics graduate students to be less cooperative, more inclined to "free ride" and to shirk group-assigned responsibilities, than are other students (Gerald Marwell and Ruth Ames, "Economists Free Ride: Does Anyone Else?" *Journal of Public Economics* 15 [1981]: 295–310.).

36. Richard John Neuhaus, "The Truth about Freedom," *Wall Street Journal*, October 8, 1993, p. A12.

in effect, do our own thing, which could not be more counterproductive for the future of mankind.

Moreover, with God individualized, not as many Americans are as concerned as they once were that they will be eternally damned for violating the Ten Commandments and other moral strictures. They can figure they won't get caught (because their God is not omniscient, omnipotent, and omnipresent, as they conceive of him) and if he were to notice their violations, he would not likely impose severe penalties (because he is made in their own image and for their own purposes).

When adherence to underlying moral precepts is totally dependent upon their assessed costs and benefits in the "here and now," there is surely an increased likelihood that adherence will dissolve (because the costs for violations are lowered). The secularization and individualization of religion is surely a means, to use David Hume's words quoted previously, a breakdown in the notion that morality "implies some sentiment common to all mankind, which recommends the same object to general approbation, and makes every man, or most men, agree in the same opinion or decision concerning it." Unfortunately, but predictably, the breakdown can be self-perpetuating, given the precepts' tenuous nature (or the lack of incentives many people may have to incur personal sacrifices required when they abide by the code).

The Liberation Culture

Myron Magnet, a former editor of *Fortune* magazine, writes in his book *The Dream and the Nightmare* that American society today is living through the consequences of the cultural revolution that occurred in the 1960s.[37] In addition to the intellectual revolution just outlined, which had the effect of making Americans, especially the poor, view themselves conveniently as victims of their circumstances, Magnet argues that the cultural revolution truncated, maybe permanently, their ability to move up and out of their dire circumstances.

He reasons that what the poor often lack is not so much "things" as it is training and inspiration for living within reasonable rules. The underclass, Magnet writes,

> are deprived of the basic socialization in early childhood that awakens and develops the conscience and fosters the belief, values, and habits of thought and feeling that constitute civility and that impose meaning and directions on individual life. Because of this deprivation, they are

37. Myron Magnet, *The Dream and the Nightmare: The Sixties Legacy to the Underclass* (New York: William Morrow, 1993).

> also poor in basic knowledge and in the skills of reasoning, analysis, and judgment needed to master the world.[38]

The liberalization of social values of self-restraint was best captured in the pat 1960s theme: Turn on, tune in, drop out. Liberation theology was manifested all too often in the blowing of one's mind and body with unrelenting exposure to the hedonistic pleasures of the moment. That cultural revolution set back all classes of people who participated. The "haves," mainly those who had a measure of the requisite socialization Magnet mentions, were able in the 1970s and 1980s to rebound from the personal and social problems they encountered in their more unrestrained days. However, many of the "have nots" (again, not to include all poor people), lacking in the required socialization skills, have not been able to recover, partly because of their lack of basic skills of reasoning, analysis, and judgment needed to master the world, but also partly because we have continued to accommodate, subsidize, and rationalize their worst tendencies to remain restrained from ultimately destructive behavior. We have failed to insist that they take responsibility for themselves and what they make out of their lives.

Spiritual Exhaustion

Former drug czar William Bennett believes that the country's problems are more related to matters of the *spirit,* or what he prefers to call "acedia," "an aversion to and negation of spiritual things," too much concern for material and worldly matter and too little concern for things that are downright wrong.[39] He suggests that Americans have simply shucked their moral mooring in hot pursuit of more income, more goods, more leisure; they have forgotten that they must work at feeding the spirit.

Many Americans no longer behave morally because basic values of right and wrong must be constantly fortified but are no longer instilled with the same vigilance by teachers in school and parents in the homes. He quotes approvingly Scottish author John Buchan, whose words were written more than a half century ago. Buchan describes the "coming of the garish age, when life would be lived in the glare of neon lamps and the spirit would have no solitude." Buchan continues:

> In such a [nightmare] world everyone would have leisure. But everyone would be restless, for there would be no spiritual discipline in life. . . . It would be a feverish, bustling world, self-satisfied and yet

38. Ibid., p. 30
39. Bennett, "Getting Used to Decadence," p. 5.

> malcontent, and under the mask of a riotous life there would be a dearth at the heart. In perpetual hurry of life there would be no chance of quiet for the soul. . . . In such a bargain's paradise, where life would be rationalized and padded with every material comfort, there would be little satisfaction for the immortal part of man.[40]

Although Bennett's claims are unscientific, perhaps exaggerated, they nonetheless ring with a substantial measure of truth for our time. While maintenance of the moral infrastructure requires continuous fortification, as a country we do seem to have lost some of our willingness to distinguish between right and wrong, to be enraged at those—young and old, white and black, rich and poor—who flagrantly violate fundamental rules of tolerably reasonable behavior and at those who make mockery of the rules of reasonable argument in and out of court. We have, to a degree, been eating our cultural seed corn, with individuals seeking to increase their current welfare at the expense of the welfare of future generations who will be deprived of a moral infrastructure that is no less important than the physical infrastructure.

Global Nets

To suggest that America has lost its moral way is a gross distortion of the forces at work in the country and the world. "America" is a rhetorical box, the meaning of which is fast becoming elusive, given the extent to which the lives of many Americans are rapidly becoming commingled with the lives of people in other countries. Moreover, the country is made up of over a quarter billion people and clearly not all—far from it—have succumbed to the cultural revolution or have jettisoned reasonable rules of conduct. Not all have given up on seeking truth, honor, and integrity. Most Americans remain diligent, trustworthy, frugal, and duty bound; are concerned about education; and accept responsibility for their actions—no less than their counterparts in Japan, New Zealand, and Hungary.

Similarly, it is equally wrongheaded to imply that the "poor" or a "minority" identified by race, gender, or ethnic background, as entire classes of people, have lost their moral mooring. Some within each group have, but most have not. Many poor people would never think of stealing, diligently work at their jobs, study hard in school, and save for a brighter future. The old divisions between the "haves" and "have nots" is no longer a clear divison, with many "have nots" as far removed

40. As quoted in ibid., p. 6.

emotionally from other "have nots" as they are from the "haves." The gulf within the "have nots" was never more evident than after the 1992 Los Angeles riots when television reporters interviewed have-not riot vicitms and bystanders who were horrified at what they were witnessing within their own neighborhoods.

Indeed, while all divisions are arbitrary to one degree or another, it seems reasonable to conclude that America is dividing, but not so much along income, class, race, gender, ethnic, or any of the other classic lines of demarcation. Hordes of people of all incomes, classes, races, genders, and ethnic groupings mix productively everyday all across the country. They do so at work, school, and many other social settings (although the extent of the mixing might not be as great as proponents of cultural diversity might want).

Admittedly, anecdotal evidence of the growing confluence and, at the same time, separation of Americans of all backgrounds can be misleading. However, all one has to do is look around. Concert-goers can be representative of everyone in the community. University students experience only occasional difficulty from mixing, mingling, studying, and socializing with others. We make a great deal these days of charges of sexual and racial harassment and discrimination, but we also observe males and females, blacks, whites, yellows, and browns working harmoniously together, and even enjoying each other's company (although rubs are inevitable).

At the same time, we can detect in the groupings commonalities that make the groupings possible. As the old adage teaches, "birds of a feather *do* flock together," but the common feather that joins people is more likely to be their generally accepted and observed rules of behavior. Where people of all colors enjoy another's company, the groups are, in a fundamental sense, colorless. They all—blacks, browns, yellows, and whites—want to get along, to produce efficiently, and to have fun when and where they can. None of those goals can be achieved without all involved seeking some common ground, some common mode of behavior that makes their behaviors consistent, predictable, dependable.

At a happy-hour gathering of faculty and staff from across my university's campus, whose color and ethnic backgrounds covered the full spectrum of American life, the conversation turned on one occasion to "cultural diversity," what the university had accomplished and where the university fell short. It was clearly evident that a black woman and I had no problem talking about this area, and we did so without regard to our skin colors. Indeed, the color of our skin did not enter the conversation and never held us back in making observations about racial stereotypes, mainly because we held high virtually the same rules of reasonable behavior. We talked much alike. We acted much alike. We expressed many of the same hopes and aspirations. We respected each other. We were of *one* grouping because we held to much the same rules of behavior. Both of us enjoyed the company at hand, but we also both admitted that there were others of all races and incomes with whom we could not associate, primarily because of the rules that separated us from "them."

At one time, not too many decades ago, Americans could be viewed as swimming in one big fish bowl. What we did or did not do dramatically affected the welfare of our fellow countrymen. What other Americans did or did not do dramatically affected us. If some Americans did not work, save, and invest (did not abide by the more general rules of reasonable conduct central to this chapter), then the country would be poorer for it, and those of us who did work, save, and invest would be materially affected. That is still the case, but clearly to a lesser extent than it once was.

Technology has enabled reasonable people of the world to unite to a degree that they never dreamed of. As a consequence, if some Americans don't work with due diligence, don't study hard, don't save, don't seek to be competitive, don't remain honorable, then those Americans who are diligent, industrious, competitive, honorable, and so forth can join with people in other parts of the world who are equally diligent, industrious, competitive, and honorable—to press forward in building their economic futures together—and in many ways leaving those Americans who are unwilling and unable to abide by the same rules of reasonable conduct behind.

For two decades now, critics have lamented the decline in Americans' saving rate. However, the country has continued to grow. The reason is simple: As shown earlier, not all Americans have failed to save. Moreover, entrepreneurs in this country (both Americans and foreigners) have been able to tap into the savings of people here *and* in other parts of the world, most notably Japan, Britain, Canada, and Germany. Similarly, with many Americans failing to make the grade in education, American firms have been able to join together with workers here and in other parts of the world to pursue their profitable ventures.

When we look at the global economy, we see transnational networks developing that are not so much based on geography (the importance of location has waned, a point made clear in chapter 6) but on unity of purpose of those involved, all of whom are following similar rules of reasonable behavior. The slaggards, the crooks, the irresponsible, the dishonorable, the unreasonable people are gradually being marginalized. Communities are emerging with visible and invisible barriers that have little to do with color or creed or ethnicity.

By way of rules of reasonable conduct, hundreds of millions of people around the would are extending their sphere of influence and order. They are prospering for the most part. They continue to dream of brighter futures. Those who are not able to link up because they refuse to abide by rules of reasonable conduct are seeing their world contract. They may see only nightmares in their futures.

Everyone accepts the fact that modern technology, which is at the heart and soul of the reorganization of the world economy, has forced firms to become more competitive, to restructure, to become more cost-effective. A growing number of people recognize (as argued in chapter 6) that the forces of technology and capital flows are forcing governments to cap their growth and to become more cost-effective. Now, people must realize that those same forces at work on firms and governments are at work on all social structures, including the rules or moral foundations of groups and whole societies. Groups must accept the fact that rules matter; behavior of their members matter to the long-term survival and prosperity of the groups. They must realize that those groups who develop cost-effective rules and are able to sustain them will prosper, while other groups will languish. In ways that were not possible during long stretches of human history, people were not able to move among groups and reconstitute their own groups. Now they can. As never before, the pressure is on for individuals, if they want to join and sustain membership in productive groups, to reassert allegiance to the groups' rules in order for groups to become more cost-effective in rules their members follow. Otherwise, many individuals and groups cannot expect to prosper, as many have not, as evident by falling incomes. People who refuse to be frugal can expect to suffer income losses in their old age, given that cuts in government aid for retirees are expected. Students who refuse to continue their school and fail to study while in school can project continuing losses in their incomes. People who do not have reputations for being honorable cannot expect to be given positions of trust within social groups and firms. There is a great deal of hope in the extant pressures, including some groups' falling incomes, to reform and compete on group and societal levels. Clearly, there are strong competitive pressures afoot to force firms and workers to reform their methods. Firms are reengineering, and unions have become less of an obstacle to work-rule reforms as their influence in the economy has begun to decline. However, there are also important, albeit weak, signs that the pressure is working in other areas. Forms of crimes (mainly, property crimes) have waned in recent years. Private school educaton is on the increase. Groups of people have begun to form for no other purpose than to revitalize their commitment to family. The divorce rate has declined slightly. The long-term deterioration in student test scores has been reversed as the number of high school dropouts has begun to decline and a growing number of high school students have begun to take tougher courses.[41]

Concluding Comments

I wish I could say that this chapter fully explains the widespread angst in America. It clearly does not do that. It seeks to explain, however, a portion of it. Many (but not all) Americans are witness to the slow crumbling of the moral infrastructure. When the crumbling is immediate, they have reason to be anxious because the lesson of the moral infrastructure is that people's futures are dependent on far more than what one or two individuals do; it depends on the willful, reinforced actions of many people to abide by the rules and to do their part in inducing others to abide by the rules. Therein lies the dilemma that we have repeatedly run up against, getting people to restrain themselves when all temptations, all logic, and virtually all incentives, point in the opposite direction.

What can be done? That's a tough question. Dilemmas have no easy solution, or they would not be dilemmas worthy of the designation. We, of course, can get rid of the institutionally imposed incentives to violate rules, for example, subsidies that encourage the filing of untrue worker compensation schemes. We can, as the city of Irvine, California, has done, wall in sections of our large communities and make them "villages," where the interests of small groups of people are turned toward the immediate others around them. We can stop subsidizing laziness, irresponsibility, and lies. We can demand more of students in school and hold parents responsible for the misdeeds of their children. We can make politics less important in society by contracting the array of issues that must be settled collectively, thus reducing the "malice in plunder-

41. The high school dropout rate declined from just under 14 percent in 1982 to 11 percent in 1993. Student scores on the National Assessment of Educational Progress rose 9 points in math and 11 points in science between 1982 and 1992. The percentage of high school students taking geometry increased from 48 percent in 1982 to 70 percent in 1992. The percentage who took chemistry increased from 32 percent to 56 percent during the same period ("Researchers Find Dropouts Down, Math Study Up," *Los Angeles Times*, August 22, 1995, p. A20).

land." We can stop penalizing saving. We can introduce a measure of realism into our welfare discussions, first of all by recognizing that compassion has its useful limits (and can have, as it has had, perverse effects). There are a host of other "policy" changes that probably come to every reader's mind.

The policy changes, however, are the easy part, which explains why so many people work on policy reforms and pay little or no attention to anything else, as if government policies are all that matter. The hard part is getting people to pay attention to the importance of the more fundamental and important moral infrastructure and the enforcement of nets they already have, to build on them, to be open to ways to improve them, to even be hard-hearted when necessary. We as individuals must rediscover the importance of harsh disapproval, even rage, and ostracism when people flagrantly flaunt rules of reasonable behavior. Those are the methods that have worked in multiple ways in the past. They might help, but I use *might* advisedly.

Being inclined to believe that our moral infrastructure will continue to evolve as it has done in the past, I am not sure how the rules will change and how we will fortify them. Neither can anyone else be sure of solutions or how the evolutionary process will unfold. The problem remains of getting people to do their part individually in abiding by the rules of reasonable behavior and of taking the necessary measures to encourage immediate others to abide by them, and that is no easy assignment. We can decide collectively to fortify the infrastructure, but we must act individually—and, again, therein lies the collective rub. People are understandably inclined, in their own actions, to stand by and let others try to maintain the rules, a logical recipe for no action by everyone. Therein lies reason for much angst. The solutions to our problems are not obvious, and cannot be.

Fortunately, morality starts in the "small," with a few people joining together to live together under agreed-upon rules. The success of those who adopt and fortify tried-and-true rules can be expected to draw others into their nets, which can give rise to an extended order that has hope of further extensions and greater prosperity. A century ago, the extended order was greatly limited by the cost of movement and communication. Our age is indeed fortunate, for technology allows us other options, really escape hatches, for creating new orders when the nets about us are fraying. We can move physically and join with like-minded others here and abroad who have established ground rules that work. We can also join up electronically, as tens of millions have already done. We can create whole new forms of communities (in cyberspace as well as in real space) where prosperity has a chance and where those who deny the validity of reasonable rules can, to one degree or another, be excluded. In short, we have new ways of leaving those who refuse to live by rules of reasonable conduct behind, albeit only to a degree. The reconstitution of the nets, and their underlying moral infrastructure, is an ongoing process but has one important, perhaps unheralded attribute: People who move physically and electronically will pressure the misguided others to reform their ways. We cannot hope for more.

9

ABUNDANT OPPORTUNITIES

All in all, there is more self-pity available to wallow in now than there was during the Great Depression when your grandparents lived in grimy little houses with newspapers stuffed in the cracks and worked so hard their bodies hurt at night. Complaining was against their religion, though. They believed that if you smile, you'll feel better.

Garrison Keillor, "Lighten Up, Graduates"

THIS BOOK has been about the presumed broad-based and growing anxiety in an economy filled with progress. We have noted that many Americans fret that their economic opportunities are collapsing. In support of their perceived dismal economic prospects, American pudits and workers stress the negatives: the broad-based downsizing of American firms, the destruction of hundreds of thousands of good blue- and white-collar jobs, and the loss of promotion opportunities as corporations eliminate tiers of middle-management positions. Because of the rhetoric of decline, many young Americans are now convinced that if recent trends continue, they will live less prosperous lives than did their parents. Plus, they fear that their children will be even worse off than they will be.

If this book has a single message, it is that many Americans need to heed Garrison Keillor's advice in the epigraph and lighten up. As previous chapters have revealed, the source of most worker's concerns has been misplaced. Contrary to all the lamentations, the U.S. economy, in particular, has performed not perfectly, but reasonably well in modern times. Growth in American unhappiness and anxiety may be grossly exaggerated. Unease and anxiety have always been a part of the American experience and will likely remain so far into the future. Granted, the country has some current economic problems that must be addressed, but for the overwhelming majority of Americans, not having enough "stuff" is not one of their more pressing problems. Having too much may be.

The book has stressed that one nontrivial source of difficulty for some groups is that too many fundamental rules of reasonable conduct are being disregarded by too many Americans, but there is even hope in that regard. Because of more income and better technology, Americans can now join together with kindred spirits from around the world to create whole new communities that can exclude those who refuse to abide by the rules of extended order.

Americans should reflect on the maxim that the late Frank Knight, a University of Chicago economist, used to convey to his students: "If it's hopeless, it's ideal."[1] I don't think for a moment that conditions are ideal, which leaves room for a great deal of hope for a better future. In this final chapter, I would like to reiterate another paradoxical thought: The fears and concerns felt and verbalized by people across the globe are more likely founded not in diminishing opportunities, but in their vast and sudden expansion. A little reflection will explain why.

No Choice as Ideal

When opportunities are reduced to only one option that is known with certainty, there is nothing to fear, because there is no choice to make, no mistake to encounter (possibly, also, no sense of success to be had). The person who has only one opportunity simply does what he or she has to do, which is the only thing that can be done. Doing that which one *must* do is ideal, given that there is no room for improvement, and even no reason to worry.

Flies and cows fret little (or, at least, they don't appear to) because there is nothing much to fret about. They know their opportunities, to the extent that they can assess them; tomorrow or even days beyond tomorrow will be much as they are today, and their decisions will be relatively simple ones, such as where to eat. There is not much they can do to change matters either; they must take what comes their way.

People can have fears about the future only when they have real

1. As often quoted by James M. Buchanan, one of Frank Knight's students.

choices, when they can make meaningful decisions, some of which will be right, but some of which can and will be wrong. When people have a multitude of opportunities, they can be expected to see many, if not virtually all, of them as gestalts, ill-defined courses of action with equally ill-defined results. People with many opportunities must strive to add definition to what they think they see. They must also make fine distinctions over right and wrong, good and bad, and they must worry that they have not perceived the gestalts properly (or as others perceive them) and that their plans will not fit with the decisions made by others. They must often break with past habits, many of which have held them in good stead (given limited past opportunities). Also, they must often give up on the remaining vestiges of hope that their past investments in education, skills, networks, and attitudes will continue to have economic value. When opportunities expand rapidly, many of the opportunities will not only be ill-defined gestalts, they will appear to overlap and intertwine, making the separate opportunities all the more difficult to identify.

The point is that opportunities present challenges, often taxing ones at that. Economists make a profession of analyzing the implications of opportunities, but they might have a difficult time appreciating the angst that people feel from expanding opportunities. Economists typically start their analyses with the presumption that the opportunities are already known by people who have them all ranked according to a clearly defined ordering. They, in other words, typically assume away *the* economic problem that most people face. Frank Knight did not let the problem of *determining* the alternatives for viable choices escape him. He once observed,

> In all the folk-lore to which human thinking has given rise, in connection with human beings themselves, perhaps the most false and misleading single item is the common notion that men "know what they want," or that there is no arguing over tastes. It would sure be much nearer the truth to say that there is no arguing about anything else, or specifically about "facts." The principal thing that men actually want is to find out what they do really want; and the bulk of what they want, or think they want, is wanted because they think that in some sense they "ought" to do so, that it is "right."[2]

2. Frank H. Knight, *Freedom and Reform: Essays in Economics and Social Philosophy* (Port Washington, N.Y.: Kennikat Press, 1969), p. 234. In another work, Knight makes much the same point with a different twist: "The problem of life is to utilize resources 'economically,' to make them go as far as possible in the production of desired results. The general theory of economics is therefore simply the rationale of

A hundred and fifty years ago, economic life was relatively simple for most Americans. Sure enough, they had choices (one of which, as discussed in chapter 2, was whether or not to move west), but the viable choices were severely circumscribed. Clearly, a hundred years ago, sons pretty much knew that they would be following their fathers into one form of farming or another. Daughters understood that they would be spending most of their working years partly in the home and partly in the fields. Life courses were challenging, and options prevailed, but the array was limited. Everyone knew that life would be tough, and very likely short (on average, less than fifty years).

A half century ago, American workers could think in terms of much longer working careers than did their grandparents, but they could also imagine that their careers would be with one firm, if the workers wanted that to be the case.

Life is no longer so simple. Secure employment is gone, and many workers are now being challenged to create their own jobs, not always a settling thought, especially when the available job options are so varied and, at the moment, unknown but, with work, knowable.

The Future as a Looking Glass

A multitude of choices, to repeat a theme developed much earlier in the book, makes life much like Alice's looking glass in front of which the world beyond cannot be known very well. People with a host of choices know that others are also beset with a similar array of choices. Each cannot know the choices that will likely be made by more than a small number of others. Accordingly, each person can only see the mirror before him or her as opaque. To get through the looking glass, each must charge ahead and be prepared to adjust and readjust her or his own actions to the host of decisions made by others.

It is no understatement to assert that the more viable choices people have, the greater the complexities the decisions at hand, and the greater the potential for adjustments that people must make. But along with

life—in so far as it has any rationale. The first question in regard to scientific economics is this question of how far life is rational, how far its problems reduce to the form of using given means to achieve given ends. Now this, we shall contend, is not very far. Life is at bottom an exploration of the field of values, an attempt to discover values, rather than on the basis of knowledge of them to produce and enjoy them to the greatest possible extent" (Frank H. Knight, *The Ethics of Competition and Other Essays* [New York: Harper and Brothers, 1935], p. 105).

more choices come more opportunities for improvement *and* for failure. It follows, not surprisingly, that the greater the opportunities, the more careful people must be in weighing their decisions, in trying to sort through the various sequences of decisions they may have to make, and the more flexible they must be to adjust to what everyone else is doing. With vast opportunities, the details of the future are necessarily less certain, less predictable, more of a pure gamble, more of an unfolding, evolving process that emerges from the unknown and unknowable actions, reactions, and interactions of many people, all of whom must respond to the details of the future as it unfolds.

But the evolutionary process at hand does not mean the future will be less prosperous, only that it *could* be less prosperous for particular people considering the choices. As argued earlier, the very fact that the future is that which cannot be imagined by any one person, because of the unknown and unknowable actions of all others, ensures that the future will tend to be all the more prosperous, in spite of the angst of individuals to the contrary. The unanticipated prosperity will emerge from the collaborative use of the aggregate brainpower that no individual has at his or her own disposal, which implies that future prosperity cannot be imagined by anyone, except in the sketchiest and broadest of forms. Opportunities lie in filling in the details.

The Uncorked Genie

Life is simply not simple when opportunities abound, and it can be made extraordinarily complex when opportunities suddenly expand, an observation that can make for a nontrivial sense of unease or fear—and, maybe, of wishful thinking that a simpler life were possible. The genie of vast and expanding opportunities, however, is out of the magic lamp, but unlike the genie in the movie *Aladdin* who had three wishes to grant, this genie offers untold wishes that people around the globe, Americans included, must consider *very carefully*. Results will not be achieved by magic. Rather they will emerge from a lot of effort, even many failures.

As discussed, past opportunities have manifested themselves in the continuing expansion of national product—even industrial production, which requires fewer and fewer workers to generate as the years go by—in most advanced countries; in the growth of international trade in real dollars and as a percent of total national production; in the growth of jobs (good and bad ones); in the growth of early retirement and people's expenditures on leisure-time activities; in the geometric increase in the number of domestic and international phone calls, faxes, and E-mails; in the escalation of patent awards; and in the increased frequency with which people are starting their own businesses—among other things.

In more concrete terms, opportunities have shown up in the expansion of new computer programs (the prices of which are constantly falling), in an endless flow of goods and services being carried by larger and larger stores, a widening range of books in super bookstores, and growth in the number and variety of work notices in local newspapers. They also show up in the expanding array of specialized shops and services in the fattening Yellow Pages of the phone book.

Times are tough in the 1990s partly because there are so many problems and so many opportunities—to succeed *and* to fail. Deciding which opportunities to take and how to take them is an arduous undertaking, fraught with immense uncertainties. But it is an undertaking that must, and will, be taken. We cannot avoid being fully employed at all times in moving into our own futures, into taking opportunities. The only unanswered question is which opportunities will be created and taken and whether the opportunities will be taken purposefully, with a sense of direction, and imagination.

The Technological Sources of Modern Opportunities

For years, Americans have been told about the miniaturization of everything (computing power in the main, but also whole firms), about the power of communication, about the integration and globalization of all economies, and about the lost economic power of former power groups through the relentless extension of competition, which implies the dissipation of economic power, not just its transfer. All of the futurists' optimistic forecasts have come to fruition in an almost unbounded constellation of opportunities partially attributed to these relentless forces, as surveyed in chapter 6.[3]

But the growth of opportunities has not stalled, far from it. The communist system has collapsed, releasing hundreds of millions of people from state bondage in the former Soviet bloc economy and the former centrally planned Chinese economy. Those workers can now join the rest of the world in contributing productively to solving the world's economic dilemmas. The American defense build-down, in response to the collapse of communism, is releasing resources to do productive

3. For an expanded discussion of the details of the economic/technological revolution underway since at least the 1960s, see Richard B. McKenzie and Dwight R. Lee, *Quicksilver Capital: How the Rapid Movement of Wealth Has Changed the World* (New York: Free Press, 1991).

things, not just to build the machinery of war that is designed mainly to destroy resources. Now, in the mid-1990s, the world economy is suffering through the consequences of rapidly expanding opportunities that come with redeployment of defense resources.

The unemployed IBM managers who once directed the production of mainframe computers can now think up new products and programs to destroy other American jobs, but we can't know exactly what they will think up. The robots that replaced the production workers at GM took away mundane jobs, but they also made it possible for the American economy to tap the released brawn and brainpower to do more complicated things, but, again, we don't know what.

"Reegineering the corporation" became a pat phrase among chief executives in the 1990s—because reegineering became practical, and thereby mandatory, for many firms. The chief issue among executives became not whether corporations would be reinvented, but how—that is, what opportunities to do more with less would be exploited. Therein lies a womb of uncertainty, given that so many people have been forced to wrestle with their newfound opportunities and the process of reconstituting their work environments.

The Microcosm and Cybercosm

People in our distant past had many opportunities, but their opportunities were then limited to this world, or rather, in this country to the Old West. We have stressed that opportunities have grown because whole new worlds—new "wests"—have been discovered and created to exploit, virtually without end. Markets are no longer confined to the physical world as we have known it, full of concrete and tangible objects. In that physical world, a major principle of economic order was the bigger the turf, the greater the power, and the greater the resource use, the fewer the future opportunities (given that fewer resources would be available for future use).

Today, opportunities exist in other virtually open-ended worlds, those of the microcosm and cybercosm. As author George Gilder has pointed out, production has historically taken place within the observable, material, physical universe. Opportunities were then constrained by the materials that were available. We had to fear that our opportunities would be closed, eventually, by the opportunities that were exploited. In that world, energy crises were a pressing concern. However, production has begun to move into a whole new universe, the microcosm, or the invisible world where space is measured by the minute distances between electrons and much production becomes, more or less, material-less. In this new economic universe where millions of people already go to work, opportunities are much more unbounded, unchecked by material constraints, because the critical resources in this universe—ideas—"are not used up as they are used," as Gilder writes. In the microcosm, the economic burdens of matter decline, ". . . [S]pace and time expand as size and power drop. In the age of the microcosm, the inventive inputs of producers launch a spiral of economic growth and productivity at steadily declining cost in every material domain: land, energy, pollution, and natural resources."[4]

The problem the microcosm presents is one of almost unchecked opportunity to create new things from virtually nothing. All one needs is a computer, the price of which continues to decline as its power expands. These opportunities seem mysterious to those who have not gone through the electronic looking glass.

Microchips have revolutionized economic opportunities because they, crystallized from sand, can be designed in so many ways. The microchip has made the future all the less knowable because any one individual or group of individuals working together cannot possibly imagine the multitude of ways the chips will be designed and redesigned or how any given design will be used and will give rise to more opportunities. Again, the microchip has made the future all the less knowable to any given mind.

One does not have to work in the space between electrons to be a part of the electronic economic order, for there is another emerging world order in the cybercosm, the multidimensional constellation of meaningful and productive economic connections that can be made through computer networks, just the other side, figuratively speaking, of computer screens. In the old economic order, economic progress was measured by the flow of resources and goods and services along established trade routes in the air and on land and sea. In this electronic economic order, new trade routes are still being established, but they differ dramatically in their nature and content from the ones in our past. The electronic trade on the emerging "nets" is not so much material, but all the more important, and is composed of ideas, knowledge, and brain power. On these trade routes, however, the cost of transport and distance has been severed. The mind can literally be everywhere (at least, many places) more or less at once. These nets have extended the opportunities for

4. George Gilder, *Microcosm: The Quantum Revolution in Economics and Technology* (New York: Simon and Schuster, 1989), p. 63.

people to link up and produce—to extend the boundaries of what can be done—in ways that could never before be imagined.

In chapter 3, I noted that American historian Frederick Jackson Turner proffered a hundred years ago that economic opportunities would be bounded by the closing of the American West, which would necessarily lead to social unrest because people would no longer have an economic escape hatch. There would be no additional turf, no more land to be taken, farmed or ranched. Turner's myopia was founded on his inability to imagine the advent of cybercosm, where there are no knowable bounds, where the "turf"—and opportunities—expands as more people inhabit its multiple dimensions. More people in this new west mean more can be done by more people separately or together.

The Rise in Opportunities

When markets are local, restricted to a few people, the opportunities for interaction are equally restricted. Two people in a local market have only two ways of producing the goods they need, separately or in tandem. There are no other ways. When a few hundred thousand people are involved in markets, the potential for trades expands rapidly into the trillions. Opportunities for working together, in other words, increase geometrically with any arithmetic increase in the number of people. Americans have far more opportunities today than ever before because they have more places to work (more turf in the microcosm and the cybercosm), because they have more to work with, and because there are far more people, in and outside the country, with whom they can work. Falling transportation and telecommunication costs have vastly expanded the array of people—the array of talents and resources—that Americans can tap in their quest to provide for themselves and their families.

Americans can do more today than ever before because they are no longer restricted to working with the people immediately around them. They can fly off to any remote city or island to meet with people who have the information and knowledge they need. They don't even have to get up from their chairs. They can phone, fax, or E-mail a multitude of potential business partners, and they can do it on the cheap, with the cost of the communication oftentimes less than the cost of a cup of coffee.

By way of modern technology, Americans can control vast amounts of computing power, which means the power to create new ideas—a crucial resource in modern production—or even fabricate goods and services without ever using any materials by way of drawings on computer screens, and they can tap into an array of resources, mental and material, at the disposal of others in remote locations on the globe. Americans have more opportunities to do things—to work—simply because they have more resources within reach, and the resources at their disposal are getting relentlessly cheaper.

More and more, Americans no longer need be constrained in what they do by the orders given by others. The "others" can hardly *make* people create, an essential task of so much modern production, because the "others" do not have the requisite information at their disposal and could not handle and use it if they could gather it all in. Modern complex production has gradually freed Americans to do their own thing in concert with others.

The angst many Americans feel is not that they can do so little, but that they can do so much, and they know that others can do likewise. The problem for some may be similar in character to that faced by a horse stuck between two attractive bales of hay, stunned, and starving, by the complexity of the decision at hand. The American workers' problem is, naturally, much more complex than choosing what to eat, given two equally attractive alternatives. The choices to be made involve a vast array of things that can be done, most of which are uncertain, again, because no one can be sure what others will be doing when any alternative is taken. They don't know what is practical, or worthwile, because so much is both possible and practical.

Economic life has always been a maze of sorts, with turns that must be made in spite of the fact that no one can be certain that a dead-end is not around the next corner. Modern economic life has become a far more complex maze in the sense that the potential turns that can be made at any point have multiplied, and the points at which turns occur have become more numerous. Moreover, the size of the maze itself is exploding as people make their twists and turns, as they open up whole new worlds of thought and mind.

Elusive Solutions

What can be done to reduce the angst? Many commentators paint a dismal picture of our recent economic past. They cite the failures, the job destruction, and the lost economic ground. They correctly identify the problem as global technological and economic forces at work. They admit, correctly, that the world has gotten more sophisticated and complex. Regrettably, they then seek to address the only question they seem to feel is worth addressing: What are *we* (the political elite) going to do to solve everyone else's problem, to create more opportunities? They don't seem to get it that the *problem* is opportunities, too many of them. There are so many in fact that political leaders, backed by hordes of government workers, can know little about them. The sophistication and complexity of modern economies should humble leaders and force them to recognize their growing irrelevancy, their growing impotency to help more than a few.

The relevant question in complex economies is "What are people—individuals acting alone and in groups—who have the requisite detailed knowledge, going to do for themselves to use the information and to exploit the opportunities at their disposal and to create their own futures?" If people's futures depended upon the brains of the political elite, they could not possibly be as bright as they will be, given that the future will evolve from the use of the brainpower of the masses, not of the very limited brainpower and information at the disposal of the politicians. As it is, markets will continue to expand, freer than ever before; more decisions will be made by individuals in new and creative relationships; and more responsibility for the decisions made will have to be shouldered by those who make them.

I have argued that opportunities for many people will likely be restricted by lost allegiance of group members to reasonable rules of contact. At the same time, I have noted the economic and societal pressures on groups to reform their ways. The reform process will, no doubt, be painful for many who resist, and who will be saddled with added costs for their failures to reform. The process will be slowed because of the resistance, but there is room for hope and optimism. Refortification of personal responsibility in society will bring its own reward.

Concluding Comments

In this chapter's epigraph, Garrison Keillor observes that "there is more self-pity available to wallow in now than there was during the Great Depression when your grandparents lived in grimy little houses with newspapers stuffed in the cracks and worked so hard their bodies hurt at night."[5] Americans should keep those words with them. They vividly remind us of just how much better life is now than it used to be for our parents and grandparents. Keillor goes on to note that his generation has

5. Garrison Keillor, "Lighten Up, Graduates," *New York Times,* May 27, 1994, p. A15.

become the generation that has popularized therapy for a new array of maladies. When his generation throws a party, he writes, they all sit around brooding about how bad things are. There is a measure of truth in the brooding, but only a measure. Most Americans don't need therapy; they need to smell the roses.

Granted, ongoing economic changes have their dark side. Change has given rise to real hardships that are undeniable. I have noted the difficulties some groups will likely experience if they don't adjust, if they cannot get their act together and abide by reasonable rules of conduct. At the same time, there is a bright side to the changes underway: My point in this last chapter is that much contemporary hardship is evidence of expanding, not contracting, opportunities.

Pessimists point to how much people do not know in dealing with the circumstances at hand. They see people as victims of external forces, not able to act creatively upon the circumstances they are given. They fret about what they don't now know and what they believe they need to know concerning how people's fears can and should be relieved. They often fail to appreciate the extent to which economic forces—markets in particular—coordinate the actions of the many.

On the other hand, optimists—and I am certainly in that camp—stress that people have a locomotion of their own, a capacity to act creatively upon the circumstances they confront, to find solutions, to work their way through the webs before them, and to adjust and readjust to the actions and adjustments of others. This is especially true now. Optimists remain confident that the future will be brighter than they can imagine precisely because the future is not dependent upon what any one person can imagine.

Many people seem to believe that the future will be no brighter than what they, and a few others, can imagine. Others remain convinced that the capacity of people to use the detailed knowledge at their disposal and to work with many others through markets will inevitably lead to a future that is far brighter than the optimists—much more, the pessimists—can imagine. That is why I remain so optimistic about the future. I am confident that my children will live a far more prosperous life than I have had. As Keillor recommends, Americans need to throw themselves a party. This time, however, they need to think about enjoying themselves. There is much to enjoy—and to look forward to.

INDEX

Italized page numbers refer to figures and tables.